Wicca Mastery

3 BOOKS in 1

Lisa Magic

By reading this document, the reader agrees that under no circumstances is the author responsible for any losses, direct or indirect, which are incurred as a result of the use of information contained within this document, including, but not limited to, — errors, omissions, or inaccuracies.

Table of Contents

Wicca for Beginners

Everything You Should Know about Witchcraft and Wiccan Beliefs Including Herbal & Moon Magic with Spells for Wiccan, Witches and Other Practitioners of Magic

Introduction – Wicca for Beginners

Wicca is a religion that many people do not understand because there are so many myths surrounding it that people have been taught and have not tried to learn the truth about. In this book, you will not only learn about what Wiccan is but what you need to know regarding herbal and moon magic.

As long as you approach Wicca with an open mind, you are not going to get yourself in trouble. Another thing that you have to remember is you cannot dabble with black magic or do anything that may harm someone else or yourself.

Throughout this book, you will learn about Wicca and how to do different spells involving herbs and moon magic. You will also learn other spells that you may want to use as you go about your journey in practicing your craft. You'll be surprised to learn that in many spells you will use herbs and a little bit of moon magic.

As someone who has been a practicing Wiccan for 10 years, I wanted to provide you with a glimpse of what you can do with your   magic.

Chapter 1: What is Wicca?

The first thing that you have to understand is that Wicca is not the worship of the devil, as many people believe. In fact, Wicca is a pagan religion that is based on the type of witchcraft that was developed in the 20th century. Gerald Gardner is credited as the one who brought the Wiccan religion to the public's attention in 1954.

Wicca is a spiritual system that is going to foster free-thought and the will of an individual while encouraging them to learn and understand the nature that will affirm the divinity that is in all living things.

Whenever you look at the Wiccan religion, you will discover that there is no central authority. Instead, it is based on traditional values and practices that Doreen Valiente and Gerald Gardner wrote about in the 1940s and 1950s while publishing their teachings so that their followers and many generations to come could read them and follow them.

As the years have progressed, there has been a multitude of generations that have come up with their own version of the Wiccan religion and it still continues to grow and evolve. Now you can find different sects and denominations inside of the Wiccan religion.

Being that this religion is decentralized, it is not uncommon that there are arguments over what the religion actually constitutes. These disputes are still happening today because some say that Wicca should be one way while others think it should be another.

However, there are a few traditions that can be seen in the Traditional British Wicca and those that follow this sect will focus on the teachings that Gardener wrote about, believing that the traditions are supposed to be observed by those following the Wiccan religion instead of the new traditions that some Wiccans follow.

How it Works

In the world that we live in it is hard to find someone who has not seen or read something that has a witch in it. There are a number of popular movies and books that are easy for us to access. The one most people think about is Harry Potter. When watching movies or reading books such as Harry Potter, it is easy to think that is how real witches work. However, this is not the case.

The meaning of Wicca is different for everyone depending on the sect that the witch falls into. There are some sects that worship the devil so that they can obtain the powers they want to do harm. But, in most cases, this is extremely far from the truth.

When you look back on the first humans that walked the earth, it was not uncommon to find that they worshipped gods and goddesses so they could have a healthy harvest and survive the winter.

Magic comes from chaos such as whenever someone becomes sick or there is a shortage of food. This is when spells are cast so the powers the gods possessed could be harnessed and used to put an end to the crisis. Most of the time, witches were females and they were considered to be healers who could use their magic to destroy or nurture the community they lived in based on what they believed.

It is because of the fact that witches can use their powers for good or bad that they tended to become isolated from others since people around them became scared of their powers and started to think that the witch would use their powers for evil against everyone. This is what started the witch hunts.

The History of Wicca

Wicca is part of the neopagan religions and is related to other neopagan religions that are based on witchcraft. Wicca first came around in the 12th century when a secret coven in England was developed so they could practice their religion based on the works of people like Margaret Murray.

Wicca became popular in the 1950s thanks to people such as Gerald Gardner who initiated the craft by a coven in 1939. The Gardner form of Wicca is known as the Gardnerian tradition and was spread around the world by Gardner himself, as well as his followers.

In the 1960s, there were new figures who rose to bring about their own form of religion under the Wiccan umbrella, such as Alex Sanders, Sybil Leek and many others who made organizations such as the Witchcraft Research Association. All of this occurred in a part of history when new religions were being moved to the United States so they did not have to be persecuted any longer for what it was that they believed in.

When the Wiccan religion came to the United States, it was adapted into new traditions and other sects of Wiccan that made sure the religion was never going to truly die out.

It was not until the 1970s that books were actually being published on the religion that encouraged others to join in the craft by describing the traditions and various other things that other people did not understand fully. As Wicca continued to rise, it became a major part of popular culture.

When the 1990s came around, there were historians that began to research the Wiccan religion and publish their findings so that others could know more about the religion.

Back in the 16th and 17th centuries, witch hunts took place which ended with around 100,000 people being killed after they were accused of being a witch because they supposedly worshiped the devil. Some historical documents even claim they ate children.

Some of the scholars who have researched the incidents have agreed that any of the victims of the witch hunts were incidents of hysteria that happened in villages that were not wealthy and were isolated. Those accused of being witches were not actually practicing anything that had to do with the religion. Not everyone believes this was the case though. Some scholars believe the victims really were practicing in the pagan religion.

A lot of Wiccans back in the early decades thought that there was a continuation of the witch cult and it was not until the 1980s that they began to see the witch cult was nothing more than a myth.

As previously mentioned, the Wiccan religion was founded sometime between 1921 and 1950. It is known as "the only full formed religion which England can be said to have given the world." The Wiccan religion actually was created from various other adaptations from religions that already existed along with some esoteric movements.

The Wiccan religion helped to prove that the people killed in the witch hunts were not worshipping Satan, but instead trying to survive in a world of pre-Christianity pagan religion. Several different historians have proven this fact through research. However, the most prominent advocate for this theory was Margaret Murry who wrote several books on the witch cult.

Debates

There are several debates that have occurred or are still occurring about where Wicca originally came from. If you look at Gardner's recalling in *Witchcraft Today*, it is a religion that managed to survive the witch cult and those who were persecuted in the witch trials.

Other theories say that the witch cult was planned along with all the trials so they can mostly be discredited. It is still very common for many Wiccans to claim they come from someone who survived the witch trials.

There are many theories on where Wicca came from originally and every sect in the Wiccan religion is going to believe in something different depending on the founder of that belief.

The one thing that has never changed in all of the decades that Wicca has been around is it is a very controversial topic and is the reason for much of the turmoil that is found in Wiccan religious communities.

Accepting the Wiccan Religion

When the religion first came around it was in a country that was dominated mostly by Christianity, which meant that it was not highly accepted that a new religion to be introduced.

Even today, many people, especially in the Christian religion, think that if someone is in the Wiccan religion they worship Satan. If that is not believed then it is believed that Wicca is a malevolent form of Satanism due to all the negative information that is out there about the craft. It does not help that many Wiccan covens and even individuals are secretive about practicing because they are scared of being persecuted for their faith.

Whenever someone comes out as Wiccan to their friends or family, it is commonly known as "coming out of the broom closet."

Doreen Valiente stated that "witches have little respect for the doctrines of the church, which they regard as a lot of man-made dogma." While this may be true for some, it is not true for all witches. There are some witches that are very tolerant of other religions and there are even some that believe in the Christian god. It is purely up to the witch and what they choose to believe in.

It is important to keep in mind that most of what is seen on television and in the movies about the Wiccan religion is not going to be accurate. So, when you are trying to choose if Wiccan is right for you, remember to try and look at the facts and not make your decision based on what has been seen on a screen.

In 1986, a legal decision was made to try and get the Wiccan religion validated as an actual religion. Despite this decision, and many other legal decisions, Wiccans are still having to fight politics and other religious organizations. One of these oppositions came from president George Bush because he did not believe that Wicca was a true religion and therefore it should not be recognized as one.

The Department of Veterans Affairs had a legal dispute in 2007 that made it to the stage where the pentagram can be added to the markers and plaques that are made in honor of the veterans that have died. The pentagram is now on the list of government recognized symbols for religion just like the cross is.

Even in Canada, the founding high priest and priestess of the Celeste coven, along with the founding elders for the church, were able to get the British government and the federal government to recognize Wiccan weddings and allow them to be performed in prisons and hospital chapels.

Types of Wiccans

As mentioned above, there are different sects in the Wiccan religion. While they all fall under the Wiccan religion, they believe in different things.

Gardnerian Wicca

A Gardnerian Wiccan is someone who follows the practices that were set into place by Gerald Gardner which is where the Gardnerian Wiccans came from. It is claimed that someone who is following in Gardner's footsteps is going to be following a religion that is straight from the New Forest Coven where Gardner first started his Wiccan journey.

A Gardnerian sect is going to typically have around thirteen members with a high priest or priestess. Any practices or rituals done by this sect are normally kept quiet from those that are not in the coven.

Alexandrian Wicca

The Alexandrian sect follows the teachings of Alex Sanders who was considered to be the king of the witches. His coven first began in the 1960s in the United Kingdom.

It is not hard to find ties to the Gardnerian Wiccans in the Alexandrian Wiccans as Sanders learned from Gardner before founding his own coven. These covens are usually more eclectic and have adopted the "if it works, use it" attitude.

Dianic Wicca

The Dianic Wiccans are more female centralized and focus on worshiping the goddesses rather than the gods. This sect is made up of several different cultures.

Witches in these covens typically focus on healing themselves from wounds that are left behind by men to reclaim their womanhood. Women in these covens are usually feminist, and they tend to celebrate the body of a woman rather than put it down.

Celtic

Just as the name suggests, this sect focuses on the Celtic religions and holidays.

The Celtic Wicca sect uses the same rituals and beliefs as most other Wiccans. Celtic Wiccans use the names of the Celtic gods and the seasonal festivals that are inside the Wiccan religion.

The Celtic Wiccans are seen as both Wiccan and a branch of Celtic Neopaganism. When you examine the Neopagan half, it ranges from eclectic to reconstructionist. On one end, Celtic Wiccan is eclectic while the non-historical forms are part of Celtic Reconstructionism.

Georgian

Founded by George Patterson in the 1970s, this sect is similar to the Gardnerian Wiccan sect except that it was founded in the United States rather than the United Kingdom. Many of the Georgian teachings come from a Celtic coven Patterson studied under.

Georgian Wiccan is eclectic and traditional as well. It is typically both males and females who have been initiated and been promoted to priesthood by the rites and rituals of the coven. Georgian Wiccans are oath bound. The lore of the tradition are only told to those that have been prepared properly. Even though the internet is a useful tool, it does not have all of the information required.

Believe it or not, Georgian Wicca is similar to Alexandrian and Gardnerian Wiccan. It's rituals are similar to those found in the books that are usually referred to as traditional Wicca.

Georgian Wiccan traditions are eclectic in multiple ways. It pulls from multiple sources including Celtic, Alexandrian and Gardnerian. It does not have a tie to any British traditional witchcraft coven. This is why it is usually referred to as a British traditional witchcraft derivative.

Discordianism

The Goddess Discordia is worshiped by this sect. Their holy book is called Principia Discordia. They believe that life cannot survive without chaos and order to balance out the universe. Discordianism says that the Greek goddess Eris is their central deity which is why they are often called Erisians. This religion places great stress on randomness, disagreement and chaos. The first rule of Discordianism is that there are no rules.

Is Wicca Right for You?

What it comes down to is: do you want to be part of the Wiccan religion? No one can say if it is right or wrong for you because it is based on your own beliefs. There are a few things you should consider to see if this is the proper religion for you:

1. You prefer natural stones to man-made ones.

2. You can recall your dreams without trying.

3. You are fond of collecting things that are found outside.

4. You would rather be outside than inside.

5. You feel like you have psychic abilities that come naturally.

These are not the only things that will help point you towards becoming a Wiccan. They are just a few indicators that will help show you the Wiccan faith is the proper religion for you.

Chapter 2: Practicing Wicca in Secret

It is understandable that you would want to hide the fact you are Wiccan because of how the outside world perceives it. However, when you are practicing in private, you have to be careful because it is hard to hide some of your spells.

The first thing you have to do is make sure that you are respecting anyone else's beliefs that you may living with. You do not want to go against their beliefs or upset them. Following from this, do not tell anyone that may communicate with your roommates. You will only want to talk to someone who you trust who knows they cannot bring it up to your roommates. If you cannot fully trust them, then you will end up being outed and that is not something you want to happen.

If you're wanting to work with stones, then one way you can hide that you are using them for magic is to say that you are interested in collecting stones because of how pretty they are.

If you are wanting a spell book, then you should get a journal that is going to keep people out of it. It is also not a bad idea to hide it somewhere like your closet or under your mattress. If you're a woman you can always get a journal that says "period tracker." If you're a man, you can try a similar tactic, only customize it so that others are not going to want to open it.

You can have herbs if you want. The best way to hide this is to have plants around that are going to make it seem less conspicuous.

You are not going to need a wand or herbs in order to be Wiccan. You also do not have to join a coven or cast spells. Remember that Wiccan is being one with nature and you can do this by going outside to meditate.

You can find a lot of information online (take some of it with a grain of salt). If you are sharing your laptop or tablet, make sure that you clear your search history. If you are printing out any information, place it in the journal you are hiding or you hide it somewhere else. Do not leave it out in the open for anyone to see! If you are not sure what to believe online, you can always go to your local bookstore and find books on Wicca or witchcraft. You can either read it there or buy it, take it home and hide it.

If you want an alter, make sure that you keep it small and put it away whenever you are done with it. If you are setting up an altar, it is not a bad idea to keep it as big as the top of your dresser or your desk. When you're done, place it in your closet or in the corner.

Do not hang up any symbols that would indicate that you are a practicing Wiccan. This also means do not get any jewelry or tattoos that will show you practice.

It will be hard for you to hide that you are a practicing Wiccan, but it can be done. Take the necessary steps to keep yourself protected and if you find that you need some support, there are support groups online that you can find and join.

Just remember that you are not alone.

Chapter 3: Witchcraft and Wiccan Beliefs and Rules

When you follow the Wiccan beliefs, you do not have to follow a particular set of beliefs. Instead, you will follow your own expectations. However, you should be advised that there are a few things that each sect of Wiccans believe in.

Beliefs

It is not required that you believe everything in the religion. Whether you are part of a cover or not, you are your own witch and you will be able to believe what it is that you want to believe without worrying about someone looking down on you.

Theology

For Wiccans, theology will cover agnostics, atheists, and theists and how they look at the religion as far as their archetypes and symbols go. Any Wiccans that are more theistic will have their own beliefs such as monotheists, polytheists, duotheistic, and pantheists.

Even though it does not matter what group the theist Wiccan falls in, they will still believe in a deity that predates Christianity. It is believed that Wicca predates Christianity by 28,000 years, if not more.

One of the most common forms of theological Wiccans that can be found are the duotheistic ones who believe in the Horned God and the Mother Goddess. How these deities are viewed depends on which sect the Wiccan falls in because every sect will have their own opinion. For instance, one sect views the Mother Goddess as the Moon Goddess and the Menstruating Goddess.

In 1959, Gerald Gardner wrote:

The Gods are real, not as persons, but as vehicles of power. Briefly, it may be explained that the personification of a particular type of cosmic energy in the form of a God or Goddess, carried out by believers and worshippers over many centuries, builds that God-form or magical image into a potent reality of the inner planes, and makes it a means by which the types of cosmic power may be contacted.

Afterlife

Just like theology, whatever you believe in when it comes to the afterlife will be completely up to you because it does not occupy a central place in the Wiccan religion. It is something that a few believe while others don't believe in it.

There are many Wiccans that believe if you do good in this life you are currently living while making the most of it, your next life will be good as well. However, it is more important for you to focus on what you are doing in this life because you never know what is going to happen in the next life.

On the other hand, there are some Wiccans that do not believe that there is an afterlife at all. Instead, they believe that your spirit will survive once your body has passed away and then it moves on to a higher plane. There is a religion found in Hawaii that says that the body has 3 souls that will survive after death. With that being said, not every Wiccan will believe in the afterlife, and some believe in reincarnation which means however you lived in this life will be based on how you come back in the next life. The more good you do in your current life, the better your life will be when you are reincarnated.

Magic

It is impossible for you to find Wiccans that do not believe in magic. Magic will play a manipulative force seen whenever you practice witchcraft.

Despite the fact that it is easy to find those that do not agree on the religion and see things differently, most will believe that magic is offered by ceremonial magicians.

Aleister Crowley once said "magic is the science and art of causing change to occur in conformity with will." On the other hand, MacGregor Mathers said "magic is the science of the control of the secret forces of nature."

As you can see, these two ceremonial magicians each believed that magic is something that can be controlled and can change something, whether it is with the will of the universe or the forces of nature.

Magic may have a different meaning for each Wiccan, but in the end it is the same thing. You will be releasing your energy out into the universe to make change happen.

You will see that the rule of 3 comes in here. Whatever you do, you will receive it threefold. So, you will want to stick to doing things that fall into the white magic category rather than black magic.

You may also see that there are two ways to spell the word magic. There is the traditional way, which is magic, or there is another way, which is magick. Magick is the spelling usually used by a witch that follows Crowley's footsteps and the way he believed in religion.

In 1970, Paul Huson stated:

The point [of magic in witchcraft] is to make the "bendable" world bend to your will... Unless you possess a rock-firm faith in your own powers and in the operability of your spell, you will not achieve the burning intensity of will and imagination which is requisite to make the magic work.

In other words, it is vital that you have faith in your own powers so that you can make the spell you are casting work properly.

Through your own research, you may discover that most spells can be done in a sacred circle that will cast a spell so that the spell works as it is supposed to. This will bring the change to the physical world that the caster would like to see.

Morality

Lady Gwen Thompson once said "bide the Wiccan laws ye must, in perfect love and perfect trust. Mind the Threefold Law ye should - three times bad and three times good...eight words the Wiccan Rede fulfill an it harm none, do what ye will."

Similar to the beliefs of Wiccans, there is no code that you must live by. However, there are rules that are known as the Wiccan Rede which is essentially the Wiccan version of the golden rule. The Wiccan Rede declares "an it harm none, do what ye will."

In simpler terms, the Wiccan Rede states that you can make whatever choices you want, but you must take responsibility for your actions, especially when it comes to harming yourself or others.

As mentioned above, the law of threefold return means that you will be messing with karma if you are trying to do something harmful to someone else. However, unlike karma, it will come back to you three times good or three times bad, depending on the spell you are casting.

Five Elements

Similar to magic, a lot of Wiccans believe in the five elements. Everyone knows what the 4 elements are (earth, wind, fire, water), but the 5th according to the Wiccan beliefs is spirit.

Rules

There are no set rules to the Wiccan religion, but there are a few rules that each Wiccan follows.

The rules and goals of the Wiccan religion have been touched on, but let's look into them a little more so that you can be one hundred percent sure that you understand them.

The Rule of Three

Ever mind the rule of three. Three times your acts return to thee. This lesson well, thou must learn. Thou only get what tee dost earn.

Just like the law of karma, whatever you put out into the universe is going to come back to you three fold so you need to be careful about what you are using your magic for or what you are saying.

Sometimes the rule of three is learned the hard way, but you are never going to get what you do not deserve despite what you have done. So, it is best to just do what you know is right and not do something that could end up coming back on you in a bad way.

Honor the Gods and Goddesses

They created life and they are there to help with the challenges that you are going to face every day.

Only allow the power to run through you in love, if it does not, then do not let it go through you.

Nothing should be done out of anger because that is when the rule of three is going to be invoked. No one needs to be harmed when it comes to doing magic because it is against the Wiccan beliefs.

This also means that you cannot make any vows to your gods or goddesses unless you are able to keep to them. If you cannot keep your vows, then you should not be making them since that is not a way of honoring your deity. It is similar to if you break a vow to your friends or family.

Do Not Bother Anyone Who is Not a Wiccan

It is understandable to be friends with people not in the religion, but you do not need to try and convert them like some other religions do.

Stick to the Vows That You Make to the Gods and Goddesses

Your word is your honor and if you do not do something that you say you are going to do, then it is going to come back on you. Any vow that you make should be honored so that the gods and goddesses do not turn their backs on you.

Do Not Use the Names of the Gods and Goddesses in Any Way Besides Love and Honor

This is very similar to the Christian's rule of do not take the Lord's name in vain. The gods and goddesses are meant to be honored and loved by all who believe in them and saying or using their name in an evil way will come back on you.

Do Not Sell Your Powers

Money should not be accepted in exchange for magic being done. You are the one who is doing the spell, therefore the consequences are going to come back on you.

There is no amount of money that is going to be worth being harmed three times what you do for someone else. Besides, you cannot control what other people are feeling when a spell is being performed nor can you control them wanting to harm someone else.

Know Your Craft

Never stop learning about the craft. Practice and never give up until you get it right. Nothing is going to go perfect the first time, but the more you practice, the better you are going to get.

Achieve Balance

Everything in the world has to be balanced and you should be balanced yourself. The more balance you have, the easier it is going to be for you to achieve your goals and keep your emotions under control when you are doing spells. Not only that, but you are going to be able to manage the good and the bad that is naturally inside of everyone.

Take Care of Yourself

Your body is a tool that was given to you by the gods and goddesses, so make sure that you take care of it to show how grateful you are for their gift.

Chapter 4: Wiccan Holidays

Just like any other religion, the Wiccan belief has its own holidays and festivals.

Major Festivals

Wheel of the Year

The wheel of the year is an annual cycle of festivals that are observed by most modern-day Wiccans. There are around eight festivals that can include the equinoxes and solstices on top of the other festivals that are observed.

Depending on the sect that you follow, you may have a different name and date for these festivals. Observing the cycle of the seasons is vital to many people, both in modern times and in the past. The only thing that has changed is the degree of celebration which will be based on various folk traditions.

It is said that Gerald Gardner took the word sabbat from a middle age term that was used for Jewish Shabbat.

Yule

Yule is known as the Midwinter Festival. This is a significant turning point in the yearly cycle because of the Stone Age. The sites of Newgrange and Stonehenge, both align during the solstice sunrise and sunset in order to help exemplify this turning point.

Whenever you look at the reversal of the sun's ebbing, you will notice that it symbolizes the rebirth of solar gods before the return of the fertile seasons.

Depending on where you are located or what sect you follow, you will celebrate this festival with gift giving, feasts or sacrifices. There are also wreaths made of greenery that are brought into the home during this festival.

Imboic

This is a festival that is on the first cross-quarter day that follows midwinter and will usually happen around the first of February. It is known as the first stirrings of spring.

It is during this time that you will do purification rituals that are also known as spring cleaning which help you get ready for the year's first signs of new life.

When you observe the Celtic Wiccans, you will notice that this festival is dedicated to the Goddess Brigid who is known as the daughter of Dagda.

The reclaiming traditions for witches is a time for pledges of the religion to rededicate themselves for the year. It is also the initiation for Dianic Wiccans.

Ostara

This is part of the spring equinox that typically falls sometime around the 21st of March. It has been said that this festival received its name from the Germanic goddess known as Eostre. Normally, you will see this festival celebrated around Easter or Passover. It is during this time that new crops are planted.

Beltane

Traditionally, this festival falls on the first day of summer in Ireland, but it is called the festival of Florais while celebrated in Germanic countries. There are various celebrations that take place during Beltane, such as maypole dancing and the crowning of the Queen of May.

Midsummer

This festival is also called Litha or Summer Solstice. This is one of the four solar holidays and is typically celebrated when the summer has reached its peak and the sun is shining for the longest day.

In the Wiccan belief, this festival follows Beltane and is followed by Lammas. There are some traditions, such as the Reckoning of Time, when a list is preserved with names for the twelve months, these names were created by the Anglo-Saxon. Midsummer falls between June and July.

Lughnasadh

This is one of the three harvest festivals that take place. This holiday is marked by the celebration of baking bread in the shape of the gods and then consuming it in order to symbolize the sanctity and importance of the harvest. This celebration will depend on what practice you decide to follow.

The name Lammas implies that it is a grain-based festival. There is a feast to give thanks for bread and grain, which symbolizes the bringing in of the first fruits of the harvest.

Mabon

This is the second harvest festival and will be celebrated around Thanksgiving. This is a festival that is meant to recognize the fruit that the earth provides and they are shared to secure the blessing of the goddess and god during the winter months.

The word Mabon was coined by Aidan Kelly in the 1970s as a reference to Mabon ap Modron which was a Welsh mythological character.

Samhain

This festival is the perfect time for you to celebrate those that have passed before you. Festivities are usually time to pay respect to the ancestors and elders, pets, friends, family members, and other loved ones that have passed before you. Depending on what practice you follow will depend on if you are part of the festival that invites those to join the festivities or not. Many times, this is known as a festival of darkness because it is used to balance the festival of Beltane.

It is during this time that many believe that the veil between this world and the next are thinned which makes it easier for you to communicate with the dead. This is similar to Day of the Dead or Halloween.

Minor Festivals

Vali's Blot

This festival is celebrated around February 14th because it is a dedication to the god Vali and it is a celebration of love. This holiday is similar to Valentine's Day because it celebrates the love that is between two or more people.

Ancestor's Blot

Just as the name suggests, this is a celebration for your ancestors. This is another Germanic celebration that takes place around November 11th. This is a day to celebrate where you come from and what is to come.

Ancestors are extremely important in the Wiccan religion because they show you where you've been and where you are going. Your ancestors look out for you and keep you protected.

Yggdrasil Day

This day is celebrated on the 22nd of April and is the celebration of a world tree that goes by the name Yggdrasil. In reality, it is a celebration of all trees and nature. Remember, this is an earth-related religion which means that nature is a massive part of what you will practice.

Winterfinding

This is typically celebrated around mid-October and it marks the beginning of winter. This celebration will fall between Haustblot and Winternights. You will find that this festival will fall right after the harvest because it is your way of asking the gods to watch over you when the cold weather comes so that you can make it through the winter.

Summerfinding

Similar to Winterfinding, you will celebrate Summerfinding at the beginning of summer between Ostara and Walpurgisnight which is sometime during mid-April. You will celebrate new beginnings with this festival.

Chapter 5: Gods and Goddesses

The concept of a deity is you have someone to worship in the Wiccan religion just like everyone else does. These deities are said to be those that produced life and continue to ensure that life is given to everything in the world. You will see that these deities are similar to what God is considered in the Christian religion.

Major Deities

The major deities in the Wiccan religion can vary but will be similar and have something to do with nature. Most of the time, Wiccan's express their beliefs in their own deities with the writings that were completed by Doreen Valiente and Gerald Gardner.

Like everything else, the gods and goddesses will have a gender polarity but will both be equal so that everything is kept in perfect balance.

The Sun God and the Horned God

This is the polar opposite of the goddess. Most of the time, this god is seen as the horned god which links him to Cernunnos a Celtic god. However, in English folklore, he is called Herne the Hunter, in Greece he is Pan, in Rome he is Faunus and in India, he is Pashupati.

Gardner attributed this god to the witches of ancient times and was supported by Margaret Murry in his theory of the Pan-European religion which has sadly since been discredited.

The horns are considered a sign of male virility and any gods that have horns or antlers are usually found in the Wiccan religion. The green man is also linked to the horned god except he does not have horns.

Depending on the time of year, this god can have different personalities such as the Oak King or the Holly King, he has even been seen as the Sun King. The Sum god is usually found around the Lughnasadh sabbat.

Each aspect of the god are for the same god but there are some Wiccans believe they are separate deities.

You can find an extensive work on the Wiccan ideas of their god in *The Witches' God* written by Stewart and Janet Farrar.

Goddess/ Triple Goddess

Many times, the goddess is known as the Triple Goddess which means that she is the maiden, the crone and the mother. The mother goddess is the most important of the three.

Murry and Gardner claimed that there was an ancient goddess that was celebrated by the witches. Just like the horned god, the goddess helps to keep the balance in the Wiccan religion.

In classical Greece and Rome, the relationship between neopagan concepts and the triple goddess were disputed, although it is not disputed that the triple goddess came from ancient religions.

For instance, take Stymphalos. Hera was worshiped as a girl, grown up, and widowed. One of the most prominent triple goddesses was Diana which was equated to Hecate. Diana and Hecate were represented in triple form when they first started to be worshiped.

Neoplatonist philosopher Porphyry was one of the first to record that there were three parts to Hecate. He wrote:

The moon is Hekate, the symbol of her varying phases and of her power dependent on the phases. Wherefore her power appears in three forms, having as a symbol of the new moon the figure in the white robe and golden sandals and torches lighted: the basket, which she bares when she has mounted high, is the symbol of the cultivation of the crops, which she makes to grow up according to the increase of her light: and again the symbol of the full moon is the goddess of the brazen sandals.

Other Gods and Goddesses

The All

This deity is regarded as unknown and is not worshipped often. This deity is credited with organizing every principal within the world, which means that he is similar to the Tao or Atman.

Star Goddess

This is the universal pantheistic deity in the Wiccan religion. The star goddess is usually worshipped by the feminist Wiccan. She is also the one that is considered to have created the cosmos. The name Star Goddess comes from the charge of the goddess which is a sacred Wiccan text. Its origins come from the Feri tradition where the star goddess or Starhawk originated.

Lover God

This title is saved for the gods that have a goddess consort along with other lovers who are devoted to him. These gods are Pan, Cernunnos and Krishna.

Sacrificial Gods

This is a title that is given to those who have sacrificed to provide life for others. These deities are the Sun gods, green gods,   Jesus,   Osiris   and   Adonis.

Chapter 6: Book of Shadows

Everyone knows of the four elements: air, earth, wind and fire. However, in the Wiccan religion, there is a fifth element known as spirit. Here are how all of these elements come into play within the Wiccan religion.

The Five Elements

Air

Air is the representation of the mind and intelligence, as well as your communication and telepathy skills. It is expressed by tossing objects into the wind or with aromatherapy.
The following are attributed to the element:

- A masculine element.

- Its direction is east while its energy is projective.

- It is found in the upper left on the pentagram.

- Things that symbolize the air are clouds, feathers, vibrations and smoke.

- The gods and goddesses of air are Aradia, Cardea, Nuit, Urania, Enlil, Merawrim and Thoth.

- The spirits of the air are Sylphys, Fairies of the trees, and flowers.

- The time of day is dawn.

- The cycle of life is infancy.

- The colors are white, crimson and yellow.

- The zodiac signs are Aquarius, Libra and Gemini.

Fire

Fire is the representation of energy, inspiration and love. This is represented by the burning of objects or love spells. This is also an element of change and its magic represents itself.
The following are attributed to the element:
- A masculine element

- Its direction is south with a projective energy.

- It is found on the lower right on the pentagram.

- Things that symbol the fire are things such as flame, lightning, volcanoes and rainbows.

- The gods and goddesses of air are Brigit, Hestia, Pele, Vesta, Angi, Horus, Prometheus and Vulcan.

- The spirits of the air are salamanders and firedrakes.

- The time of day is noon.

- The cycle of life is youth.

- The colors for air are red, crimson, white, orange and gold.

- The zodiac signs are Aries, Leo and Sagittarius.

Please note: be careful using this element. Do your rituals that deal with fire in an open space rather than the house.

Water

Water is for the representation of emotions and purification. It is represented by brewing water or pouring water over objects. The following are attributed to the element:

- A feminine element.

- Its direction is west with a receptive energy.

- It is found on the upper right of the pentagram.

- The symbols for water are oceans, rivers, springs and lakes.

- The goddess and gods for water are Aphrodite, Isis, Marianne, Mari, Tiamat, Yemaha, Dylan, Ea, Osiris, Neptune and Poseidon.

- The spirits are nymphs, mermaids, fairies of the ponds, lakes and streams.

- The time of day is twilight or dusk.

- And the cycle of life is maturity.

- The season is autumn.

- The colors for water are green, indigo, black, grey, turquoise and blue.

- The zodiac signs are Cancer, Scorpio and Pisces.

Earth

The earth element is for strength and stability. It is represented by burying objects and making images out of stone.
The following are attributed to the element:

- A feminine element.

- Its direction is north with a receptive energy.

- It is found on the lower left of the pentagram.

- Symbols for earth are rocks, soil, salt and clay.

- Gods and goddesses of the earth are Ceres, Demeter, Gaea, Mah, Mephtys, Persephone, Rhea, Adonis, Athos, Arawn, Cernunnos, Dionysus, Mardyk, Pan and Tammuz.

- The spirits are gnomes, trolls, and dwarfs.

- The cycle of life is aged.

- The season is winter.

- The colors are brown, black, green and yellow.

The Zodiac signs are Taurus, Virgo and Capricorn.

Spirit

This is the element that is for providing space and balance amongst all the elements. It is represented by a sense of joy and union.

The following are attributed to the element:

- A universal element.

- No direction.

- It is found on the upper part of the pentagram.

- The god and goddess of this are the Lady and the Horned God.

- The cycle of life is eternity.

- The season is the wheel of the year.

- The color is white.

Altar and Book of Shadows

Important tools of any Wiccan's rituals are going to be their altar and their book of shadows. Below we're going to go over what you'll need for your altar and how to set it up, as well as what your book of shadows "should be."

Altar Tools

This will be discussed in more detail in a later chapter.
Your altar is going to be where you conduct most of your rituals and where you "worship." There are a few tools that you're going to need to have on your altar even if you do not use them constantly.
Some of the things that you're going to want to make sure you have are:

1. The Athame (a ceremonial blade)

2. A bell

3. Candles for every direction

    - North: black, brown, green

    - South: orange or red

    - West: aqua or blue

    - Center: white, gold, silver or a god or goddess candle

- East: white or yellow

1. Pillar candles

2. A chalice

3. Images of your deities

4. A libation dish

5. Offerings

6. Pentacle

7. Salt water

8. Scent or feather

9. Stones or crystals

10. Your wand

You may also want to include your broom, cauldron, a working knife and a sword.

Your Book of Shadows

This is your bible essentially. There are not sacred texts for the Wiccan religion like there are in other religions. However, your book of shadows is going to include your spells and different things that you have gone through while on your journey.

In order to start your book of shadows, you're going to want to pick a book that you are comfortable working with. It can be a journal or it can be a spiral notebook. It is all a personal preference.

Make sure you label the book as well as set the purpose and energy of the book before you begin to write in it. On the first page, you're going to want your personal blessing before you go on with the rest of your book of shadows.

Here's how to set up your book:

- Book title and date

- Book blessing

- General index

- Sections

    o Magickal rules and principles

    o Goals and aspirations

    o Dream and divination records

    o Research

    o Classes and experiences

    o Spells, incantations and prayers

    o Rituals and ceremonies

    o Herbal remedies and potions

    o Closing   thoughts

Chapter 7: An Intro to Witchcraft

What is Witchcraft?

Witchcraft is the belief in and practice of magical skills that are either exercised by an individual or a group of people. It is believed that witchcraft is a complex concept that varies between societies and cultures.

The term witchcraft should be used with caution depending on which culture you're talking about because it is not a cross-cultural term that means the same thing in each culture.

However, witchcraft can actually share a common ground when it comes to things such as sorcery, magic, superstition, paranormal, necromancy, shamanism, healing, possession, spiritualism, occult and even nature worship.

Witchcraft often plays a religious or medicinal role when it comes to societies or groups that believe in magic.

What Witchcraft is not

There are some misconceptions about witchcraft as there are with many things in different religions. These things are misunderstood mainly because people simply do not know anything about the religion or they have been taught it for so long that it is ingrained in their brain.

However, witchcraft is not all that everyone believes it to be. Here are some common misconceptions about witchcraft:

1. Witchcraft gives you ultimate power: This comes from Hollywood and the way they portray witchcraft in the movies that have witchcraft in them. While magic is real

and can be used by people, it will not give you the
ability to do things such as:

    a. Call up cyclones on demand.

    b. Turn people into toads.

    c. Or any other childhood fantasy that we have had.

These kind of misconceptions come about when people only
take what they know about the Wiccan religion from watching
movies. Actually, practicing the religion is multitudes different
than what you see on television and in the movies.
Sorry to say, you are not going to be lighting anyone on fire
with your mind anytime soon.
Magic is more of a spiritual awareness in which you can work
miracles by using your own energy. You are placing your
energy out there into the universe to accomplish something.

2. <u>Wicca and Christianity are utterly opposed:</u> This belief
mainly comes from the ancient prejudices that we see in
the Old Testament due to people not understanding or
being able to accept those that were different than
them. Those who actually follow the teachings of the
Christian god do not have a problem with anyone who
follows another religion.

When you look at the Wiccan religion, there are a few
similarities when it comes to the Christianity. Just like with
every religion, there are pieces of all religions in one another.
This is because each religion is slightly based on the others by
taking the pieces that they like and evolving them to meet
what they want to believe in.

3. <u>Witchcraft is Satanism:</u> This is probably one of the
biggest misconceptions of witchcraft. When you look at
it, Satan is not actually a Wiccan deity. The devil is a
Christian construct that was used to reflect the fears of
those in ancient times about those who practiced other
religions.

In fact, Wiccans do not recognize Satan as a real at all. However, there are certain people in society who worship Satan and they are known as Satanists.

4. <u>Witchcraft is black magic:</u> Black magic is known as magic used to hurt someone or something. However, those in the Wiccan religion generally live by the rule of threefold and do not do harm to others. There are those that do practice negative magic in the Wiccan religion, but they are very few and far between.

5. <u>Witchcraft involves demonic possession:</u> The belief in demons is up to the individual. However, those in the Wiccan religion generally do not consort with demons, or any negative energies for that matter. Is it possible that some Wiccans actually do deal with demons? Yes. But, it is not part of the actual craft.

Science and Magic

Is there a tie between science and magic? Yes, there very possibly is. But it is not something that anyone can determine because the belief in magic all depends on the individual, not to mention how you consider magic.

However, you have to think about some of the things that we have been able to accomplish as a human race. Would we be able to do this without magic? This would be things such as flying, going to outer space, communicating over long distances, fighting diseases and much more.

So, is there a tie between the two? Who knows. Ultimately, it is up to you to decide if there is or not. No one can disprove the existence of magic because each person's magic is something different.

Ritual and Spell Work

Rituals and spell work are actually two very different things. Many people believe that they are the same thing because you can do spell work during a ritual, but they are actually very different. Here are some of the differences between the two:

- Spell work is a specific formula that you are going to use to shape your circumstances or in order to get a specific outcome. This usually takes you between space and time and is an act of creation.

- Spells are used to instruct, craft, weave, mold and swirl the different synchronicities.

- Spells are used to create something while embedding it to a life force within the living matrix.

- Spells add more energy to the energy web that surrounds us all.

- Rituals are the fostering of a connection between your mind, body and soul.

- Spells can be either simple or complex but are usually meant to touch something deep within your core.

- Rituals are prayers that are set in motion to make a physical gesture that merges within or even without but it is always something that integrates with your presence.

- Rituals are held in a space that helps you to maintain an internal state until it becomes a default space for you.

Ultimately, rituals are going to give you a structure that provides you with a safe space in which you can open up to your innermost self, whiles spells are going to transform you so you go from one state of consciousness and to another.

How to Become a Wiccan or a Witch

This is not something that you're going to wake up and decide that you're going to do one day. You are also not born with it. More often than not, it is something that you're going to accidentally come across one day unless you happen to have grown up with it being practiced around you.

The only way that you can actually become a Wiccan or witch is to do your research and decide if it is even the religion that is right for you. Make sure you understand the beliefs of the different practices and you believe in what the Wiccan faith is about.

Ultimately, the choice is yours to decide if you want to follow the Wiccan religion. Listen to your inner voice and see if you believe this is the right path for you. Do not let anyone pressure you into doing it because if you do then you may come to regret your decision. Not only that, but the ritual of becoming a Wiccan or witch is something that needs to be yours and yours alone.

It is important for you to design your ritual the way that you want it because you are dedicating yourself to the craft. You're going to want to make your dedication ritual one that you never regret.

Chapter 8: Tools You Can Use

Witches require the proper tools. Your alter tools do not have to be expensive or complicated. In fact, you can use what you have on hand. However, there are a few customary tools that you may want to get to fill out your alter.

Ritual tools are the tools that you will use to help with your rituals. It is important you know what the basic tools are and how you can use them.

This chapter will explain all of the altar tools and other tools that you should have on hand to help you better cast your spells.

Altar Tools

Each altar tool has a symbolic meaning. You should know the symbolic meaning of each tool so you are using it properly.

- Athame: A ritual knife that is one of the prime Wicca altar tools. An athame is typically black handled and will lie in to the east which is the direction that represents mind, choice and thought.

Athames do not have to be metal. You will be able to find ones that are made out of wood or carved from stone. It will not be used as a physical knife, but rather a symbolic one.

Athames hold the God (yang) energy. They will be used in directing energy and casting ritual circles as well as recalling them. They can also be used to cut energetic ties.

- Bell: Bells are said to be like the voice of the Goddess. Whenever you ring a bell it will bring the divine's attention to you and your attention to the divine. Bells that have lovely tones will call beautiful and healing energy to you. They can also be used to clean energy out of a space.

When you finish a ritual, it is a good idea to ring a bell. If there is any unwanted energy around you while you are performing a ritual, you can use a bell to get rid of it.

- Candles (directional): There should be one candle for every direction and each direction will be color coded. Candles are used in invoking and holding the powers of each direction.

  - *Center* - If you do not use a god or goddess candle, you can use white, gold or silver for your center candle

  - *North* - Black, brown or green

  - *West* - Blue or aqua

  - *South* - Red or orange

  - *East* - White or yellow

- Candles (God and Goddess): These are typically large pillar candles that are used to represent the God and Goddess. They are set on each side of the pentacle or somewhere near the center of the altar.

Some of the other options that you have are to place a large candle for the Great Goddess or even three (white, black and red) representing the Crone, the Mother, and the Maiden.
It will be up to you to place them, but be sure to place them somewhere where they are not going to drip on anything too delicate or catch fire. These candles will invoke the energies of the divine.

- Chalice: The chalice is one of the most important tools for your altar because it signifies the Mother Goddess. This is also known as a "yin" altar tool.

There are some Wiccans that place fancy bejeweled cups on their altar but that is not necessary. Any type of cup or wine glass will work fine, a bowl will work as well. As long as it can hold water and is rounded, it will work. Silver is always a good idea when you are placing something on your altar for the Goddess.

The chalice should be placed in the west which is the direction of the water. The Wiccan chalice is used for ceremonial drink, offering libations to the Divine.

- Deities: Any image or representation of the god and goddesses that you are worshipping is welcome to have a place on the altar. These images are not considered to be "altar tools," instead they are a reminder of the divinity. Statues of your gods and goddesses can hold actual vibrations of the divine. Your altar is a living temple where the divine will dwell.

- Libation dish: A bowl, dish or cup should be placed in the middle of your altar so you can place your offerings there. This can be your chalice or your cauldron. After your ritual, you will pour or bury your offerings in the earth or in living water so that they can be carried to the divine.

- Offerings: When honoring the divine with a gift you should bring them to the altar. Most of the time, flowers are kept on your altar as an offering, you can also use something that is beautiful and special or symbolic to you.

Offerings should not be anything that can be harmful in any way. Since the divine lives in all things, anything that is harmful to you will be harmful to the divine. Pragmatically, you will be placing your offerings in the earth later.

Offerings are usually overlooked in the Wiccan practices today. However, it is an aspect that can increase spiritual power and importance.

- Pentacle: This is a 5 point star that is surrounded by a circle and is usually placed in the middle of the altar. The pentacle is important because it offers protection and power.

- Saltwater: A small bowl that contains saltwater used for cleansing. This should also be placed near the middle of your altar or your chalice can hold the saltwater.

Water and salt are both considered purifying agents in the physical realm and the energetic realm. Saltwater also represents the energies tied to the earth and water as they unite.

- Scent or feather: The representation of air is usually marked by incense, essential oils, smudges, or a bird feather. This will go on the east side of your altar since the east represents air.

Sacred scents are used in cleansing the area's energy as well as calling in powers. It can also help you to shift consciousness. Feathers can be used to cleanse energy fields or spread incense or smudge smoke.

- Stones and crystals: For your earth element, you need to place stones or crystals. These will help bring you earth energy as well as help ground you. Crystals can help bring you energies that you may need to cast your spells.

- Wand: Wands are portable versions of brooms. The original theory was that one instrument could be used to perform all the purposes that are done by two today. Wands can be made up of any material that is natural. Wood is the most traditional because each wood is going to have unique powers, so you will want to choose the wood that is going to suit your needs.

Wands are also great for divination and channeling magical energy. You can cast and recall circles instead of using an athame. Your wand will go in the south because it represents yang.

Other Altar Tools

These are extra tools that should be kept near your altar but not necessarily on it.

- Broom: Brooms are not classified as altar tools, but they are great for when you have to get rid of any unwanted energy. You can keep your broom near your altar since it is too big to place on your altar.

- Cauldron: Most cauldrons are cast iron and have three legs. They come in every size. Cauldrons are handy to have around in case you have to burn items and that's why it is one of the most common tools to have on your altar.

Place incense charcoal at the bottom and sprinkle herbs and powders on it to create a pagan incense (Make sure you are careful when burning anything). Thanks to the legs on the cauldron, it should keep heat from the surface that it is standing on, but always make sure that it is. Also, try to keep anything flammable away from the top of the cauldron, especially your hair or your shirt sleeves!

Cauldrons can also hold any witch brews you may make. These brews will be magical spells in liquid form. This can range from saltwater to more complex spells.

- <u>Working knife:</u> This knife will be used to cut things and draw lines in the earth or runes on your candles. Most working knives will be white handled. The knife has to be distinctly different from the athame so that you are not confusing the two. Not every witch will have a knife as one of their altar tools, but it is a rather functional implement.

- <u>Sword:</u> Most people prefer to use a sword when it comes to casting in groups because of emotional or physical safety. The symbolic hostility that is in swords can be hard for sensitive people to cope with, especially when it comes to intimate situations such as rituals. Swords can be awkward when placed on an altar which is why some are kept near or under the altar to hold in the magical aura.

Other Ritual Tools

- <u>Altar cloth:</u> The altar cloth is optional but can be helpful. When you choose one that has the proper color or design, you will be setting the stage for the energy that flows around your altar. It will also help keep drip from scarring the top of your altar. You will want to choose a cloth that is not hard for you to remove wax from or will not be too expensive in the event that it gets ruined.

- <u>Anything charged with magical energy:</u> You can charge anything by placing it on your altar for a period of time, it is recommended that placing it on your altar for a full cycle of the moon is best. This can be spells, crystals, new altar tools, symbols of something you would like more of in your lif, or new deities statues.

- Book of shadows: If you have a book of shadows, it should be kept on your altar. This is one of the most important tools to be placed on your altar. However, if your altar is not private enough or you cannot keep it there because of space, it can be kept under your altar. Other books that you use for reference for spells or rituals can be kept under your altar. It is better to keep them close by rather than get up from your cast circle.

- Spells and spell casting materials: Any materials or spells should be kept under your altar if you are not using them when you first cast your circle.

- Songbooks: If you have a collection of songs or chants that you would like to use in your circle, keep them close by so you don't have to leave your circle.

- Tokens of helpers: Your altar is a great place for symbols and offerings to guides or special beings that help you throughout your magical journey.

Where to Find Altar Tools

You do not have to spend a lot of money on getting your altar tools. In fact, you can make your own tools or buy tools from other witches. If you do not want to do that, you can also find altar tools in alternative bookstores or in New Age shops.
Another option is to purchase them online. If you are doing that, there are Wicca altar starter kits that can be purchased online.

Chapter 9: Herbs You Can Use

Botanist have put in place a specific set of characteristics that set herbs apart from other plant life. For those that are cooks, healers or witches, the word herb includes any plant that can be useful to humans. This means trees, fruit, shrubs, flowers, vegetables and grass are considered herbs.

Interestingly enough, witches and herbalists use the word herb for any plant that has physical benefits to the body, including those that can be deadly such as belladonna and henbane. If you have any knowledge about herbs then you can understand that there is no plant that is good or bad, it just depends on what it is being used for in relation to the human body.

In the event that you are just starting out with herbal magic, ensure that you are heeding all warnings that regard toxic herbs because some of the old traditions use them. However, it is better to be safe than sorry, make sure you find an appropriate herbal substitute that is non-toxic for these recipes and spells.

Herbs That You Can Use in Spells

Herbs are vital for witchcraft because they can be used in a number of spells. Not only that, but they are required when you are doing herbal magic. In this chapter, you will see a list of some herbs you should keep around for your spells and what they can be used for.

- Camphor: A pain reliever, heals skin and burns. An herb sacred to the Goddess and can be used in full moon rituals as an offering to the Goddess. It purifies and promotes celibacy while heightening physical energy.

- Catnip: Helps to treat colds and reduce fevers. It can also aid in indigestion while curbing flatulence. It helps in strengthening the psychic bond that can be seen between humans and their animals. It is also used for courage, true love and lasting happiness.

- Cayenne: This is a great herb when it comes to first aid. It does not burn your skin or inner tissues even though it feels as if it is. Cayenne helps to coagulate the blood both internally or externally. If you are bleeding, it can be sprinkled on the bleeding cut to help it stop bleeding. It can also be used if you are suffering from heart disease.

- Chamomile: You can use chamomile to soothe your mind and body. It can be used as a sedative before you go to bed or as a pain reliever when placed in a compress. You can also use it for good luck or to change your luck.

- Clove: You can use this to soothe toothache pain or calm stomach pain. It also helps to banish hostility or negative energy while increasing personal gain.

- Coltsfoot: Relieves pain and is a cough and allergy suppressant. When used in spells it can help with prosperity and love.

- Comfrey: An extremely nutritious herb that soothes stomach pain, heals sprains, strains and fractures. It also can be used in protection spells.

- Diamiana: This herb is an aphrodisiac and improves digestion while relieving coughs. It can also be used in sex magic or for divination.

- Devil's shoestring: Protection and good luck.

- Fennell: Helps with digestion and can be chewed or placed in coffee. Helps to prevent curses while imparting strength and sexual virility.

- Galangal root: Cleanses your system internally and should be taken at the onset of a cold or flu. Can be used in sex magic, hex breaking and helps with psychic powers.

- Garlic: Good for hair and skin. Also helps to lower cholesterol and blood pressure. Can be used in magical healing and exorcisms.

- Ginger: A relaxing stimulant. Helps to settle stomach issues while inducing perspiration for sweating out a fever.

- Ginseng: Promotes longevity and can be used as an antidepressant. Can be used in love spells, healing spells and beauty spells.

- Heal All: This is an all-purpose healing herb. When gargled with cold water it can soothe a sore throat or can be used as a poultice for cuts and minor contusions. In spells, it can be used for success in gambling.

- Hibiscus: An antispasmodic that can also help to relieve hives as well as sweeten breath. When used in spells it can attract love. It can also be used for dream work and divination.

- High John the Conqueror: You will use this herb to conquer any situation that you may be faced with such as finding lost items or seeking protection.

- Jasmine: Calms nervous tics and can be used for snakebites. In spells, it can attract money and love. It can also be used to charge crystals or for moon magic.

- Kava Kava: A very powerful aphrodisiac and can help you with astral travel and protection when you are traveling.

- Lavender: This is almost an all-purpose herb. it can be used for stomach problems and it can also help you to find inner peace. It can also be used to relieve stress, find love, money or attract good spirits and faeries.

- Lobelia: This is an antispasmodic and anticonvulsive herb. It can also help to soothe any withdrawal symptoms you may be facing. Note that this is a poisonous herb and should only be used in small doses.

- Mugwort: An appetite stimulant and a digestive aid. You can use it for strength in traveling as well as clairvoyance or to boost power in your scrying tools.

- Patchouli: This herb will reverse spells and can be used in sex magic, divination and will help you to manifest and draw in money.

- Pennyroyal: You can repel insects with this herb and it can also be used in consecration rituals and exorcisms. Note that you should use this herb only in small doses.

- Peppermint: Can help to soothe heartburn and can also calm motion sickness. It will also promote peaceful sleep and boosts psychic abilities.

- Plantain: A blood detoxifier and also a treatment for poison ivy and bee stings. The juice of the leaves can be used on bites and stings. You can also make it into a tea or chew on the leaves.

- Raspberry leaf: Improves kidney function. It also helps with diarrhea and colds. It can help to promote peaceful sleep and can be used in protection and love spells.

- Rosemary: This is a nerve stimulant and helps to aid in memory and soothes headaches. You can also use it for protection, purification and healing.

- Rose Hips: This is a nutritious herb that is high in vitamin C. It can also be used as a mild laxative. When casting spells you can use it for good luck or to summon good spirits.

- Sage: You can use this as an antiperspirant. When gargled it can heal sores in your mouth and on your gums. You can also use it in your spells for wisdom, protection, money, healing and longevity.

- Sandalwood: You can use this as a poultice for bruises and contusions. You can also use it to stimulate sexual urges, healing spells and purification work.

- Skullcap: This is a tranquilizer and even an anti-insomniatic. It can help to relieve anxiety while promoting a peaceful feeling.

- St. John's Wort: Immune system booster and headache relief as well as a way to ease menstrual cramps. You can use it for protection, courage and exorcisms.

- Tonka beans: Can be used for good luck and attract material desires. Note that you should only use this externally.

- <u>Valerian:</u> A sleep aid and helps to treat nervous conditions. This is also an herb that is used in love magic and black magic.

- <u>Vervain:</u> This can be used for minor pains and arthritis. You can also use it in spells for protection, consecration and creativity.

Keep in mind that there are a lot of herbs that can be poisonous when taken in certain amounts. This is why you have to be extremely cautious when handling these herbs. Always make sure to consult a physician or even a horticulturist before you ingest something that you are not 100% sure of.

Chapter 10: Herbal Magic

Since the plants on Earth have been developed for millions of years, even before humans came around, it is fair to say that herbs are some of the oldest tools you can use for magic. For millennia, we have known that herbs have beneficial properties both physically and spiritually. There are many different plants that have been incorporated into the spells that healers, shame, and other medicine men and women used in the old days which is where herbal magic originated.

In the days before medicine was separated from magic, physical healing was usually accompanied by a ritual and a prayer. This was to ensure that the patient was treated with an herbal decoction along with a smudging ritual and incantation to the spirits so they could experience a speedy recovery.

In today's society, the ritual of enjoying herbal tea can have spiritual and emotional effects along with nutritional benefits. Combining healing and magical properties can make herbs powerful tools for modern magic. In fact, there was a study that showed patient practices for herbal magic to be the most rewarding form that a witch can discover.

Elemental Power of Plants

When you look at magical symbols, plants embody the power of 4 different Wiccan elements that work together to create and sustain life. First, they start out as seeds in the Earth where the minerals they need to grow can be found. From there, they interact with "fire" or sunlight, which helps to convert carbon dioxide into oxygen which affects the quality of the air we breath.

Air helps to foster more plants through the form of wind, which helps to stimulate the growth of stems and leaves which also helps in scattering seeds so the cycle can continue. Last but not least, all plants have to have water to live which is why plants play a crucial role in regulating the water cycles by purifying water and then moving it from the soil back into the atmosphere.

There is no better illustration that can show you how the classic Wiccan elements (earth, water, fire, air) can come together than to examine the cycle of a plant.

Plant Intelligence

Aristotle believed that plants had psyches, which is a word typically used when describing the quality of a human soul. Most Wiccans today would agree with his beliefs. In fact, there are some scientists that have begun to realize that plants have a consciousness.

Plants are able to communicate and interact with each other and other species. In the forest, trees and other plants have the ability to exchange information through an underground network of roots and fungus. This way of communicating allows them to exchange nutrients and help any plant that may have a shortage of nutrients at any point during the growing season. In other words, they are borrowing eggs from their neighbor while giving it back later with interest.

Plants are equipped to warn each other about any predators that may be nearby. So, if a leaf is nibbled on by an insect, then a chemical is released that will repel the insect while alerting the other plants to release their own chemicals.

These discoveries all demonstrate how intelligent Mother Earth is. No matter what part of the plant you are working with, you can tap into this magical energy when you are incorporating herbs into your spells.

Versatile Magic

When it comes to connecting with the earth's energy, nothing is going to beat working in a garden you plant with your own hands. Growing and harvesting your own herbs can keep you in touch with the Earth's powers as well as the elements. It also keeps you in touch with the role that insects and other animals play in the plant cycle. On top of that, gardening allows you to charge these tools with your own energy.

Herbs are one of the most versatile tools when it comes to hands-on magic. You can use them to create your own crafts like dream pillows, spell jars, sachets and other charms. There are some people who enjoy making their own oils and incense with their herbs which helps to add more magical power to their work.

If you do not want to make your own crafts, then you can also do "kitchen craft." This is where you make magical teas, potions, baked goods and tinctures.

Herbs are able to be used in many spells along with candle and crystal magic. Smudging is the ritual of burning dried herbs in order to purify or bless a space. It is one of the ancient traditions that has survived throughout the ages and made it into contemporary witchcraft.

Whenever you look at rituals, there are some Wiccan practitioners that use special herbs to mark their circle before they begin a Sabbat ritual. There are others that use herbs to honor their patron deities such as lemon balm which is sacred to the Roman goddess Diana.

Herb magic is incredibly practical and can be done with ingredients that are already in your kitchen!

Getting Started using Herbal Magic

The amount of information that you have access to on herbal magic can be overwhelming when you are first starting out. Just keep in mind that you do not have to be a master gardener or a botany expert to practice herbal magic. To get acquainted with the magical properties of herbs, you should only use one or two at a time to better build up your relationship with the energies that can be found in the plant world.

Some of the most popular magical herbs can be seen in the spice section of your favorite grocery store.

Chapter 11: Herbal Magic Spells

As you saw in the previous chapter, herbal magic primarily focuses on using herbs for your spells. In this chapter, you will see several herbal spells that you can do. Remember to be cautious when you use herbs since some of them can be dangerous when used wrong.

A Charm to Open Up to Love

If you have ever wanted to do a spell to bring new love into your life, then this is the place to start. Most people have a desire to attract a solid relationship but find that they have a blocked flow of energy when it comes to bringing love into their life, and they don't even realize that they are blocking their energy.

This herbal magic spell will figure out what is blocking you so that you can resolve any issues that are lurking under the surface. Be careful because this process can end up being uncomfortable emotionally. Just remember that when you release these blocks, it is going to be worth it because you will be able to find a solid relationship.

Charmed herbal sachets are perfect for you to carry around or wear. It is recommended that you use a small drawstring bag that is made of cotton or silk which can be purchased at a craft store. If you do not want to purchase one, then you can always sew your own.

In the event that you cannot get a hold of each herb on the ingredients list, use a greater quantity of the herbs that you are able to get a hold of.

Note: This spell also uses candle magic.

What you need:

- A pink candle
- 6 cloves (whole)
- A small bowl
- 1 tsp of dried mugwort
- 1 tbsp rose petals
- 1 tsp lemon balm
- ¼ c chamomile flowers
- 1 tsp St. John's Wort

What to do:
Once you have gathered all of the ingredients that you need, place them on your altar. Light your candle and take a few deep breaths to still your mind.
Move your bowl in front of you and mix your mugwort, St. John's Wort, lemon balm and chamomile together with your fingers. Make sure that you are gentle while mixing the ingredients together. From there pour your mixture into your sachet. Sprinkle the cloves in followed by the rose petals and finally close the sachet.
Hold your sachet in your hand and close your eyes. You should imagine your entire body is suffused with a white light that starts at your heart and moves outward. As you hold onto this vision for a while, allow a pink light to shine from your heart as it mingles with the white light. While you do this, recite the following spell (or something similar) at least three times.
As below, so above,
I release every unseen block to allow love in.

As above, as below,
My heart is healed and allows love to flow.
You should allow the candle to burn out on its own. Now you will keep the charm near you as often as possible which includes keeping it by your bed at night. Whenever you feel that its energy has fulfilled its purpose, you will bury the charm or you can open it and sprinkle the herbs back into the Earth.

All-Purpose Charm

This charm can be completed on any number of spells. For instance, take any herb that suits your purpose and tie it into a bundle that can be carried with you. Before you do that, you should place them on your altar. Small pouches can also be sewn with dried herbs placed in them. If you are seeking extra power, use fabric and ribbon in colors that are related to the intent of your spell.

A few examples for protection bundles can be made of garlic and parsley. You can use garlic and rosemary for purification or rosemary and marjoram for love.

To bless your herbs, say your own version of the following chant:

Enchanted herbs both brown and green.
Herbs for magic and the power be.
Goddess bless everything that I do.
For the good of all, I will do no harm.
With herbal spice, this spell is done.

Spell to Remove Bad Vibes

Take your kitchen salt and pour about an inch into a bowl. The next thing that you will do is squirt lemon juice onto the surface while repeating this chant.
Lemon juice and white salt
By mixing thee, I shall feel no bad vibes.
Remove despair and negativity
Goddess please, so shall it be.

Prosperity Spells

In a bowl mix together a teaspoon of cinnamon, half a cup of sugar, and a teaspoon of allspice. Next, you will pour it into a glass jar and screw the lid on lightly. You will empower the mixture using this charm. While you speak the charm, visualize your wish.
Sugar and spice and everything nice.
A bit of magic and a pinch of charm.
May my intent turn out as I want.

Prosperity Tea

Herbal tea has the ability to give you a financial boost. This spell can help bring you prosperity. You will most likely have all of these herbs in your kitchen and you may also find that you need to add some honey to sweeten your tea. Do not worry because it is not going to affect how well the spell works.
What you need:

- A sprinkle of ground flax

- A pinch of cinnamon

- A sprinkle of nutmeg

- A pinch of ginger (minced and fresh)

Boil a cup of water and add in all your ingredients. Stir them into the hot water and allow it to steep for around 10 minutes. As it steeps, you should visualize that you need extra money and envision how much better your life will be with the extra money. While the tea steeps, you will repeat a chant similar to the one below.

One coin here and one coin there.

Prosperity everywhere.

I need some wealth,

to fix my financial health

but I only need my share.

After the 10 minutes has passed, strain out the bits of ginger and other herbs. You can add some honey to the tea as mentioned earlier. Make sure to drink the whole cup before it gets too cold.

Bless This Kitchen

This charm can help you to bless your kitchen to enhance your powers.

What you need:

- Rough twine or string

- A large sprig of rosemary (fresh)

- Orange rind

- Bay leaf (whole)

You will tie your bay leaf and orange rind to the base of the rosemary. Make sure that you wrap it around enough times that it is not going to come apart. Once you've done this, you will want to hang it up somewhere in your kitchen that it can purify your space while bringing in positive energy.

Chapter 12: Moon Magic

Moon magic refers to any ritual that is performed using lunar magic. It will establish a connection between where the moon is positioned and the magic ritual being performed.

As you most likely know, the moon revolves around the earth. As it makes its revolutions, there are times when the earth comes between the sun and moon which is when the sun appears to be brighter than normal, these are called "full moon days."

On the other hand, when the sun comes between the earth and the moon, these are called "dark moon days." It is between these two points of a full and dark moon day that the moon will wane and wax which is known as the phases of the moon.

The moon is considered to be one of the most significant heavenly bodies when it comes to the Wiccan practices. Depending on the phase of the moon will depend on what role it plays in your rituals. This is because the energy levels of the moon will vary based on which phase the moon is currently in. The amount of energy that is found in the moon will be vital when it comes to performing your rituals. According to the most general principles of magic, the wax moon will be the time for new beginnings while the waning moon is a time to reflect and to alleviate negativity.

Moon Phases

Waxing

A waxing crescent moon is when the left side of the moon is darker than the right. There may be times that the moon is tipped so you are not sure if it is right or left that is dark. During the waxing moon, you can perform drawing, increasing and growth spells.

The waxing crescent will rise right after sunrise and then set just after sunset, it is only able to be seen in the night sky for a short period of time once the sun goes down.

Every night that the moon rises in the east, you will be able to see that the thickness of a waxing crescent will get bigger until the shape appears to be a half circle. This will be known as the first quarter or a waxing half moon. The left side will be dark and the right will be bright. You can continue the increasing, growth and drawing spells.

The waxing first quarter moon comes out around noon and does not set until around midnight.

From there the moon will appear to look as if it is pregnant because it will be round on the right side and have some darkness on the left side. This is known as a waxing gibbous moon. You are still going to be able to continue to do growth spells, increasing or drawing spells.

Waxing gibbous moons rise in the afternoon and set just before sunrise.

Full Moon

It takes around 14 days for the moon to completely grow or wax. The light from the moon will be reserved for light works and any dedication that you have to benevolent lunar deities. You can also use the full moon for prayers for peace and celebrations.

The full moon rises at sunset and sets at sunrise.

Waning Moon

Once the moon has gone through its 14 days of waxing, the entire process will reverse causing the moon to decrease in its size. After 3 days of appearing to be full, the moon will start to go dark on the right side. This is known as a waning gibbous moon and it will look as if it is perfectly round on the left side and then bulged on the right. This will be the time that you should do repelling, waning, reversing or decreasing spells.

A waning gibbous moon will rise early in the evening and set after sunrise.

Each night the moon rises in the east later and the thickness of the waning gibbous will get smaller until it appears that the moon is half a circle. This is called the last quarter moon and some call it the third quarter moon or a waning half moon. It will be dark on the right side and brighter on the left. You will want to continue to do any spells that have to do with reversing, decreasing, waning or repelling.

A waning last quarter moon will rise about midnight and set at noon.

While the shape continues to get small as the nights move on, the moon will become a waning crescent which means that the right side will be bigger than the left. You will want to continue repelling, waning, reversal or decreasing spells. This is also one of the most powerful times for you to remove curses or send back any evil to those that sent it to you.

A waning crescent moon will rise between midnight and dawn but will slowly fade once the sun has risen.

New Moon

Once the moon completely vanishes, it is known as the dark side of the moon or a new moon. This moon phase is strictly reserved for dark works and dedications done to dark deities. On new moon nights, there will not be any moon to see because it rises at sunrise and sets at sunset.

Waxing Moon (Again)

After up to 4 days, you will begin to see a small piece of the moon reappear in the sky at sunset. There are some people who call this the first crescent moon while others call it a Siva moon because of the Hindu god Siva. This is the time for you to start attraction, growth, drawing and waxing spells once again.

The first crescent moon will rise just after sunrise and set just after sunset.

From there, the moon will grow to the man in the moon type of crescent moon where you can continue your growth, attraction, waxing and drawing spells. From there, the cycle will start over where we started out.

How to Tell What Phase the Moon is In

To tell if the moon is waning or waxing, go outside when the sun is setting and look for the moon. If you cannot see the moon, then go out later and check again. You can also check during the day.

If you see the moon in the sky during the evening, the moon is in its waxing phase. Each night it will rise a little earlier and appear to be more full. Once the full moon rises, it will be able to be seen right as the sun sets.

If you cannot see the moon when the night falls but can be seen later in the night, or if you can see it during the day, then the moon is in its waning phase. Each day it will appear in the sky a little later and appear to be a little thinner.

A new moon will rise right when the sun does which means you cannot see it at all, no matter how hard you look.

Moon Energy

For every month of the year, there is a single full moon. However, if there are two full moons a month then it will be known as a blue moon. Every year there is at least one blue moon. Every month's full moon has a different name.

January: The January full moon is known as the Wolf Moon. This will be the time to shed any unwanted energy and cleanse yourself. The old year should be released so that a new energy can flow through you as the new year begins. This is the perfect time to release yourself from the past so you can start anew.

February: The full moon in February is known as the Ice

Moon. This is the perfect time for you to do some soul searching or to take a journey examining yourself.

March: The March moon is called the Worm Moon and this is a time to start new beginnings and explore new territories.

April: This moon is called the Growing Moon. You will want to gather and grow this month. It is also the perfect time to start things that you have been putting off.

May: The Hare moon is a time to nourish yourself emotionally, mentally and physically. You will need to pay attention to your needs and the needs of those you love.

June: The Mead Moon is the integration for the yin and yang that is inside all of us. This is the perfect time for attunement and understanding.

July: The July moon is called the Hay Moon which is the time that you should take to look at your life and think about any plans involving the future and look at the things that you should pay closer attention to.

August: The Corn Moon is the time to let go of any old emotional pain that is weighing you down. You should release it during this time and move on while making sure that you are more open and flexible.

September: The Harvest Moon is the time for you to start tying up any loose ends and trim up stray edges. Make sure you pay attention to any things that you have left undone. Start to examine your future with a clean slate and a clear conscience.

October: The Blood Moon is the time for you to build or start something that will flow into your new way of being as you get rid of old habits you no longer need.

November: The Snow Moon is the time for you to examine the things that bother you and reassess what is actually working for you in your life. If it isn't working, then it is time to get rid of it and find a new way to make your life go in the direction you want it to go.

December: The Cold moon is a time for you to cut away anything that you do not need in your life. Think of it as pruning a plant so that it can grow new shoots. You are not going to move forward if you have things that are weighing you down.

Chapter 13: Moon Magic Spells

You've learned that the moon has magical properties depending on what phase of the moon you are currently experiencing. In this chapter, you will learn about several different spells you can use by harnessing the power of the moon. Remember, some of these spells will require a specific phase of the moon in order to work.

Full Moon Money Spell

This is an extremely simple way for you to attract money. Ensure that you pass on some of the good fortune so that the flow of the universe is not interrupted.
What you need:

- Patchouli or Sandalwood oil (optional but is recommended)

- Green Candle

On the candle, you will need to write the names of each person that is taking place in the spell. If you want to anoint the candle with the oil that you chose, as you do this, recite a version of the following chant.
Now is the time that we weave our wills.
As the Gods and Goddesses reach down and lend us their strength,
we take it and place it to use.
We cast our energies out into the universe in order to create
our destinies as we wish them to be.

Now, you will light your candle and focus on the energies that are being sent into it so that they can be transformed and released through the smoke. The flames will be the power you need to do your bidding while you recite a version of this chant.

Full moon bright and full moon's light,
please grant me my wish this night.
Bring wealth into my life to stay,
so all my problems may melt away.
Allow money to come to me now
With harm to none,
so mote it be.

You will need to allow the candle to burn out on its own.

Moon Money Spell

This simple chant will help bring money into your life.
What you need:

- Paper money

This spell can be done from a full moon or new moon, you will need to go outside and identify the phase of the moon. Once you've done this, you will stand outside and place a dollar in each palm and repeat the following three times:

Moon moon, beautiful moon.
Fairer than any other star by far.
Moon moon, if it so be,
bring both money and wealth to me.
So mote it be.

Once you've done this, you may begin to notice that there is a change in your finances.

Moon Power

You can perform this spell outside or inside. You will be representing the moon with a piece of paper or a flower. In this incantation, the moon will be represented as a white swan. You should do this at a full moon to harness the energy of the moon.

What you need:
- Paper Moon (white) or flower (white)

- Bowl of water

Place your paper moon or flower into the bowl so that it is floating. Raise the bowl up towards the moon and repeat the following.

Hail to the white swan on the river. The present life, turner of the tide. Moving across the streams of life, all hail. Mother of new and old. To you, through you, this night I cling to the aura you present. Pure reflection, total in belief, touched by your mere presence. I am in awe of your power and the wisdom you hold. Praise to your power, the peace you give, my peace and my own power. I am strong. I praise. I bless.

Place the bowl on your altar and stand in silence, appreciating the power that the moon holds. This spell is an incantation to the moon which is why it is very simple. There are no other tools or skills needed except for the moon to be present. The water is a sacred tool to the moon which is why you offer it up to her because it belongs to her.

Snow Moon Spell

This is a simple spell that is going to awaken your new purpose in life.

What you need:
- A full moon in February (AKA Snow Moon)

- Violet candle

The full moon in February during Colonial American was called the Ice Moon because this was typically a time of fierce blizzards. Some people would call this moon the Quickening Moon because this was the time that nature started to reawaken. Despite the fact that the snow crocus would bloom, most of the land was still covered in snow.

During the Ice Moon, you will ask the Ice Moon to help you when it comes to making more positive changes in your life. Just like nature will awaken after winter has passed, you will also be able to awaken with a new calling.

When the Ice Moon is in the sky, you will need to declare your magical intentions to it. You will need to take your violet candle, which is your token of thanks, and light it as you begin to speak to the Ice Moon.

As the earth is covered in a sheet of white,
in icy splendor, you guard the night.
Allow me to make the changes, and let me be reborn.
As I plant this seed of magic, I will be transformed.
Allow your candle to burn out on its own.

Blood Moon Lunar Eclipse

This spell is going to call upon the Triple Goddess in order to grant you a wish or provide you with the power you need. This spell can only be done during a blood moon eclipse.

What you need:

- A calm mind (you should meditate before)

- Yourself

You should meditate as you take a ritual bath. As the bath water drains, you should invision all of the negativity from your day being washed down the drain. Once you're done, you should go outside a few moments before the eclipse and locate a place where you can see the moon clearly. After the moon is fully eclipsed, you should say:

I summon the Triple Goddess by all of her names, faces and forms. The Maiden, the Crown, and The Mother I summon and ask you to grant me a wish. I wish (insert your wish here and make sure that you are explicit). I thank you dear Triple Goddess. As I will, so mote it be.

Make sure to be careful about what you wish for.

Moon Water

What you need:
- Full moon

- Water

- Container to hold water

After the sun sets and the moon rises, take the container that you have chosen and fill it with water from a natural source. You can also use bottled spring water if you do not have any safe natural water sources close by.

Place the open container full of water outside and allow the moon's light to shine on it. Ask the Goddess to bless the water. The container should be left there as long as the moon is up. Once you're done, you will want to carefully close the container and keep it for any spells that require water. This can be done every full moon so you have a supply of freshly blessed water.

Full Moon Wishing Spell

This spell is good to use when you want to make sure that your wish will come true.

What you need:
- A glass of juice or wine

Under a full moon, you will need to go outside with your glass of juice or wine. Stare at the moon and tell her what it is that you wish for, you should visualize your wish coming true while you do. You need to be as specific about your wish and give as many details as humanly possible.

Whenever you have completed your wish, you will toast the moon goddess and repeat this chant:

Lunar goddess, look at me
This is the goblet that I offer to you
It is yours for everything that you do
Gracious one in silver hues.

After you're done, you will need to pour out your cup into the soil believing that your wish will be granted.

Moon Wishes

This spell will use candles as well as meditation. You can do this at both new and full moons so you can harness the moon's energy. By meditating before you go to bed, you will open yourself up to allowing your higher self to influence you.

What you need:

- A colored candle that represents your wish (it is recommended that it is in the color of your astrological sign)

- 5 white candles

Before you do this spell, you need to make sure your mind is free of clutter. It is also highly recommended that you meditate to ensure that you have clarified your wishes.

Next, place the white candles in the shape of a pentagram in a spot where they will burn safely. If you do not want to do that, you can light them according to the connecting lines found on the pentagram starting at the top.

While you do this, say the following incantation:

Moon above that glows so bright
guard my sleep so it may be deep this night
I pray to you with this one request

my life works out at my command.
You should allow the candles to burn for around half an hour before blowing them out and allowing yourself to go to sleep. When you wake up the next morning, light another candle and meditate while you think about what you wish for, this should take around 30 minutes. You need to spend some time visualizing what life is going to be like once your wish has been granted. This process should be repeated for 3 nights.

On the 4th morning, relight all of the candles and allow them to burn out as you listen to music that means something to you. In the last hour while the candles continue to burn, you will need to reconsider your wish and make any realistic adjustments necessary.

Full Moon Love Spell

This is a basic homemade spell that will increase your chances with the person of your choosing. You have to do this spell under a full moon.

What you need:

- Invoke the deity of your choice

- Meditation

- Pen

- Full moon

- Intent

- Casting circle

- Visualization

- Calling on the elements

- Paper

- Basil and cinnamon

- Stones (to increase your spell)

- Candle (pink)

You will need to focus your intent on what it is that you want. Why do you want the spell to be done? Make sure you cast your circle and call upon the elements while invoking your chosen deity that corresponds with romance or love.

Make sure to meditate with energy to charge your candle with that energy. At this point in time you should have cast your circle and called on the elements along with invoking your deity. Here is when you will anoint your candle with the herbs that you've gathered.

Light your candle and write your name and then the targets name on top of yours. Visualize that the flame holds your completed goal so that you can get with the person you want to be with. You should make a crystal grid around your candle to increase the energy flowing around you.

Once you've done this, repeat this chant:

It is on this blessed night
that I ask the goddess (the name of your goddess)
to unite these two souls in order to allow them to find
happiness
and romance.
May this romance warm the hearts of the couple and others with
the power that is inside these herbs and stones.
So mote it be.

Make sure that you thank your deity and leave an offering for them.

Chapter 14: Easy Spells for Beginners

Things to Consider Before Beginning

There are some things that you're going to want to consider before you even begin to do spells. Even without intending to, you can end up harming yourself or someone else because of the emotion that you have while practicing. It is important to remember that you need to be careful with each spell as well because each spell will have its negative effects if you do not do it properly.

Remember, do not cast any binding spells without being willing to accept the karma that will come your way. Do not cast any spells that will harm anyone without being willing to accept the karma. And do not cast any personal gain spells, rather cast spells that will give you the means to achieve what you're wanting to gain.

There are three questions you might want to consider before you begin any spell:

1. Have you tried everything to resolve the situation without using a spell or magic?

2. Is this spell going to harm someone else or bend someone's will to what you're wanting?

3. Are you prepared for anything that may come from doing this spell?

Beginner Love Spell

Everyone wants love, and it depends on what kind of love you are trying to attract that will determine how you're going to cast this spell. For this, we're just going to go over the simplest spell that we can find that any beginner should be able to do. What you need:

- Pen

- A pink candle

- White paper

The best time to do this is on a Friday night. **So,** when Friday night comes around, light your pink candle.

Using your favorite pen or favorite color, write your name and your lovers last name on the piece of paper. Next, draw a circle around the names and close your eyes in meditation so you can focus on the two of you together.

Next you're going to repeat these words three times:

Our fate is sealed, we are one. So mote it be. It is done!

Next you're going to watch your pink candle for about fifteen minutes all the while meditating on the person that you're wanting. If you can, you should meditate until your candle goes out.

If you use a larger candle than a tea candle, you can do the spell every night for seven nights making sure to meditate for fifteen minutes every night when you do the spell.

Beginner Prosperity/Money Spell

Money, who doesn't want it? We all do. In this section we will go over a basic money spell that you can try to see if you can raise your level of prosperity. What you need:

- Athame or wand

- Dish of salt or earth

- Basil

- Chamomile

- Sage

- Cup of water

- Caldron and burning coals

The best time to do this spell is on a Sunday or Thursday during a waxing moon.

Cast your circle. Invite the lord or lady to your circle. Cast the herbs onto the burning charcoal while visualizing your goal. Next, sprinkle a few drops of water and salt upon the charcoals. While moving your wand or athame over your cauldron in a clockwise motion, use these words:

By the powers of air, fire, water, and earth. I
release this spell. I ask for Divine guidance as I seek
help this day. With harm to none, this spell be done.

Spend several moments in meditation as you imagine the smoke carrying the energy out of the circle and into the universe.

Thank your lord and lady for the assistance, release the circle and ground and center yourself.

Beginner Health Spell

Health is important to everyone. And just like everything else, there is a spell that can help you with your health. It is important that you are not using this spell to harm someone else's health because then you're going to have to deal with the law of threefold.

This spell is meant to help you with your own health.

There are multiple health spells that you can use, but this one is to alleviate headaches.

What you need:
- Glass of full moon water

- Clear quartz crystal

- Lavender scented candle

- One teaspoon lavender flowers

First you're going to want to dim the lights while taking a few moments to center yourself.

Boil a cup of full moon water until it reaches a full boil, drop in your lavender flowers and inhale the steam and aroma while saying :

Purple flowers heal my head; I will not take to my
bed. The pain will flee oh rising steam take the pain
with thee.

Then you're going to strain the liquid and sit while sipping the tea. Allow the warmth of the liquid to seep into our body while calming your headache.

When you are down to one sip, you're going to put the crystal over what is left and say:

Crystal bright, bring your shining light. Take this
pain to keep me sane. Right now I feel no mirth.
Your power is from the earth. Send this pain away
and make my day.

Now remove your crystal and place it over your third eye. Lie down a few moments and let the crystal absorb the pain.

Take the crystal to the sink and wash it under running water while watching your pain go down the drain.

Chapter 15: Protection Spells

Everyone wants to be safe, and with a protection spell, you are going to get the safety you are seeking. However, this is not the kind of protection that is going to stop intruders from coming in your front door if you leave it unlocked all the time. Make sure you are using some common sense in working your spell.

Sprinkling of Protection

What you need:
- Garlic powder (about a teaspoon)

- Salt (a handful)

First thing you do is mix the garlic and salt together (using garlic salt is not going to have the same effect so it should not be used). Next, you will take the mixture and put it around each threshold in your house. Make sure to get the windowsills as well. In doing this, you are going to be keeping all the negative energy out of the house.

Bury and Banish

Sometimes people come into our lives that we just need to get rid of. There is a spell that can help with that.
What you need:
- A black piece of paper (construction paper will work so you do not have to spend too much money)

Write down the name of the person on the paper. You do not have to be able to read it. Fold up the paper into the smallest square that you can get it into. Bury the paper in the ground somewhere outside. After you have it covered up, repeat this spell:

Into the ground
You cannot be found
You are not around
I cannot hear your sound.
Finally, step over the burial place of the paper. You should be able to see the person that you want to be rid of leave your life. After this spell, watch the person slowly fade out of your life.

Watch Your Step

This spell is meant to keep harm away from you as well as negative energy. This is a spell that will ensure that negative energy cannot cross the threshold of your home.

What you need:

- 1 garlic clove

- 3 pieces of broken glass

- 1 rusted nail or screw

Step outside your front door and dig a hole, it needs to be about six inches deep. Place all the items in the hole making sure that the garlic goes in last. Cover it up and stand on the small pile. Say this spell:

At this point,
all negativity in my life stops.

Do not remove the items from the hole as they are going to keep any negative influences away from your home.

Shield Spell

There is negative energy out there everywhere, and it is hard to avoid. But, you can shield yourself from it so that you no longer need to attract so much and carry it around with you.

What you need:

- A white candle

Cast your circle as you always should before you start a spell. Call upon your guides. Staring into the flame, visualize this flame wrapping around you and creating a shield from the negative energy that is floating around in the world. Say this incantation as you continue to stare at the fire:

Craft the spell in the fire.

Weave it well, weave it higher.

Weave it now of shining flame.

None shall come to hurt or maim.

None shall pass this fiery wall.

None shall pass, no! None at all!

Protecting Your Loved Ones

Your loved ones are those that you hold dear to your heart. They do not necessarily have to be family, they can be friends or anyone else that you want to protect. To make sure that no harm comes to those that you love, you can use this spell to put a barrier of protection around them and shield them from negativity and people that may be out to harm them.

What you need:

- A picture of your loved ones

- Candle (white)

- Protection incense

Light your candle and allow it to smoke. Placing the picture or pictures of your loved ones on your altar, put your white candle on top of them. Light the candle. Meditate and visualize a white light surrounding your loved ones with protection while reciting this spell.

O Goddess, shield my loved ones every day,

As they rest and as they play. Assist them to

Always smile bright, and keep them safe in

Your warm light. Protect them from evil

And from all they dread, for they are the ones

That I hold dear. I thank the Goddess for

Helping me. I trust in her aid, so mote it be.

Allow the candle to burn out on its own and go about as if your spell has already come to manifest in the physical world.

Chapter 16: Beauty Spells

We all want to be prettier, skinnier or whatever our goal is to feel better about ourselves. It can be hard to be happy with who we are because of the media and other outlets constantly telling us that we are not good enough. Magic is not going to make you supermodel beautiful overnight, but it can give you the boost you need to achieve your goal.

Melting Weight Loss Spell

There are not many individuals out there that can say they are happy with how much they weigh. If you are not happy with it, then you are going to want to change it. While the spell is not going to be the only thing that you can do, you are going to get some assistance from it to lose those stubborn pounds.
What you need:

- A brown candle

With a sharp object, carve how much you currently weigh at the top of your candle. At the bottom, you are going to carve what your goal weight is. Whenever you get ready to go to bed, light the candle. Allow the candle to burn for about fifteen minutes. As the candle whittles down because of the lightings, the closer to your goal you will get.

Grow Hair

Is your hair too short or you just want it longer? Without having to gather anything, you can say a spell that is going to help your hair to grow longer. Say the following three times a day:
My hair shall grow like weeds,
My energy will be like little seeds.

It will grow longer,
It will grow faster,
To my tailbone, it shall be.
This is my will,
So mote it be!

Weight Loss

What you need:

- A blue topaz stone

Charge your stone during a waning moon with this incantation:
Help me in my diet quest,
Bring me new strength and zest.
Take these extra pounds from me.
As I will, so mote it be.
Carry the stone with you and watch your weight drop.

Sleep Spell

Getting enough sleep is important to making you feel good inside and out. If you discover that you are having trouble sleeping, you can say this spell before you go to sleep so that you feel more relaxed and your sleep comes to you more easily.
Goddess above, queen of the night, help me sleep in
your healing light. Restful sleep come to me, relax
my body and let my mind be free. Grant me calm
and peace tonight and let me wake in the gods'
golden light.

Cleansing Bath

With a cleansing bath, you can wash away all the negativity that is attached to you and make yourself feel like a new person.

What you need:

- Lime (fresh)

- Candle (white)

- Rosemary

- Sea salt

Run yourself a warm bath. Add the sea salt into the water so that it has a chance to dissolve a little. Light your candle and place it next to the tub. Any artificial lights should be turned off.

Sit in the tub and try to relax, allowing all of your troubles to melt into the bath. As you relax, focus on the flame and think about yourself being renewed as you soak in the bath.

How long you stay in the bath is going to be a personal preference, you can soak in it as long as you want.

Before you can get out, you will need to knock the candle into the tub so that the flame goes out.

Refrain from using a towel to dry off, instead allow yourself to air dry, so you may want to stay in the bathroom if you have other people living in your home. It is wise to let others know that you are going to be taking time to spend in the bathroom if you only have one bathroom in the house. You are not going to want to be disturbed while you perform this spell.

Take your rosemary and the lime wedge rubbing them over your skin. Finally, drain the bath and visualize any impurities and troubles going down the drain with the water.

Chapter 17: Trouble Spells

Troubles tend to dominate our lives and when they do, we often tend to be forgetful and things in our lives tend to go downhill and then more troubles start. However, with some simple spells, we can at least get these troubles out of our mind so that we can continue with our lives and keep things going as they are supposed to.

Knot Your Troubles

It does not matter what trouble you are having, all you have to do is find the color that is best suited to what you are going through. You can look at the color chart that is located in the first chapter.
What you need:

- Yarn in the proper color (12 inches)

Hold the yarn taunt while you meditate on your problem. As you think about your problem, begin to tie knots in the string. Think of your problem being tied in knots as your fingers tie the knots.
Tie as many knots as you want or until you feel that you have tied enough. Bury the knotted rope once you are done to keep your problems away. Make sure you use a single color of string. One color per problem.

Clearing Up an Argument

Whenever you get into an argument with a friend or loved one, you may feel like there is something that is blocking you from making up with them. With this spell, you are going to be able to clear the air and move past it.
What you need:

- Candle (yellow)

- Paper envelope

- 1 bay leaf

Enscribe your name on one side of the envelope. Use the other side to write the name of the person you are fighting with. Put the bay leaf in the envelope and seal it shut. Light the candle as you hold the envelope over the flame, allowing it to burn. Ensure that you have a bowl of water to drop the paper into so that you do not burn your fingers.

Removing Anger

You are not going to have to set anything up for a ritual and you can teach this to other people because you do not need anything special.
What you need:

- A stone

Place the stone in your hand and visualize the anger that you are feeling moving through you and into the stone.
At that point in time, you will feel like all your anger is now sitting inside of the stone. Throw the stone away from you. It is best if you throw it into a body of water to ensure that the stone can become cleansed.
Repeat the following spell to ensure your anger has been removed:
Great guardians of the west
Who watch over the sea and ocean,
Let this anger disperse through space and time,
Make it disappear forever.
So mote it be.

Ending Heartbreak

Heartbreak is difficult to get over, especially when you really loved the person. But, if you cannot get over the heartbreak, you are going to be stuck in a place that is not good for your mental health. Therefore, you have to protect yourself and end the heartbreak so that you can move on with your life.

What you need:
- Cauldron

- Candles (one for every element)

- White sage (ground up)

- Rose incense

Cast your circle. Place your candles where they belong around the circle as they would appear on the pentacle. Light all your candles going around the circle. Now you can light your incense. Lastly, take the sage and burn it in the cauldron. Say the following incantation:

My fault it be not,
Forever he/she forgets me not,
He/she blames me for their inner strife
Left me heart broken with doubts of life.
My strength returned
His/her dominance slipped.
I will be my own person,
Strong, cleansed, and pure.
With harm to none
This spell be done.
This is my will
So mote it be.

Spirit Vanishing Spell

If there is an entity in your house that you no longer want there, you are going to have to banish it so that it knows that it is not wanted there.

While you have probably seen the television shows that depict a big elaborate process in getting rid of a spirit, it is nothing more than a show. You do not need anything but your voice to get rid of the spirit so that you can take charge of your house once more. There is no need for you to live your life in fear or with a spirit that you are not wanting in your life.

Stand in the middle of the chamber and speak these words three times in a row with conviction.

Evil spirit standing tall, it is time for you made your greatest fall.

Return to hell thou evil plight; I banish with this holy light!

Now go away and leave my sight and take with you this endless   night!

Chapter 18: Luck Spells

Luck, we all need it, and it is something that is hard to come by. If we can get ourselves a little bit of luck, why do we not do it? This chapter is where you are going to find all of your luck spells.

Simple Wiccan Luck Spell

At times where you find one bad thing happening after another, you can use this spell in order to turn your luck around.

What you need:

- Oil (cooking oil, herbal essence oil, or frankincense)

- Black candle

Take a drop of oil on the tip of your finger and wipe it across the candle. You are going to move your finger up and down three times while saying this incantation.
Black candle, turn my luck around. Bring prosperity and joy abound.
Give your thanks and light your candle. Moving your hand to your heart chakra, you are going to say a new chant.
Flame and fire, candle burn. Work to make my luck return.
Be sure to meditate on you having good fortune and being happy while the bad luck is lifted off your shoulders and banished. Should you decide to keep the candle, you are going to need to make sure that you do not use it for any spell that is not a luck spell. This is because it is charged with a particular energy that should not be transferred off to other spells.

Reversal Spell

In using this spell, you are going to be reversing any bad luck that may be placed on you.
What you need:

- Spoon

- Your circle

- Bowl

- A white candle

- Rosemary

- Basil

- Pepper

- Cinnamon

- Mustard

- Garlic

Mix all the spices you gathered together in your bowl. Light your candle. Think of the bad luck spell that may be placed on you to make it vanish off of you. Light the spices on fire. Once they begin to smell, toss them away. Blow your candle out and ground any extra energy you may have. You are now free to close your circle.

Luck for a Day

Need just a little bit of additional luck for the big meeting that you are having or the exam that is coming up? This is a good spell for you.

What you need:

- Chamomile tea

- Belief

- Cabbage leaf

- Clover leaf

- Alfalfa leaf

If getting alfalfa is difficult for you, you can still do the spell. Ground up the leaves well. After they are ground up (you may want to make sure there are no big chunks left) sprinkle a little bit into tea.

You will say this incantation over the tea:

Fortuna, Tyche, Goddess of luck. Award me your guiding hand for one day, so I may succeed. You are a glory, the maker of luck. Support me, though I do not deserve to be in your proximity. So mote it be.

Once you have finished your spell, drink your tea and ensure you drink all of it. Also, make sure that you say thanks to the Goddess even if you do not feel as if you are having good luck that day.

Easy Luck Spell

What you need:

- Your voice

Say the following chant:

The winds of change I feel tonight,

The waters are calm, and the sky is bright,

Luck be mine, come into me,

My desires are true, so mote it be.

Luck powder

What you need:
- Calamus (1 part)

- Vetivert (2 parts)

- Nutmeg (1 part)

- Allspice (2 parts)

Mix all your herbs together. Next, sprinkle the powder around your home or around your desk at work.

Triple Gemstone Luck Spell

This spell should be done whenever the moon is waxing.
What you need:
- Frankincense incense stick

- Small wooden box that has a lid

- Green candle (1)

- Gemstones (3)

- Pen (green)

- Piece of paper

Cast your circle while you prepare your altar for the spell. Get all other thoughts out of your mind so you can focus on the task at hand. Putting both hands on the box, say the following:
By the powers of the earth,
By the powers of the air,
By the powers of the fire,
By the powers of the water,
I empower this spell box
This will assist me in my spells.

So mote it be.

Light your green candle and then your incense. Now with your paper, write down a paragraph about something good that has happened in your life. Relive that memory in your head and allow the joy that you felt at the time to flood through your body.

With each of your gemstones in hand, you are going to repeat this incantation:

Powers and energies

Send good luck my way.

Now put each gemstone into your box. Blow your candle out. Over the course of seven days, you are going to repeat the steps listed above. After seven days, you will open your box for an hour to release the energy that has become trapped inside. When you want to attract good luck, carry the stones with you.

Chapter 19: Spells for Dreams and Wishes

Dreams and wishes are part of everyday life. There are some dreams and wishes for which we just need that bit of an extra push to make it come true or to where we can make our dream or wish a bit more clear so we know exactly what we want.

Wish Spell

It is best that you do this spell before you go to bed.

What you need:

- Pen

- Candle

- Piece of paper

The color of your candle needs to match what you wish for. The candle needs to be a candle that has never been used before. Make sure your wish is clear. After you have worked all the details out in your wish, write it down on a piece of paper. Place your candle on top of the paper where your wish is located.

Clear your mind so you are not sending mixed signals into the universe. Lighting the candle, you need to only be thinking of your wish and   how it is going to look when it comes true. Allow for the realization of that wish to permeate all of your senses as if it has already come true.

Take about ten minutes to visualize this before taking that same piece of paper from under the candle and burning it.

Repeat the following:

Candle shining in the night
With your flame enchanted,

By the powers of magic might
May my wish be granted.
When the candle sheds its gleam
At the mystic hour,
Let fulfillment of my dream
Gather secret power.
Flame of magic, brightly burn,
Spirit of the fire.
Let the wheel of fortune turn,
Grant me my desire,
One, two, three – so mote it be!

A Simple Wishing Spell with Incense

If you are in a hurry, then this is a good wishing spell for you. You are going to want to do it when the moon is either waxing or full.
What you need:

- -a stick of incense of your choice

- An incense burner

Your mind should go into a state of meditation as you light a stick of incense. Moving your focus to your heart, you should feel as if you are being filled with joy. Here is where you will begin to imagine what you are wishing for to come true.

You want to imagine as much detail as possible to avoid mixed signals. You should also think of it as if it has already happened. Focus on how you are going to feel once the wish has come to pass.

Once you have gotten yourself into a spot where you can actually believe that your wish has come true, say the following chant ten times:

Magic herbs burn in fire,

Bring me my heart's desire.

Dream Spell

This spell will best be used when you are trying to enchant your dreams. You may also find this spell allows you to dream walk, but that is no guarantee. There are no special objects that are required to do this spell. Repeat this incantation:

Lady of the night,

Bless my soul with your light.

Queen of the moon,

Let your magic fill my room.

Silver dust of the bright stars,

Heal my wounds, erase my scars,

Let me wander into your realm free,

Nurture my body like a healthy tree.

Career Spell

Your job is a major aspect of your life and if you are not doing what you love, why are you doing it? Use this spell to be able to find the perfect job for you or to get your foot in the door towards getting the job of your dreams.

What you need

- A candle (green)

- Pin

Carve the title or type of job that you are seeking. Light the candle and say the following spell:

To do for me this deed

Bring to me this job I need

Your candle needs to burn out on its own, so ensure it is in a safe place where it cannot be knocked over.

Chapter 20: Spells for Health and Wellness

Our health is very important. If we are not healthy, then we are not going to be able to keep going with our lives which is not ideal. There are times a bit of help is needed when it comes to making sure we stay healthy.

Simple Health Blessing

Everything that is used in this spell is not supposed to be used as a medical cure. They are simply objects that symbolize health and vitality.

What you need:

- Candle (white)

- Glass of apple juice (organic if possible)

- Cinnamon stick

Put your juice in your glass, stir it around four times with the cinnamon stick. Set fire to the candle. Drink a little bit of the juice. Say the following incantation:

Goddess bless body and soul
Health and wellness is my goal
Drink the rest of the juice and then blow your candle out.
At any time that you feel like you may be getting sick, you can do this spell. Or, if you want to ward off any illness before it comes on, drink it every morning.

Happiness Candle Spell

Your mental status is just as important as your physical health. If you are not content, then you are not going to do the things you want to do. This spell is going to assist in bringing some joy to your life.
What you need:

- Dried lavender

- Candles (Orange, 2)

Taking the lavender, place it on your altar between your candles. Light your candles, hold your hands up   to   feel the warmth of the flame. Say this incantation seven times in a row.

This spell, please bless

For my happiness

Allow the candles to burn down on their own. Feel happiness spreading through your body as the flame that had just been burning.

Confidence Candle

How you view yourself is a big part of how you live your life. With this spell, you are going to gain a little insight on how to love yourself.
What you need:
- Pure water

- Pink candle

- Rose petals (red and white)

- Rainwater is ideal for this spell but if that is not something that you feel comfortable doing you should buy a bottle of spring water. Try and avoid using tap water unless you absolutely have to.

On your altar, take the flower petals and make a ring around your candle. Before lighting the candle, think of a few of your best qualities and meditate on those. Now that you have those thoughts in mind, you can light your candle and say the following spell:

May my own light shine
With love divine.

After you have said your spell, you are going to drink the water to rid yourself of any negative thoughts that you have in your head. Allow the candle to burn out on its own.

Healing Candle Spell

What you need:
- Light blue candles (3)

- Pin

Carve your name or the name of the person you are casting the spell for into the candles. Place the candles in their holders on your altar. Light your candles and then say this incantation:

Healing light

Shine tonight

The power I feel

Be used to heal

Meditate on the condition that needs to be healed. The candles should be allowed to burn out on their own.

Simple Motivation Incantation

As mentioned in a previous spell, your mental health is just as important to your well-being as your physical health. This is a spell that does not require you to gather any objects together, all you are going to need to do is say the following incantation to improve your motivation so that you can get things done.

Speak these words whenever you feel like your motivation is lacking and you need to get a task done:

May these words bring me comfort

And rekindle my interest in this moment,

I invoke the higher power.

Among the hindrances these hours

To rouse the motivation in my heart.

As visions of great return,

And the spark of positivity is lit,

And the strength rises within me.

It is my wish; please guide my steps

During this moment.

May this incantation

Push me forward,

So mote it be.

A Spell to Increase Patience

It is easy to find yourself being impatient throughout the day, but being impatient does not do you any good as you have most likely found out. So, why not bring a little more patience into your life so things go smoother throughout the day whenever it comes to dealing with other people, whether they be at home or work.

What you need:

- Essential oil (palmarosa, lavender, jasmine)

- A cup of water

- A candle (blue)

Be sure to cast your circle before you light your candle. Focus on the flame as you take in around ten deep breaths so you can steady yourself. Each time that you breathe in think about inhaling the peaceful blue of the candle. Every time that you exhale think of all your frustrations and impatience being lifted out of your body and taken away from you.

Once you have finished your breathing, you will move on to the cup of water. Three drops of the oil that you have chosen should be dropped into the water. After you have done this, you will place your fingertips in the water and stir it while saying:

Blessed waters cool my spirit,

Fill me with your soothing peace.

Like the river, I shall flow

Patiently, with joy and ease.

At this point, you can close your circle and blow out your candle. Be sure to keep the cup of water on your altar so when you begin to feel impatient, you can inhale the water and redo your spell.

Spell to Restore Health and Vigor

After you say this chant, you should begin to feel refreshed. What you need:

- Your voice

Say this chant or something similar to it:

Sky above me stars so bright

Hear my plea upon this night,

Restore health and vigor in me,

The spell is done, so mote it be!

Health Spell

Everyone wants to be healthy and have their loved ones healthy. But, you cannot ask for health in a spell, you need to ask for the tools that are required in making sure you can stay healthy or become healthy. No one's health should be placed in jeopardy when this spell is done lest it comes back to you threefold.

What you need:

- Teaspoon of lavender flowers

- Glass of moon water (full moon)

- Lavender scented candle

- Quartz crystal (clear)

Dim the lights and center yourself. Boil the moon water, do not do anything with it until it is at a full boil. Drop in the flowers. As you breathe in the steam and scent, you need to repeat this saying:

Purple flowers heal my head; I will not take to my bed. The pain will flee oh rising steam, take the pain with thee.

After saying this, strain the liquid into a cup and sit down to sip the tea. Let the warmth of the tea overcome your boy as your headache becomes calmed. After one sip, you will place the crystal over the remaining liquid and repeat the rest of the spell:

Crystal bright, bring your shining light. Take this pain to keep me sane. Right now I feel no mirth. Your power is from the earth. Send this pain away and make my day.

Place the crystal over your third eye. Lay down and allow the crystal to take away the pain. Now wash it in the sink under running water as you imagine your pain going down the drain.

Depression Banishment

In modern times, it is hard to find someone that does not

suffer from some sort of depression. You do not want to allow depression to take over your life and a good way to do this is to use this spell while you focus on the good that is in your life. It is hard to do this sometimes, but keep trying. You are strong!

What you need:

- 2 candles (pink and yellow)

Light your candles and repeat the following words:

Blessed Goddess of love and light

Please come help me on this night.

My heart is heavy, and my feelings are blue,

My soul is sad I do not know what to do...

Help me banish the pain I feel,

This lackluster feeling has no appeal.

Help me see the love begin and

Feel my heart be light again,

Let me climb up from this hole,

And be with you heart, body and soul.

I ask thee Goddess on this night, please

Help me make myself alright!

So mote it be!

Chapter 21: Money Spells

Money is hard to get and even harder to keep. We all need it to survive, and some need it more than others depending on their situation. However, we all need it, and there never seems to be enough to go around. With these few simple spells, you can hopefully get some of that green that you need.

Pagan Money Attraction Spell

What you need:

- Silk or cord colored green or gold (13 inches)
- Green candle (1)

Tie a knot in the cord you have while saying this spell:

With knot one, this spell has started.

With knot two, plenty of tasks to do.

With knot three, wealth comes to me.

With knot four, opportunity is tapping on my door.

With knot five, I am and will succeed.

With knot six, financial problems will be fixed.

With knot seven, success will follow.

With knot eight, increase is great.

With knot nine, all of this is mine.

The best time to do this spell is either during a full moon or a waxing moon as you are trying to increase your financial holdings.

Money Wish Spell

This spell is best done on a Thursday, Friday or Sunday of a full moon or a waxing moon.

What you need:

- Visualization skills that are honed in and powerful
- A special coin or something you consider a good luck charm

Visualize yourself with the amount of money you need. Be sure to visualize yourself receiving this money. The more you visualize, the more charge your coin is going to have.

As you clutch the coin in your hand, say this chant or something similar to it:

Silver and gold, return unto me

By the witchy powers of three hundred times three

The money I require is mine to keep

Make your way to me, immediately.

Keep this coin with you and forget about the spell.

You can give thanks to the Goddess or the universe at the end of your spell if you want to. It is a personal option. However, it is highly recommended that you give thanks to your goddess so that she knows that she is appreciated for helping you.

Everything Under the Moon Money Spell

This money spell should be done under a full moon on a Thursday if possible.

Before you do this spell, meditate and try and forget about your money problems or else you are going to end up causing the spell to go astray. It is best that you are not in desperate need for money.

You need to do the spell and forget about it with the faith that the Goddess and God are going to provide for you as they see fit.

What you need:
- Silver coins

- Cauldron

- Water

- Candles (1 white and 1 green)

Place the water in your cauldron until it is about half full. Toss the silver coin into the cauldron, quarters usually work best. Put the cauldron near a window so that it can absorb the moonlight. As you glide your hand over the surface, think of it as you are trying to pick up the silver that is reflecting off the surface of the moon.

Chant the following:

Lovely lady of the moon, deliver to me your wealth right soon. Fill my hands with silver and gold. All you give me, my pockets can hold.

You are going to want to repeat this spell three times.

Step away from the bowl and leave it there for the entire night so that it gets all of the moonbeams. Upon waking up the next morning, dump the water out into the earth but be sure not to put the coins with it.

Grow Some Wealth

What you need :
- Dried patchouli (sprinkling)

- A houseplant (one that is thriving is best)

- A coin

It does not matter what kind of plant you get. However, basil plants work best. Put a little bit of the patchouli into the soil but not enough to choke the plant off from water. Taking the coin, stick it into the soil as well, but leave part of it out where you can see it.

Should you get some money, you are going to want to spend the coin in the soil as soon as possible, replacing it with a different coin. Continue the process until you believe you are satisfied.

Spice Up Your Wallet

This spell is very simple and is going to be used so you can get some extra money in your life.

What you need:
- A paper money

- Ground cinnamon

Pick a Thursday and rub the cinnamon on your fingers. Taking the fingers with cinnamon on them, leave five different smudge marks on the bill. Place this bill into the space where you keep your money. Leaving it there is going to attract new wealth.

A Simple Prosperity Spell

The purpose of this spell is to assist in bringing some inner peace and prosperity to your life.

What you need:

- Cinnamon (a pinch)

- Bundle of sage (1)

- A bowl

- Green candle

Light your candle on your altar. Take your sage and sprinkle some on the flame as well as around the candle. Think only of positive things such as achieving inner peace and prosperity. Watch your flame grow before you start to sprinkle your cinnamon on your flame saying this incantation:

I embrace prosperity and inner peace.

Your candle should be allowed to burn out on its own. Once the flame is extinguished, bury it so that your spell can be manifested into reality

Spell for Money or Prosperity

Money is the root of all evil, or so we've been told. But, money is needed to ensure that you can take care of yourself or your loved ones. With this spell, you are going to raise your prosperity so you can gain more money and be able to survive in a world that revolves around money.

What you need:

- Caldron with burning coals

- Athame or a wand

- Water

- Dish of salt or soil

- Sage

- Basil

- Chamomile

You will want to do this during a waxing moon on a Sunday or a Thursday.

Cast your circle. Invite your deity to your circle. Put the herbs that you have gathered into the burning coals as you visualize your goal. Sprinkle just a few drops of water and salt on the charcoal.

As you move your wand or athame over the cauldron, be sure to go in a clockwise motion while saying your spell:

By the abilities of air, fire, water, and earth. I release this spell. I ask for divine supervision as I seek help this day. With harm to none, this spell be fulfilled.

Continue to meditate on your goal while you imagine the smoke taking the energy out of your circle and spreading it throughout the universe. Thank your deity for their help in the spell. Release your circle. Center yourself before you leave your circle.

Chapter 22: Other Helpful Spells

These spells will be helpful to you but cannot be put into a specific category. If you place these spells in your Book of Shadows, you may discover you will have to make a tab that is special to miscellaneous spells.

Finding What Has Been Lost

It does not matter how long or short your spell is, if you put your entire heart into it then it is going to bring you the results that you are looking for.

With this spell, you are going to be trying to locate something that you may have misplaced in your home.

What you need:

- A white candle

Light your candle and place it on something that is going to be easy to carry around without dropping.

Walk room to room saying this incantation:

I need what I seek

Give me a peek

Draw my eyes

For my prize.

As you go into a room and say your incantation, look around the room so you can see if you are feeling drawn to where the object may be located.

Hushed Moment

Whenever some peace is needed in your life so you can smooth out what is happening around you, this spells is one that you can use.

What you need:
- White thread (several inches long)

- White feather (1)

You need a quiet place to do this spell, even if that means that you lock yourself in the bathroom to do it. Tie the feather to it to the white thread, but do not use all of the string for this. Hold the end that is not holding the feather and place the feather in front of your face. Breath out and watch as the feather swings until it comes to rest.

As the feather is swinging, whisper these words:

Still, quiet, hush

I am not in a rush.

You are going to repeat your spell once again after the feather has come to rest.

Altar Dedication

After you have your altar setup, you will need to cleanse the space so that it becomes dedicated to your magic work only.

What you need:

- Ritual tools (The tools that were discussed in a previous chapter. These tools are optional)

- Altar candles (2)

- White candle

- Incense

Burn a little bit of incense around your altar to ensure that the space is cleansed. The candles should be placed on opposite ends of your altar. As you begin your spell, light the candle that is on the left before lighting the one that is on the right. Lastly, light the white candle before picking it up.

Walking clockwise around the space that is set up for your altar, you are going to say this chant:

By the light, which cuts through darkness

By the fire, which burns within

By my will, which stirs the elements

Let nothing harmful in.

Upon the completion of your circle, place your candle in front of the altar before saying the end of the spell:

So mote it be.

With your space dedicated, you can do any spells or cleansings that you need to do. Once you have finished, you need to take the white candle up once more and walk the opposite direction while saying your spell

By my will, which called the elements.

By the fire, which burned so bright.

By the light, which lit the darkness

I leave you for tonight.

Blow your candle out. Extinguish the other candles first right then left. Finish off by saying:

So mote it be.

Calming Spell

It is hard to calm down once you have gotten yourself worked up or if you just feel as though you need a little bit of support. With this spell, you are going to be able to find the calm that you need.

What you need:

- Noise of some kind of keep you calm such as white noise or classical music (or silence if you prefer)
- Crystal (amethyst is good for calming rituals)
- A bowl filled with water
- A candle (color choice is yours)
- Incense or oil in a scent that is appealing to you or is associated with your intent

Light your candle along with your incense if you are using some. Ensure there is clean water in your bowl before placing your crystal in it. Work towards clearing your mind of the chaotic thoughts that may be swirling around your head and focus on positive calming thoughts. Once you have control of your thoughts, project your calmness to the water so that it may absorb that calming energy.

At the point in time that you feel like you have gotten enough calming energy into the crystal that you are using, you will remove the crystal from the water. If you have chosen to use oils, dab a little bit of oil on your rock. If you are using incense, hold your rock over the smoke so that it may absorb the smell that you associate with being calm. The last thing you do is hold your crystal over the flame of your candle for it to dry.

Keep your crystal with you, and at any point in time that you begin to feel anxious you can hold it or rub it in order to feel the calm energy that was absorbed into it through your ritual.

Full Body Blessing

In doing this spell, you are going to be connecting your physical body to your spirit as well as opening up your readiness channel. You will need to do this during a full moon so that you can see the moon.

What you need:

- Pine incense

- White candle

- Sandalwood incense

- Bowl of water

- Pinch of salt

Light your candle and incense. Sprinkle the salt into the water. Standing at your altar, you will touch each part of your body saying the following:

Eyes: bless my eyes that I might have clarity of vision.

Mouth: bless my mouth that I may speak the truth.

Ears: bless my ears that I may hear all that is spoken and not.

Heart: anoint my heart that I may be saturated with love.

Feet: bless my feet that I may find and walk my own true path.

Allow yourself to be filled with the understanding and love being offered from the Goddess After you are done, you will extinguish your candle and let your incense burn down. You will want to dump the water into the earth so that any negative energy it may have captured is released back into the earth.

Wand Blessing

A wand is not a required tool for doing your spells and rituals. However, it is something that you may decide to use from time to time. If you elect to use a wand, you are going to want to bless it so it can be blessed, charged and ready for its intended purpose.

What you need:

- Your wand

Holding your wand, say the following incantation to charge it so you can use it for your spells:

Through the strength of the elements

Light of the sun, empower this wand.

Splendor of fire, empower this wand.

Speed of lighting, empower this wand.

Swiftness of wind, empower this wand.

Depth of the seas, empower this wand.

Stability of the earth, empower this wand.

Firmness of rock, empower this wand.

I charge and empower this wand.

So mote it be.

Chapter 23: Tips and Tricks

Tips and tricks are going to make your spells that much easier. Learning which spells work for you and which ones do not will be a journey and will be one you will have to take on your own.

However, it is a great idea to have some advice or some tips and tricks from fellow Wiccans. Don't forget to share with other Wiccans so you can help make their journey a little easier.

- Salt: Placing a circle of salt around an area helps to prevent negative entities and demons from entering that space. You may also use salt to make a line on doors or window sills so that they become impassable to malicious spirits.

- Iron: Iron helps to repel evil which is why Wiccans place an iron object at the entrance of their home to deter any unwanted visitors. Hammering three iron nails into the frame of a window or door (1 at each side on the bottom and 1 at the top in the middle) will help to keep malevolent spirits from entering the home. It is believed that most spirits cannot cross railway lines since the iron creates an impenetrable wall for them.

- Silver: Silver is a symbol for the moon and the Goddess. Using silver for jewelry makes it easier to enchant as a talisman for protection. Silver pentagrams are powerful objects of protection even without having a spell placed on them.

- The pentacle: A five pointed star that symbolizes the five elements and can be traced anywhere as a symbol of protection.

- Light: Lesser demons typically avoid any area that is bright and will only attack when it is dark. However, this does not work for demons who are of higher rank.

- Fire: There are some spirits that are afraid of fire, especially those that are related to ice or water. This is what makes a candle a tool for protection.

- Crystals: Quartz crystals that are blessed by a witch can help to create a circle of protection. Arrange them in a circle so spirits find it hard to cross. The circle can protect you or can be used to trap spirits in the middle. The circle will be stronger if the crystals are placed at the cardinal points.

- Gemstones: Stones and gems are going to be very useful in magic and can be used for protection. Tiger's eye will reflect negative energies while amethyst blocks any manipulative spirits and helps to decrease the effects of harmful potions. Magnetite can entrap lesser demons and opal can lock higher demons up for a short period of time. Onyx and obsidian are able to cancel out various negative energies like necromancy. The mineral that is used most often is a clear quartz, but it has to be blessed first to be effective.

- Orgonite: This is an energy healing tool that is usually made up of resin, gemstones and metals. It can be used in re-balancing negative energies. There are a lot of people who use orgonite for protection against any harmful electromagnetic pollution. It can also be used for powerful spiritual protection.

- Incense: There is a great variety of incense that can be used to repel negative energy. If you have the proper quality incense, you will be able to keep them away.

Some of the most common protection incense are sage, sandalwood, frankincense, patchouli and myrrh.

- Plants: There are several spices and herbs that have protection qualities. Garlic is able to repel any creature that drains their victims. Saffron and thyme deter flying spirits that are usually tied to the wind. Rosemary repels evil spirits linked to water. Sage, when it is burnt, is cleansing and intolerable to any negative spirit. Henbane and aconite repels demons violently because they are extremely toxic, which means that you have to be careful when you handle them. Lilacs, when they are planted near the house, will deter any wandering spirit who passes by. The branches of a thorny plant like a rose can be as effective as a salt line when placed along a door or window sill. Myrrh helps to strengthen any spell or protective talisman.

- Athame: Most Wiccans do not sharpen their athame because it is never used to cut anything. However, because it is a knife, it should be handled with caution. The athame is a phallic symbol which makes it a symbol of the God. Athames that have been blessed properly can be used to draw a circle of protection. Point it in the air and draw your circle's boundaries. On top of that, the atame can hurt demons and spirits despite the fact that they have no physical body.

- Broom: This is a symbol for cleaning and brooms that are placed at doors prevent weaker spirits from entering. Should a dangerous spirit enter the house, brooms will fall to the ground as an alarm signal.

- Dig deep: Before you start planning what you want manifested, you have to dig deep. This will apply if you are asking for something that you have not gotten before.

For example, if you constantly ask for an apartment or job, but despite your wishing you continue to run into roadblocks, you probably feel as if you are not being listened to. Remember that the universe will provide you with anything that you want, you may just not know exactly what you want.
You have to be careful what you wish for because once you get it, you may not want it after all. Keep in mind that everything has 2 sides which is why you must explore the downsides to the wish that you are asking for.

- Imagine: Imagine how your life will be once you get what you wish for. There are often things that hold you back, one of the biggest things that will hold you back is the feeling that you have to have everything planned out while still wanting mystery. You have to be willing to let go and allow the universe to flow through you as it is supposed to.

- The power of three: Before you start manifesting what you want, you have to ask if it is going to harm anyone or yourself? If it could potentially harm you or someone else, you should not try to manifest your wish.

Chapter 24: Wiccan Myths Debunked

As you know, there are a lot of myths about the Wiccan religion. In this chapter, we will debunk some of the myths that people commonly believe.

- Wiccans are witches: This is true. However, Wicca is different from witchcraft. Witchcraft is the practice and belief of magic while Wicca is based in nature. Each will compliment each other, not every Wiccan practices magic while not all witches are Wiccan. There are even some in other religions that have been known to practice magic.

- Wiccans use magic to hurt people: Sadly, this is true. There are some spells that have the ability to cause others harm in some way. However, not every Wiccan is out to get those that are not in the religion.

In fact, as you have seen, the first rule is "harm none, do what you will." Basically, this means that Wiccans are usually peaceful people. When you combine this with the rule of three, Wiccans know that when they go out of their way to harm someone, they will eventually receive a worse treatment. This is why when most Wiccans cast spells to harm someone else, they only do it out of self-defense or to right a wrong.

- Wiccans worship the devil: This is the furthest thing from the truth. The idea of satan came from the Christian religion which is why it does not make sense for Wiccans to worship satan. They also believe that the pentagram is an image associated with the devil. However, it's Greek roots come from Pan and is used as a symbol for protection and magical energy.

- Wiccans are always naked and participate in unsafe sex: False! There are a few ceremonies that Wiccans have where they participate in nudity, but they do not walk around naked like nudists do. For their nude ceremonies, they find a secluded place where they can practice in peace. There are some Wiccans that view sex as a celebration of fertility and life but they practice safe and private sex just like everyone else.

- Wicca is a cult: Wrong! It is a religion. Yes, like every other religion, there are those that are considered "weird." The only reason people believe that Wicca is a cult is because they are mysterious and often practice in secret.

- Wiccans have sex orgies: Not even close. Even though some Wiccans are liberal about their sexuality, they do not participate in orgies. Everyone in the Wiccan religion is an adult so they do not care if you are gay, straight or polyamourous.

- Do Wiccans cast spells?: Yes! As you've seen in this book, there are a number of spells that a Wiccan can cast to manifest their wishes. This is not Harry Potter magic. There are some spells that are nothing more than prayers sent up to the gods while others are going to be based on your intent.

- What is the difference between Wiccan and pagan? Almost every Wiccan is pagan, but not all pagans are Wiccans. In other words, pagan is an umbrella term for a group of different spiritual paths.

- Why do people want to become Wiccan? There are a number of reasons that people decide to become Wiccan. Some want to become Wiccan because they are not happy with any other religion. Others decide to study various religions and decide that Wiccan is the one that is most compatible with their beliefs. No matter what their reason, every Wiccan says they chose this path because it was what was right for them.

- How are new Wiccans recruited: They aren't! The information is shared with those who want the answers, but Wicca does not recruit people into the religion. Wiccans only want those that truly want to be in the religion on their side.

- Are you worried about going to hell? No, as you saw earlier, Satan is a concept from the Christian religion so is Hell. This is why they do not worry about going to hell because they focus on the good things as they believe that what is done in this lifetime will echo upon the next one.

- Do you believe in God? Most Wiccans are polytheistic which means that they believe in more than one deity.

- You have to come from a family of witches: Having a family member that is in the religion will help you, but that is not required. There are many people that make the decision to become Wiccan because their beliefs line up with the beliefs of the Wiccan religion.

- You have to be initiated in order to become a witch: Nope! If you decide to join a coven, then you will be forced to go through initiation so you can show how much you know about their traditions. But, for informal witches, you can mark your progress with a small ritual.

- You have to cast spells naked: Some people choose to cast them naked, but this is not required. If it is part of a festival then you may cast them naked. However, if you are in a coven and they are advocating that you do something that makes you uncomfortable, you should leave it. You should never feel coerced to do something that you do not believe is in your best interest.

There are a million different myths that have been put out there by those that do not understand the religion. If you are serious about wanting to join the religion, if you have not already, it is best for you to find someone that can help you to understand what you do not understand. It is always a good idea for you to understand everything before you jump head first into the Wiccan religion.

Conclusion – Wicca for Beginners

If you are just starting out with Wicca, then this book hopefully helped you figure out where to get your start. Herbal magic and moon magic are going to be the easiest places to start. Once you are able to harness the power you can gain from those, then you will be ready to move on to more complicated spells.

If you are a practicing Wiccan and were looking to expand your skills, then I hope that this book was able to show you a new magic that you may not have thought about before.

The Wiccan religion is extremely fascinating and there is always something else that you can learn about it. Not only that, but the Wiccan beliefs can help you to feel as if you are in control of your life and that you are able to keep going when you feel like you can't go anymore. This is thanks to the spells you can perform or the support system you'll get from a coven.

The hope is that no matter what level of Wiccan you are, you are able to take what you learned in this book and put it to good use. And remember, no matter what you do, do no harm!

Blessed Be! And good luck on your journey.

Wicca Book of Spells

The A Step-by-Step Guide to Practicing Wiccan Magic with Candle, Crystal and Herbal Spells

Introduction – Wicca Book of Spells

The Wiccan religion is considered to be a branch of Paganism; therefore, we can say that it is merely one of the many traditions associated with Paganism as a historical and spiritual phenomenon. Even though the Wiccan religion is relatively young, it has already intrigued many, and there are rumors that surround it, especially those that connect Wiccans with Satanism. However, this is an entirely incorrect interpretation of Wiccan teachings, just like many other things that you might read or hear from those who lack facts.

After more than ten years of practice, I have seen and heard many different views of this religion. Many of them were not only wrong, but filled with hatred towards something that those people didn't understand. That is why through this book I will address some basic misunderstandings about Wiccans, and I will try to explain basic terms and uses of Wiccan magic practices. You will see that the purpose of this guide is not to convince or convert, but to educate and encourage those who want to enter the world of profound spiritual journeys. This contemporary Pagan religion is based on the premise that you can become the best version of yourself, and it teaches you that you can achieve anything if you use your spiritual and physical power in combination with self-discipline. The Wiccan religion doesn't revolve around one authority, nor does it have temples that you need to visit in order to practice and sustain your beliefs. It worships the power of nature and the elements that surround us, and nurtures a belief that everything is energy and everything is connected. You can find some sources that say that Wiccan tradition is a basis for Paganism; however, it is the other way around. In fact,

Paganism is a basis for Wiccan teachings, and it combines modern spiritual teachings with ancient Pagan ideals.

In order to become Wiccan, you need to become one with the Earth and to believe in the magical properties of everything that surrounds us. Still, there are many who abuse these beliefs, and that is one of many reasons why you might hear negative things like Wiccans are Satanists and so forth. In order to become Wiccan, one must be ready for many temptations and responsibilities that such a decision bares. Wiccan religion isn't something that can be defined in one sentence, and it represents different experiences.

The Wiccan religion is very unique, especially since many of us are used to monotheistic, monolithic religions like Christianity. All Catholics believe the same tenets, for example. However, this doesn't ring true for Wiccans. In fact, freedom of beliefs is one of the most important aspects of the Wiccan religion. Take note not to insult the beliefs of other Wiccans, because in the grand scheme of things, they're just as valuable and justified.

It is also not a religion of hatred. While curses and such do exist, they are very rarely used, and are recommended only as a last resort, rather than being the first thing you turn to in a moment of trouble. Never believe that having the ability to curse someone gives you the right to, for that would be against everything for which Wicca stands.

That is why it is important to understand what the fundamentals of its teachings are, and to work towards your individual goals. In the end, the goal of unlocking the magic and releasing it into your life sounds amazing and tempting. Therefore, here is a simple introduction to the magic world of Wicca.

Chapter 1: Wicca and Witchcraft

Influential Practitioners

Wicca appeared in the 1950s and quickly gained attention from modern society. The most important role in Wiccan development was played by Gerald B. Gardner, whose work was dedicated to spirituality and esoteric knowledge. Attention from big media sources also helped Wicca to become one of the mysterious occurrences during the transitional post-war period. Of course, many practices that were introduced by Gardner through his works weren't new or invented by him. There were many beliefs in those publications that had been practiced throughout the centuries. The novel that provoked interest for the witch cult, called *High Magic's Aid*, was published in 1949. In this novel, Gardner wrote about Wiccan teachings, and it had a great impact on the development of the so-called "witch cult."

It is important to note that Gardner only formalized Wicca, and did not create it. In fact, many Wiccans don't practice the kind of religion Gardner was a proponent of. With that in mind, it can still be useful to start off with his teachings, as he formalized much of what we consider to be modern-day Wicca.

This rich number of works can be viewed as the fusion and continuation of many books and writings throughout history. Undoubtedly, there has been a wide range of people throughout history who have explored spirituality and magic, and there is a great selection of sources that talk about esoteric orders or practices that existed in the past or still exist today. This is especially applicable at the end of the 19th century and the beginning of the 20th because of the boom of folklore studies and anthropology. One of the studies that was important for the development of the Wicca practices was the book titled *The Golden Bough*. In it, James George Frazer, the author, explained relations between religion, rituals, and myths. Frazer was exploring the cultural patterns from the globe in order to find the common behaviors that would connect these three areas of society.

In this book, he tried to explore all the different kinds of rituals, myths, and beliefs that people held. Naturally, he was not able to explore them all. Even today we are unable to do that, despite all of our modern technology. Despite that, he did do a great amount of work, and helped form what Wicca is today.

One of the most important people in the development of contemporary magic is, unarguably, Aleister Crowley. He is an important figure not only to Wiccan teachings, but to every aspect of magic as a whole. Crowley was a practitioner, researcher, and writer of magic for nearly fifty years during the twentieth century, and he became a person who influenced and contributed not only to magic practices, but to Wicca in general. He was very well connected to other practitioners and always corresponded with them, or some other interested and talented magicians, explaining his experiences in detail. In one of the letters that he wrote to his disciple Frater Achad, Crowley explained that the society matured enough for a natural religion to appear. According to Crowley's letter, people had always liked ceremonies and rituals, and they did not want to talk to hypothetical gods anymore. He told his disciples that they should insist on the belief in the Mother-Force, in the Moon and the Sun, and so forth. That way, as Crowley saw it, we could connect to the full current of life by celebrating and worshipping these forces, and unifying them. Crowley believed that religion should be a joy, but it also has to treat death as an initiation that is worthy and dignified. He advised his disciples to start a pagan cult that would celebrate all these things and make people joyful by adding noble things that inspire, but also add festivals of wine and corn that would be dedicated to the forces of nature. This was one of the first writings that encouraged the traditions of magic that are similar to today's Wicca tradition.

In the book called *The Gospel* there were also similar allusions. Crowley talked about the cult formed by John Barleycorn and considered it religion that had its worship renewed.

Crowley explained that the celebration of the ancient rite had sprung up through the whole world. According to some research, this talk could be referring to the order called Ordo Templi Orientis, or O.T.O., for short. This order later became one of the biggest and most influential orders in the 1920s. However, there are no connections to this claim from the Oto Templi Orientis, so it is believed that this cult was actually the Astrum Argenteum (A.A.) that Crowley established to promote the teachings of Thelema. Thelema, which is a Greek word meaning "the will," is actually a philosophy formed by Crowley. At its core is the teaching that one's true will can only be found through the religion of the new age that is dawning. This premise is formed from the text called *The Book of the Law*, or *Liber AL vel Legis* in Latin. Thelma's laws and teachings became very influential in the later Wiccan tradition. With the formation of the Astrum Argenteum, Crowley believed that this religion would be empowered. The person who helped him with this work was his fellow magician George Jones. Jones introduced Crowley to the Hermetic Order of the Golden Dawn, which was a milestone for the Astrum Argenteum inauguration in 1906. The most famous scholar of the Golden Dawn, J. W. Brodie, wrote that if we left prejudices aside and looked at things objectively, we would see that the witch cult is something that is as old as humanity itself, and that it is as strong today as it was in previous centuries.

Considering all of the above, we can conclude that witchcraft is not a religion, but a teaching, and Wicca, formalized by Gerald Gardner in 1957, is a tradition of witchcraft that some people see as a religion.

Keep in mind that witches can be spiritual, but they are not religious in their practices. Some of them are even atheistic. This means that they don't worship any particular deity, and they work for themselves by honoring the sacred life and the power of Earth. Witches are usually Pagan, but that doesn't mean that all those who are Pagans are witches, too. Also, take into consideration that not all witches consider themselves Wiccan. This means that one can practice magic and witchcraft, but he or she does not have to believe in or embrace Wiccan teachings. According to Scott Cunningham, witchcraft is actually the craft of the witch. It is magic that uses the power of the person and conjoins it with the energies that exist in herbs, stones, and other objects of nature. According to him, even though it has spiritual overtones, witchcraft in this manner cannot be considered a religion. Cunningham adds that being Wiccan does not mean that you are a witch, and vice versa.

Early Origins

In the early Christian period, witchcraft was considered sorcery that had been practiced since ancient times, and in that period, it wasn't related to the devil or demons. In Anglo-Saxon practices of magic, for example, spells involved simple medications that were even sometimes mixed with Christianity, so it was possible to hear people praying to God while they prepared a potion. During the early period of Christianity, divine relics and saints were just a step away from Pagan practices, and they were introduced so people who could be potential Christians would feel more comfortable with magic on a daily basis. It was also a good way to establish Christianity as a form viewed as superior to Paganism.

St. Augustine of Hippo in the 5th century proclaimed that magic and Paganism were the Devil's invention and that they were made to make people stray from God and the real Christian path. He also preached that there was no such thing as supernatural powers and that no one was capable of invoking magic. He believed that magic was a Pagan error that made people non-believers of the one and only God. According to this, witches were powerless and the Church didn't need to be bothered by their magic rituals and spells. Thus, they didn't need to track the practitioners of magic. However, that is exactly what happened in the Middle Ages when the church persecuted witches for several centuries.

One of the most influential Bishops in the 7th century, the Bishop of Lyon, preached that witches were dangerous and that they could fly during the night, make storms and bad weather, and be shapeshifters. In the 8th century, it was further established that the existence of witches themselves was an un-Christian occurrence. By the 9th century, witches were punished by death until the Frankish king made a decree that abolished it. Still, the Church was very influential during the 7th and 8th centuries, and that period is known through history as a time of persecution of the witches. Many anti-witch laws were introduced during that time, and it was a period when the Latin expression "maleficium" was introduced. This meant that everyone who practiced magic was guilty of malevolent doings that were connected to the Devil. During this period, magic was considered heresy and a crime against society. It was considered a crime against God, and this belief was so strong that, in 744, a "List of Superstitions" was made. This list was a prohibition for saint sacrificing, and it demanded that the person must renounce their work for "demons," especially Thor and Odin. According to medieval lore, weather makers, otherwise known as Tempestarii magi, existed amongst ordinary people. It was believed that these magi could change the weather at their will; they could make a storm, or prevent it. They are one reason why others hated, feared, and respected these people all at the same time. The Church, however, had an explanation that, in this case, God gave permission to the Devil and the practitioners of witchcraft to do this as a form of punishment for those who are wicked in this world. Still, the Church did not allow any remedies against it because they were considered Pagan. Their prescription, so to speak, was to pray and to invoke the name of God instead.

Before the 13th century, witchcraft was defined as a collection of practices and beliefs that included spells for healing and predicting the future through clairvoyance. During this period in England, for example, there were "witch doctors." People believed that these doctors had curative magic. There were other names for this type of person, like the "white witch" or the "cunning man." There weren't only the witch doctors; there were also "toad doctors" who could remove malevolent magic, too. Even though they did not actually qualify themselves as witches, people often came to them for services such as healing from bad witchcraft or cursing someone. These doctors were considered an important part of the community at the time.

At the beginning of the 13th century, the Catholic Church began to label witchcraft as "demon worship." An open attack on the heretics called Cathars was incited by Pope Innocent III. The Church wanted to discredit the Cathars' belief that both Satan and God had supernatural powers, but that they were at war. This is when the Church proclaimed that the Cathars were heretics who worshipped the Devil, and that they even had devil-worshipping rituals that empowered their evil deity. During this period, many heretics had to emigrate to Savoy and Germany. All of these people fled to escape the inquisition that was trying to suppress those committing heresy against the Church. Theologian St. Thomas Aquinas, one of the most significant figures in the Church in the 13th century, believed that the world had many demons and that evil lurked everywhere. This evil, according to Aquinas, tempted people through sexual relations and witchcraft.

One of the most recognizable occurrences during the Middle Ages was The Inquisition. The Catholic Church wanted a way to punish heretics and change the beliefs that opposed the Church. In the 1230s, people trained to execute the Inquisition were hired by Pope Gregory IX. The Pope assigned the training and the inquisitorial duties to the Dominican Order. This Order had the authority to act in the name of Pope, and in later years, the Pope even authorized them to use torture. The influence of Inquisitors was so strong that eventually every church and every court was persecuting witches. History suggests that the era of Inquisition can be divided into four phases: the Papal Inquisition (the 1230s), the Spanish Inquisition (1478-1834), the Portuguese Inquisition (1536-1821), and the Roman Inquisition (1542-1860).

Meaning of the Word "Coven"

Now, in order to understand Wicca and witchcraft, it is also important to understand what "coven" means, since we will refer to covens multiple times throughout the course of this book. There are many definitions of the word coven through the literature. The Internet, however, offers descriptions related to all sorts of things. You can find covens mentioned in rock and roll music in Poland, and then you can find online covens or popular witch role-playing. This is why modern society often has a blurry image of the real meaning of the word coven. In the next paragraphs, we will give you our version of the accurate definition and description of the coven.

The coven represents a group of witches or Pagan followers (at least three) that have a similar goal or similar interest. A coven isn't a random gathering of practitioners; they need to choose to get together and act as a community with the same purpose. There are some general characteristics that every coven has. To become a functioning coven the group must have at least some criteria that form their foundation. First of all, a group of practitioners needs to exist. Secondly, that group needs some members, and if you want to respect tradition, then we are talking about thirteen practicing witches. This is not a rule, per se, but it is typical for covens. Once you have the members, you need to work on the group's ability to become a family and act like one. Another thing that a coven needs for its existence is a tradition. However, all of these things are useless if the coven does not have trust between the members. If there is no loyalty and commitment to the coven's shared goals, the coven won't be strong. Witches or Pagans that form a coven also share a bond that rests on conviction, honesty, and confidentiality. The purpose can be different from coven to coven, which means that their beliefs and their ethics can differ, too.

So, the main definition is that a coven is a group of witches that practices magic. While the Internet can show some different collections of magical practices that can or cannot be seen as a coven, the fact is that a coven isn't a group of weekend teachers or nature lovers. We are talking about more than three people who worship and celebrate the same ideas and same deities. We are talking about those who embrace teachings and traditions, Wiccan in this case, and act together, sharing and building their knowledge in performing rituals and spells. Keep in mind that, if a group of Wiccan people gathers over conversation or food and coffee, it doesn't mean that they are a coven. A coven involves only practicing witches. It requires effort and dedication that is more than just being a believer.

In addition, if there is a very small gathering of the practicing witches, it is not necessarily a coven. Every coven strives toward self-sustainability. For example, if there are only three witches in the coven, and one of them leaves, the coven ceases to exist. This is why it is important to have a decent number of practicing witches in a coven. In case something happens, the coven prevails and keeps functioning normally. Another good example of this is the loss of a member due to any kind of betrayal of the coven. Without enough practitioners, that coven is doomed. That is why we say that a coven is a group of at least three practicing followers.

Once you enter a coven, you start to consider it your family and it becomes something like your second home. To be clear, this is not a family you are born into; this is a family you choose. It is a family that shares the same Wiccan beliefs and connects with you on a mental plane, rather than a blood connection. Entering a coven means that you will expose yourself to your group, and you will talk about yourself, your fears, and your attitude toward things. You will also hear other people's sincere exposures, and you will have an insight into the needs of other members of the coven, and they will know yours. That is why a coven can't be a random gathering of strangers who practice magic. They can call themselves a coven, but that is not the real deal. Opening yourself to others and receiving the same response strengthens the bond, and enables a coven to have better results and perform stronger and consistent magic. That is why functioning like a family is an important part of every coven.

It is believed that every coven needs their own, unique tradition. It will create a distinction between their followers and those who follow already established traditions, such as the British tradition or the tradition of Cornelian Nativists. Covens should be able to create a tradition that is specific to them. The concept of tradition, or rather the concept of making your own specific beliefs and practices and using them alongside already existent ones, is important for the definition of your purpose as a group. It helps in setting the specific goals of the coven, and it is useful to determine the so-called ways of the coven.

It is significant to set the tradition because sometimes individuals tend to work on their own, which can distract the group from forming the identity that a coven needs to survive. If everyone just did whatever they wanted, it wouldn't be a coven; it would just be a bunch of practitioners who want to show off their skills.

Being a part of a coven is not easy. It requires hard work from everyone. If the coven wants to be active and strong, its members need to show that they are loyal. They also need to prove that they can commit. This means that they will follow the plans of the coven, even if sometimes you have something else that you'd rather do. Commitment means that you will show up for the scheduled ritual even if you planned to go on a vacation, and following the coven's scheduled activities even if sometimes it is not about a big spell or a ritual at all. Loyalty and commitment mean that you will follow the things you pledged to achieve with your group.

That is why another important role of an active coven is to set up regular meetings. These meetings help members keep track of their progress and results. If the same people show up to these meetings regularly, they will create a stronger bond. This won't be the case if you just have a random meeting and there are always different people. During these meetings, covens usually try to introduce people by stating their expectations and reasons for joining the coven. This leads us to the main purpose of every coven and that coven's ultimate goal. The goal of a coven is to set its path for the future. Every witch needs to know what it is that their group wants to do, and what they need to do to achieve what they want. This is how a coven sets a direction and gathers practitioners with the same vision.

Historians, Researchers, and Literature

The field of folk magic was introduced in 1999 by Brian Hoggard, who wrote a book originally titled *The Archaeology of Folk Magic*. This book was important for the Wicca tradition because it was closely connected to the witchcraft and physical remains from the era in which white witches performed rituals in order to protect properties from black magic. There are many sources, especially from the 16th and 17th centuries, that are related to the archaeology of protection rituals. Over the years, historians have improved in their witchcraft research and their uninformed views of witchcraft as a primitive religion, superstition, or heresy. In 1959, author Rossell Hope Robbins wrote one of the most valuable works when it comes to witchcraft called *The Encyclopedia of Witchcraft and Demonology*. In this book, Robbins discusses the awful tortures that occurred, but he doesn't compare this witch persecution to the other similar horrible events or genocides from history. On the other hand, books like *Religion and the Decline of Magic* talk about the practices of the cunning people in detail. It also describes early witchcraft from modern Europe through collections of important articles that talked about witchcraft from Iceland and fights amongst spirits.

Some of these historians even initiated themselves into the coven in order to learn more about witchcraft. Historian Tanya Luhrmann was one of those people. She wrote the anthropological study in which she tried to show the importance of witchcraft in village communities. In her work entitled *Persuasions of Witchcraft*, she wrote about the role of rituals and other witchcraft practices in the community.

Other historians argue about Wiccan claims that all witches in England at the time were burned. Diane Purkiss was one of the historians who explained that the "burning times" never existed in England because witches were usually hanged. Still, in her book *The Witch in History*, she acknowledged Wicca as a religion that exists as an alternative response to Christianity, which is considered the mainstream world religion. Many authors consider that the fear of witches is a phenomenon produced by ruling elites during the era of witch persecutions. It is said that the belief that witches fly on their broomsticks during the night developed at the time of mass executions of the witches and that, at the same time, the rituals of Sabbath emerged as a response to the Christian rituals. In the book called *The Stripping of the Altars*, Eamon Duffy talks about beliefs in Christianity that can be considered superficial and that, when combined with the beliefs of regular people, easily became something that we can consider as pre-Reformation. This means that, in that kind of parish, worshipping the saints or polytheism could exist at the same time as Christianity without issue. A good example of this is provided by Anton Wessels, who talked about something that he called "pagan-animist" nature. According to him, this is something that is broadly connected to this particular nature and not to Christianity.

There are many books that have copies of documents related to witchcraft verdicts or similar reports through history. One of the best examples of these kinds of books is called *Witchcraft in England 1558-1618*, in which we can find one of the most consistent and detailed descriptions of the studies of witchcraft. On the other hand, we have writings such as *Witchcraft Papers - Contemporary Records of the Witchcraft Hysteria in Essex 1560-1700* that contributed a lot to the debates and further research about witchcraft.

All of this literature shows an effort to explain the real nature of witchcraft practices and what really happened during these centuries, not only in England but throughout the whole world. Many people only know about these practices and traditions through movies, cartoons, or TV series, and it is recommended that you truly educate yourself before you decide to enter the world of witchcraft.

As we explained, all of these works are just examples; there are many others that talk about this phenomenon, and they all represent a part of witchcraft anthropology. There are many other authors who wrote about it, but they were usually just using their findings to confirm other formerly-established theories, not creating new ones that were specifically related to witchcraft. An example of this is a work by Ralph Merrifield, who wrote about magic and rituals from the Neolithic period up to the 19th century. In the entire book, there is only one chapter that discusses witchcraft. Even though there are many other works that you can find, Merrifield best described the most common events where people used witchcraft. He explained that people usually used it in order to protect themselves from black magic, but he never actually says much about what the rituals that witches performed to accomplish such protection actually were. He does mention objects, such as dried or mummified cats or bottles with potions, and these objects were always connected to the protection rituals that prevented demons from entering or doing harm to people or their houses. This suggests that witchcraft is a part of a very old system of beliefs that can tell us a lot about its origins.

As mentioned previously, the proclaimed father of Wicca is a practitioner named Gardner. He initiated and worked with many people, practitioners, and high priestesses, and he helped in forming a large number of covens that would develop and gain power in the following decades. Other important names include Alex and Maxine Sanders who, in the 1960s, promoted the Wiccan teachings through mass media and helped Wicca become established as a recognized tradition worldwide. The Sanders engaged their beliefs with their audience and did enormous work in forming a Wiccan community. Over the next few decades, they provided training and initiations to many members and brought Paganism back to life by reviving its teachings and practices.

When we talk about the difference between old witchcraft and the Wiccan religion, the fact is that witchcraft is much older. For example, witchcraft was practiced in America decades before the Wiccan religion came. Wiccan teachings were brought there by authors such as Raymond Buckland and Sybil Leek. Pagan scholars sometimes don't acknowledge the difference between the magical practices that were previously popular even though the neo-Pagan Wiccan religion has even more followers.

Wiccan religion is based on worshipping the Horned God and the Triple Goddess, and Wiccans invoke elements of nature for their spells. Wiccans are known to cast a circle for their magical acts, and they use a combination of ceremonial magic, known legends, and their beliefs and devotion. As previously mentioned, the strongest influences in Wiccan teachings were brought by folklorists who were studying old witchcraft and principles of magic. Wiccan teachings have their roots in pre-Christian myths, magic that was used for different ceremonies in ancient times, and rituals that are practiced even today.

Many rites are used by both Wiccans and other magic apprentices. Some Wiccans believe that many rites that they use today were created in the territory of today's Great Britain. Also, it is believed that many ceremonial magic rituals were connected to druids and their worshipping of nature. If we compare rites and rituals of European covens and American covens, we can see the parallels between the Wiccans on both continents. The main difference is that European covens use Gardner's books as their reference in general, while in America *The Common Book of Witchcraft and Wicca* is most often used. Many Wiccan followers in America say that they learned their spells from members of their families or from their acquaintances from the "old continent."

Still, Wiccan practices in America and Europe have many common characteristics. Several rituals and spells on both continents are the product of the synthesis of beliefs and rites of indigenous cultures. This is especially prevalent in American covens which use a lot of Native American aspects in their magical performances.

On the other hand, Gardner's work represents a collection of European folklore tales, legends, dances, or magical ceremonies that were usually performed in rural areas until the 1940s. The development of the media encouraged Wiccans across the world to exchange their experiences, whether they belong to covens from Europe or America, or if they are just individual practitioners.

Chapter 2: Gods and Rituals

Wicca is not like Christianity. This means that the Wiccan community does not celebrate monotheism; their worship is dualistic. This means that Wiccans believe in two gods rather than in just one. Their separation of gods is based on gender, so they worship different gods and goddesses. Wiccans believe that humankind is created from the love between different deities and their affairs. It is not only Wiccans who believe in duality. Taoism is also a religion based on dualism. Yin and Yang are opposite sides that represent the god of the Sun and the goddess of the Moon. On the other hand, the Wiccan religion is also known to celebrate two deities; one is the Triple Goddess and the other is the Horned God. They believe that this goddess and this god are lovers who are in charge of keeping their followers in line, and that those followers spread into this world. Even though they don't influence their followers in their daily lives, they are the ones who grant power for the completion of the spells, and those who perform these spells call upon their deities for help. Still, there are some Wiccans who believe in many other deities; therefore, they are not considered dualistic, but polytheistic. According to their belief, they can call upon not only two deities, but many, in order to complete their spells. They say that one god cannot assume that much responsibility and one god cannot control everything, so there are many other deities, higher and minor, who can enable them to perform spells of different strength. Wiccan religion does not limit you to be a dualistic or polytheistic believer; you can choose what suits you, which is why we will discuss all major Wiccan deities in the following text.

Worshipping Gods and Goddesses

As we already explained, dualism represents the belief in two deities. This means that this religion doesn't have one, but two gods. Wiccan religion is not the only one that has elements of dualism because we can find it in many religions that have two sides – one good and one evil. In many of these religions, humans were born from this balance and they have to maintain it with the existence of good people and bad people. According to these teachings, every person has both good and evil inside them and it is up to them to choose which one to follow.

The Triple Goddess

The Wiccan goddess has many names. The most common one is the "Triple Goddess," but you can find her by the name "The Goddess" or "Mother Goddess." The Triple Goddess is who Wiccan followers call upon to give them the power to perform healing spells or love spells, or any spells that are connected to the forces of nature. Wiccans believe that the Triple Goddess has three aspects: the Maiden, the Mother, and the Crone. In the Wiccan religion, the Mother controls all moon phases and its rotations, and she is in charge of the earth and everything that grows on it. Wiccans say that the Triple Goddess created the tides in the oceans. They consider her to be a goddess of love and fertility, and she is mostly called upon by women because, according to Wiccans, her influence is stronger on females.

Still, men can also call upon the Triple Goddess since the feeling of love is very powerful, and even men need it in order to perform spells of higher class. There are many unknown things about the Triple Goddess, and it is believed that a reason for that is because the deities do not like to share much about their existence. The interesting thing about worshipping the Goddess is that there are no sacred rules that commit you or prayers that are necessary on a daily basis. There are no commandments or regulations, and the threat of hell doesn't exist if you are not a believer. Worship is a matter of choice.

The Horned God

The Wiccan God is known as the "Horned God," and he is one of the main reasons why people connect the Wicca religion with devil worship or Satanism. The Horned God is the god of the Sun and he is unrelated to the Devil, otherwise known as Satan. According to Wiccan teachings, the Horned God controls our animalistic nature and is in charge of all animals on the planet. He is portrayed as a god with bull horns and he takes care of men and helps with protection spells in general. That is why all protection spells that are performed by Wiccans use the Horned God as an anchor for the energy from which they draw power. He is not only invoked for protection spells; since he represents the Sun, the Horned God is called upon for all light spells, too. Many historians connect the Horned God to the Greek God Pan, who was also an animal god. The lore says that Pan still lives in different realms and that, in fact, he is the one who guides Wiccans and gives them strength for their spells. It is said that the Horned God is the symbol of pubescence for men and that there are many interpretations for his appearance and power. However, there isn't much information solely on the Horned God since he is usually portrayed in a comparison of other religions with similar deities. This is one of the reasons for Wiccan polytheism. They think that, by having more deities, there will be less confusion and fewer cases of mixing deities and humans.

Polytheism represents the belief that there are many gods, not just one or two. According to the followers of polytheism, many different deities have control over the elements, nature, and religion in general. This belief is formed on the premise that, if there are more deities, the deities will have less trouble in providing guidance and power to the ones who call upon them. Wiccans view this as a system in which every god or goddess has their own field and spells they control, and they do not cross into each other's territory. That is how they keep balance. Wiccans say that this is the only way in which these deities communicate with humankind. There are many people who are not Wiccans but who still believe in polytheism rather than in monotheism or dualism.

Other than the Triple Goddess and the Horned God, there are two other deities who will be discussed in this chapter. Of course, there are many other smaller deities, but since these additional two are the most important ones, we will discuss them in more detail.

The Star Goddess

The first one is the Star Goddess, also known as the "Dryghten." Wiccans believe that she is the goddess who created the cosmos, and if you ever made a wish upon a star, the Star Goddess was the one who heard it. It is said that the Star Goddess is vengeful and not very fond of humans because the Triple Goddess forbid her to have any contact with them. The reason for this is because the Star Goddess wanted to sleep with humans, and the Triple Goddess was against it. She thought that if the Star Goddess happened to have a child with a mortal, then that child would be against their laws. Since she was unable to communicate with humans, the Star Goddess felt bitter, and this could be the reason why some wishes are not granted. Still, some wishes can be an exception, and the only way to make them come true is by winning the Star Goddess' heart. According to Wiccan teachings, this can be done by worshipping her as a real deity.

The One

The other important deity in Wiccan polytheism is a god known as "The One." The other name for this god is "The All." Wiccans believe that the One controls all other deities and is above all others in the entire Wiccan religion. It has the ultimate power and cannot be defined by gender or level. It is omniscient and all-knowing. One can be compared to the faith of Christianity. There isn't much information about this deity; the only thing that is known for sure is that polytheistic Wiccans see the One as the most powerful deity. It is the god above all others and it makes sure that all of the other gods and goddesses do their work and stay in order. It is especially connected to the main deities, the Triple Goddess and the Horned God, and makes sure that they perform their duties properly.

These four deities are the main ones, whether you decide to choose a dualistic or polytheistic Wiccan path. Still, different covens have different minor deities that you can learn about. The number and the nature of those deities depend on the coven, and they are usually specific for each one. The Triple Goddess, the Horned God, the Star Goddess, and the One are the biggest deities in the Wiccan religion and they all influence followers in different ways. If we consider the number of covens throughout the world, we can say that there are countless minor deities that help perform different spells and rituals for different covens. On the other hand, you should keep in mind that there are many beliefs in the Wiccan tradition that do not include deities at all. Those are usually ritual beliefs, and they are connected mostly to celebrations of important Wiccan events or other kinds of rituals that are believed to be of the utmost importance. These rituals also represent the core of Wiccan teachings and traditions.

The Wheel of the Year Ritual

When we talk about the Wiccan rituals, it is necessary to mention one of the biggest ones: the Wheel of the Year. This ritual is actually a celebration, and it is not just one. The Wheel of the Year consists of eight celebrations, or Sabbaths, that are held during the course of the year. All of these celebrations are important for Wiccans because they represent the opening of the gates between the mortal world and the magic one, and they invoke excitement and a lot of magical performances during that period. There are covens that do not celebrate all eight Sabbaths, only four or six of them. According to these covens, the remaining two parts of this annual ritual are actually an invitation for dark magic, and they don't want to involve their white magic with it. Solstices are also a part of the Wheel of the Year ritual. They represent important celebrations because that is the time when magic is most intense and Wiccans can draw more power from all objects of nature. The magic is strong and flows through all elements during solstices, and if a Wiccan follower misses them, they also miss a large magical recharge. This can present as a problem in an individual's Wiccan practices during the rest of the year. Solstices are great for recharging crystals and can bring out their full potential, too.

Sabbaths represent the eight celebrations of the Wheel of the Year ritual. These celebrations are sacred to Wiccan religion, and their importance is undoubtedly maintained on multiple levels. Wiccans say that this ritual in particular should be treated with respect and that people should stop making a commercial type of holiday out of it. All Sabbaths are celebrated during either the equinoxes or solstices. However, there is one exception; one of the Sabbaths occurs on a day that is neither a solstice or equinox. Sabbaths happen over the course of the whole year which means that they start at the beginning of each New Year and they continue until the end of it.

First Sabbath: Candlemas

First Sabbath is called Candlemas and it happens in the spring. Candlemas represents the first and true signs of spring and it is celebrated as such. This Sabbath happens on February 1st or 2nd if you live in the northern hemisphere, and August 1st if you live in the southern hemisphere. First Sabbath celebrates the Triple Goddess; it praises her with the prayer that she brings life to the earth and drives away the coldness. Wiccans ask for the flowers and the bees to begin the garden circle as they celebrate Candlemas and worship their goddess.

Second Sabbath: Ostara

The second Sabbath is called the Ostara. It is also a celebration of the spring, but Ostara celebrates the vernal equinox rather than the first signs of spring. The second Sabbath is celebrated on the 22nd of March or the 22nd of September in the northern and southern hemispheres, respectively. Wiccans pray to their Mother Goddess during Ostara also; they ask her to bring fertility to their women and to their animals. This Sabbath is important because it celebrates life and the revival of things that were dead during the cold winter. Ostara is about new life and female fertility.

Third Sabbath: Beltane

Third Sabbath, otherwise known as Beltane, is the Sabbath that is celebrated on the 1st of May in the northern hemisphere, or the 1st of November in the southern hemisphere. Beltane represents the celebration of full spring and its bloom. It is the time when Wiccans ask for the prosperity of their land and their gardens. It is believed that Beltane is an extremely important time to please the Triple Goddess, otherwise she can be vengeful and destroy the harvest. This is one of the reasons why Wiccans try very hard to celebrate the third Sabbath magnificently, and they hope to please their Mother Goddess so she can fulfill their wishes.

Fourth Sabbath: Litha

The fourth Sabbath is called Litha, and it represents the celebration of the summer solstice. It occurs on the 21st of June in the northern hemisphere, or the 21st of December in the southern hemisphere. It is the time when Wiccans ask the Horned God to provide them with the strength to fulfill their duties during the summer and to finish all their hard work that will eventually bear fruit. It is also a celebration in which men ask their Horned God to provide them with virility for that year.

Fifth Sabbath: Lammas

The fifth Sabbath, or Lammas, is connected to the first fruits of nature for the year. It is a celebration dedicated to the Triple Goddess where Wiccans thank her for giving them enough crops and other successful fruits of their labor. It is believed that, if the Triple Goddess is pleased during this celebration, she will give people a better harvest. The fifth Sabbath is celebrated on the 1st of August in the northern hemisphere, and the 1st of February in the southern hemisphere.

Sixth Sabbath: Modron

The sixth Sabbath is known as Modron, and it is a celebration of the autumn equinox. This Sabbath happens on September 21st in the northern hemisphere and March 21st in the southern hemisphere, and it is the time when the harvest occurs. During Modron, Wiccans thank both their deities, the Triple Goddess and the Horned God, and they worship them for the prosperity they gave. There is a tradition to take a part of your crop and burn it as an offering to the gods who helped you have a successful and fruitful harvest.

Seventh Sabbath: Samhain

Seventh Sabbath is called Samhain. The popular name for this celebration is Halloween, and it occurs on October 31st in the northern hemisphere, and April 13th in the southern hemisphere. Samhain represents the veil that lifts between the realms of the dead and the living. It is the night when many Wiccans talk to those who are not amongst the living, and it is important to keep in mind that, if this isn't done properly, it can cause many problems. This one Sabbath out of the eight does not celebrate a season. It is considered to be one of the most dangerous among the Sabbaths dedicated to the Wheel of the Year. There are certain covens that don't celebrate the seventh Sabbath at all, and they believe that this celebration is used to draw dark magic and corrupts their fellow Wiccans.

However, being Wiccan means that one should use its full potential, and it is recommended to celebrate all the Sabbaths rather than just picking ones that seem harmless. The recommendation is to cast a circle while you are paying respects to the gods, and to make sure that the circle is closed while doing it. This is of the utmost importance if you want to try talking to those in the realm of the dead. There is a belief amongst the Wiccans that, if you don't close the circle, anyone can answer your call, demons included, which is how many Wiccans end up starting to use black magic.

Eighth Sabbath: Yuletide

The winter solstice represents the last Sabbath, Yuletide. On the day of the winter solstice, Wiccans celebrate the rebirth of the sun and the fact that the year is almost finished. It is a time when followers show their gratitude to the Horned God since this Sabbath is dedicated to him. Yuletide occurs on the 22nd of December in the northern hemisphere and on the 21st of June in the southern hemisphere.

In order to complete the Wheel of the Year, there are some rituals and spells that require the cycles of the moon rather than Sabbaths. These moon cycles are known as "esbats," and if the spell is not done during this period, the results of the Wheel can be nullified or even go wrong. Esbats are connected to fertility and the tides, and it should be kept in mind that the phases of the moon can influence the spells and rituals, too.

Chapter 3: Elements and Other Wiccan Beliefs

Elements are one of the most important parts of the Wiccan religion, and some even consider them to be one of the core Wiccan beliefs. They are used in every Wiccan ritual or spell, in every description, and in every energy channel. Elements are the anchor of every Wiccan performance and they give them strength and connect them to their gods. Many people believe that there are four cardinal elements, but in the Wiccan religion, there are five. The elements are the force of life, things that sustain and balance energy and existence itself. They give us the ground we walk on, the oxygen we breathe in, and fluids to maintain our bodies; they keep us warm and give us souls in order to survive in this world.

When casting any spells, Wiccans always draw a circle and they call upon the elements they need. It is important to face north while calling upon the elements, and then turn clockwise to every element separately before you move to the center and call upon the one you need the most. You must not leave the circle while casting any spell because once you draw it, the elements form a protective shield around it. Elements cannot protect the person outside of the circle.

The Five Elements

Air

The first of the five elements that we'll talk about is air. It is also the first element to call upon when you are faced north in your circle getting ready to do your spell. Air represents our breathing and the winds that move everything around us. There are many chants that can be used to call upon the element of air, but as a beginner, it is recommended to start with the simple ones that are proven to work. For example, fill your lungs with a deep breath and gently say "I welcome you, air!" Other combinations can be used, but the important thing is to keep the chants simple and concrete, and to make sure that you feel comfortable while saying them.

Fire

After air is summoned, the next element to call upon is fire, which is located on the right side of the circle. Fire represents warmth and is an important part of our food preparation. The same principle of chanting is applied to the fire summoning. An example of a chant is: "Our hearts are warm as we are with desire; you sustain our lives, I welcome you, fire!" If this is not the most comfortable chant, it can be changed according to your preferences. The only important thing is to keep it simple, the same way that you did with the air summoning.

Water

The third element that is summoned in the circle is the element of water. Water is one of the most important elements in nature. It provides us with the water that we drink and it makes up more than two-thirds of our body. It is considered to be the element of life and the one that we must rely on in order to survive. The element of water is found on the south side of the circle, directly opposite from air, since they represent a balance together. The incantation needed for the water summoning works in the same way as the previous two. One of the simplest examples is the chant that says: "You fill the bodies of your sons and daughters; keeping us whole, I welcome you, water!" You can do the same thing as you did with the other two chants and make your own version. Just remember to keep it simple.

Earth

The fourth element for summoning is the one that balances fire. It is the element of earth. Earth represents our grounding; it represents the thing that we are born from, and it is also our final destination when we die. Calling upon the element of earth is also done through a chant similar to the others, and the simplest example is: "We are born from you and return to your dirt; you are our foundation, I welcome you, earth!" Like the chants of other elements, the same concept applies if you want to change it, as long as it is not complicated.

Spirit

The final element that the Wiccans call upon when they cast a spell is the fifth element, or spirit. Spirit represents our will. It is the thing that keeps us alive and conscious. It represents our literal inner being and what is left of us when we die. When a Wiccan follower wants to complete the circle and call upon the final element, they move to the center of the circle. That is the first step. The second step is to say the chant. The chant can be: "You give us will we never want to lose; it is all we have when we die, I welcome you, spirit!"

As in every summoning, you can use different chants; the important thing is to feel the connection with the element. If some other chant connects you better with the spirit, that is the one you should use every time you call upon it. It is important to work on the chants and element summoning because that is the strongest shield you have while performing different spells and rituals. Elements are there to provide protection, and they represent the forces you should be thankful for while closing the circle.

Other Wiccan Beliefs

Even though the main beliefs of the Wiccan religion are available and well-known to many, there are some beliefs within this religion that are not that common. Many people don't know that some parts of the Wiccan community believe in these things. It is not mandatory for every coven, but many of them follow these beliefs.

Reincarnation

The first one is the belief in reincarnation. Reincarnation means that, once when you die, you have the chance to be born again, and you are reborn as another person. You get a new body. Reincarnation is very controversial, and some would argue that it causes disputes. Some covens argue fervently about this belief, and it sometimes leads to chaos. Occasionally, a coven may divide when many practitioners decide to leave it and practice for themselves.

Some Wiccans believe that if you were doing good during your lifetime when you die, there is no reincarnation; you just die and the suffering stops. On the other hand, there are some who believe that, if you did well while you were alive, there are two choices: either you will be reincarnated, or you will go to the "Isle of Souls." The Isle of Souls represents a kind of heaven for spirits in the Wiccan religion. It means that, when you die, your soul travels to this isle and it becomes liberated from all of the pain and the worries of this world. It is an eternal place for you to remain free and painless. There are some who believe that your soul will be reincarnated if you led a pure life, and that only the souls of the bad or evil don't get the chance to be reincarnated. This belief has provoked many debates because some followers say that being forced to live a mortal life over and over again is a punishment rather than a reward for your good deeds.

Many argue that there is no such thing as death and that we all get the opportunity to be reincarnated at some point in time. This belief is based on the premise that every person born gets to have multiple lives over multiple periods of time. The event of death is actually just the final step before we can be born again and live our lives all over again. This kind of reincarnation has another term that is directly connected to this belief. It is a realm called "Limbo." Limbo represents a place where a soul goes in order to wait for its turn to reincarnate. Some religions define Limbo as a realm, or purgatory, that exists between life and death. It is believed that

Limbo represents the neutral zone in which souls dwell, and these souls are neither all good nor all bad. It is further explained that, if you break any rule of Limbo, the punishment is immediate death and you ruin your chance to reincarnate. On the other hand, if you follow all the rules, you enter the world once more as a soul connected to another body. According to this belief, once they are reborn, spirits don't remember their previous lives. The only way you might remember is to have short flashbacks about your previous life while you are still a small child. This is why some people say that children sometimes know things and their answers come out of nowhere. Wiccans believe that the only rational explanation for this situation is that a child is a reincarnated spirit that remembered something from its previous life.

Afterlife

Another Wiccan belief that is spread among followers is the existence of an afterlife. Afterlife is a life given to a person once they die, and the person has the ability to live it without being reincarnated. However, Wiccan religion does not have the same definition of the afterlife as Christians do. Wiccans do not believe in Paradise, nor do they have it.

For Wiccans, when a person dies, their soul goes to a place where it can relax for eternity. Their spirit does not live in the golden streets of Paradise; it rests and has the opportunity to be reincarnated if it finds eternity boring. Wiccan religion is the only religion that considers the possibility of returning to the realm of the living once your spirit leaves the Earth. Followers of the Wiccan traditions believe that energy is an unstoppable, evermoving force; a spirit is built from pure energy and, thus, is able to come back to life.

Animism

Animism is also a Wiccan belief that involves the possession of the spirit. According to the Wiccan religion, everything on the earth has a spirit, whether it is a plant or some other inanimate object. They see everything as a living thing and worthy of our respect since they have feelings. Animism is based on the fact that Wiccans consider the Earth as a sacred element that should always be respected. That respect includes not only humans and animals but also grass, plants, and trees; that is why some Wiccans say that they feel the tree's spirit while touching it. It is said that, if you call upon the earth element and you touch the plants or trees, the Earth connects you to them and you are able to sense their feelings. Wiccans connect this to one of their main deities, the Triple Goddess, who is also referred to as Mother Earth.

In order to sense this connection, it is best to go to an area that is wide and clear, preferably outside of the city, and lay down on the earth. It is important to touch the earth with your skin and not through your clothes. The best thing would be to remove your shoes and wear summer clothes if the weather is nice enough. Focus on your breathing while you lay down touching the earth with your face towards the sky. When you slow your breathing, say the companion chant for calling upon the element of earth. The companion chant is not the same chant as the one used for the element circle. This chant asks elements to join you rather than protect you. You can use a chant like this, or similar to it: "Earth, I call you in the hope that you will come to help me see the pain you hold; show me the damage that was done." By showing the element that it has a choice to refuse the assistance, you show that you care and the element will most likely answer your call. Keep in mind that any sign of excitement can ruin your call; you need to breathe calmly and deeply since earth does not respond well to excitement.

If you want to try to do a similar thing with some other element, like with water, for example, you should not immerse yourself fully as there is a danger of drowning. The safest thing would be to put your legs in the water and focus with your eyes closed while you try to match the rhythm of your breath with the water. When you establish the synchronization, then you can say another companion chant in order to call upon the assistance of this element. An example of this companion chant is: "Water, I call you. I ask you to join me. Show me the problems; show me all I need to see." If the first try isn't successful, you should do it a couple of times and then you may feel a connection with the water. Water is an element that is easier to share a connection with, while air and fire are much more difficult to link to. Fire can be really dangerous, and if you are not careful enough, it can burn you. That, however, doesn't mean that you shouldn't at least try summoning them using the same principles as with the first two elements.

Wiccan religion doesn't prohibit other groups or occult communities, and some of them are even considered good by the Wiccans. However, they do believe that there are many of these groups that represent themselves as good, but they are not. The reality is that many occult groups use black magic and they lack the knowledge and possibilities of the Wiccan tradition. Wiccan religion is formed from various occult groups; that is why they don't have negative teachings about them, and, in some situations, they even exchange and learn different magical rituals and spells from other Pagan communities. Wiccans consider this kind of open relationship important because they can influence others to avoid using dark magic and reassure the use of the Wiccan tradition of doing good. Keep in mind that this attitude is common for most of the Wiccan covens, but does not include all of them.

Chapter 4: Wiccan Magic - Black and White Magic

The Wiccan tradition rests on one rule: you shouldn't bring harm to other people. However, there are many sources, especially on the Internet, that connect magical resources with the use of dark or black magic. There are many websites that even promote black magic, referring to it as necessary and very powerful, while there are others who label black magic as something that causes harm, brings negative energy, and negatively impacts the people around us. In Wiccan religion, causing harm with your magic means that you violated their only rule and that you do not understand what being Wicca actually means.

There are many practitioners of magic that believe in the existence of white magic and black magic. To them, black magic means that you are doing dark spells, while white magic is good and is usually performed by Wiccans. According to these practitioners, Wiccans' magic benefits all living things, and they even note a difference between the black witches and white witches. In this comparison, Wiccans are considered to be the white witches while the others who perform dark spells are condemned to be the black witches. Even though we can conclude that black magic is connected to the dark spells and white magic isn't, the question remains, what is the real meaning of black magic and where this magic does come from?

This is where we go back to the point of history in which Christianity marked any spiritual practice as "black magic." At that point in time, everything that wasn't Christian was considered evil, and those who were performing any kind of rituals that weren't approved by the Church were labeled as sorcerers, or worse, if they were respected by the other members of their communities. When the inquisition started, sorcerers, and non-Christian people, in general, were considered to be the cause and source of any bad situations in everyday life. If the harvest was bad, the Church blamed them; if the animals got sick, the Church blamed them, and so forth. Practitioners of any kind were persecuted and portrayed as negative and evil entities that cause harm just by existing. Women were labeled as witches most of all. They were accused of summoning demons and other evil beings for centuries. The stories often say that these evil witches were able to provide curses to people for money and that they didn't have any moral standards. That is why, when a person thought that they were cursed by an evil witch, they went to look for a white witch to undo the curse. During that time, any bad thing that happened to anyone, including plagues, injuries, or any kind of misfortune or illness, was described as a curse or the deed of a black witch, and people of that era believed that only the white witches could counter the effects. Keep in mind that, in those centuries, medicine wasn't developed, and the scientific discoveries that could explain many things they considered witchcraft had not been realized yet. This is the reason why superstitions were a strong compass for human behavior and why this kind of irrational propaganda was well-received. When you added the influence of the Church, which wanted to suffocate every non-Christian movement, you would get the stories of boiling bodies, people turning into frogs and bugs, and many other scary stories about the black magic rituals that they connected to their so-called heretics.

If we fast forward to the 20th and 21st centuries, we will see that Pagan followers in this era have a different attitude about magic, and these old stories about witches and witchcraft being the cause of all evil were nothing more than myths and superstitions that caused a lot of harm and prejudices. Still, the existence of black magic is not erased, and there are practitioners who still embrace it even though they don't typically use it for evil causes.

This can be explained through the example of curses and hexes. Wiccan tradition suggests that curses and hexes are black magic and that they shouldn't be used. On the other hand, witches who are not followers of Wiccan teachings say that curses and hexes can't be labeled as black magic because they are usually used as self-defense against those who want to hurt them. These curses and hexes are not destructive like burning houses or harming people; they are an act of protection if someone wants to cause the witch harm. This is the attitude and view of non-Wiccan witches. A true Wiccan, however, has a different point of view. They say that, if you try to protect yourself, you should focus on a spell that will protect you yet not cause harm to the person who wants to hurt you. Wiccans believe that negative energy is unnecessary. There is always a way to create protection spells without using curses and hexes and causing negative effects on the person who threatened your well-being. Thus, they exclude all forms of black magic when handling any situation.

Some Wiccan practitioners take this one Wiccan rule of causing no harm very seriously. As a matter of fact, they take it so seriously that they start every spell with phrases such as "I am calling upon the spirits for the good of all" or "In order to harm no one." One of the most used phrases from this kind of Wiccan practitioner is "For the good of all and harm to none." They believe that, by expressing the intention this strong, they can actually make an impact on this reality and invoke positive consequences for various individuals, whether they see it or not.

Most of the spells that are considered to be a part of the black magic legacy are spells for revenge or spells for controlling others. There are people who act angry and vengeful when they are feeling hurt. If someone provoked them or made them feel like they were victims of some kind of injustice, they would turn to spells to get back at those people. The other case is if they are unlucky in love and they want to get their desired partner to love them back; they use spells to control that person's emotions and desires.

Even though all these emotions are known to all sorts of people, including Wiccans, they understand that feelings like desire, revenge, anger, or hatred are not the right reasons to cast a spell or use any kind of magic. Wiccan religion is even against the love spells because they believe that it is dangerous to manipulate another person's will. If it isn't done properly or if the real connection doesn't exist between the two people, this kind of spell can only make the situation worse. It can corrupt the person or even produce an opposite effect, and the person who was the victim of the spell could either end up obsessed with the caster or end up hating them.

There are many Wiccans who label themselves as white witches; therefore, they are practitioners of white magic only. Still, there are many others in the Wiccan religion who don't make a distinction between black magic and white magic. The only criterion that matters according to these Wiccans is the criterion of doing no harm. They say that a practitioner either follows this rule or doesn't; it is unnecessary to label magic with a color, since colors are only used as one of the tools in practicing magic. Colors are important for crystal or candle choice, but they don't define the magic being performed as white or black. In this context, black is the color that symbolizes protection and power, and it is something that every witch wants and uses.

Black is also one of the most common colors that witchcraft communities choose for their clothing. This being said, black magic or white magic is not defined by color, but by the intention of the one who uses magic and casts the spell.

Chapter 5 : Meditate and Visualize

As with every religion, Wiccan religion has important daily practices that help its followers to create powerful and consistent magic. Two of these practices are meditation and visualization. These represent some of the most important elements of daily routines for the Wiccans. Without the proper execution of both powers to visualize and to meditate and focus yourself, a person is not able to achieve their full potential and become more powerful. Meditation is extremely important because it allows you to practice your breathing and to be calm at all times. It is a way of connecting yourself to the divine forces and enables you to alter consciousness and use the full potential of the energy inside and around you. Visualization is equally important because it represents the process of picturing the energies that you are able to sense during meditation. Visualization helps you pull energy from the astral to the physical realm and manipulate it in order to make a change that will affect reality. Mastering these skills takes a lot of time and effort and it can be difficult at first. However, it is a part of a Wiccan practice that cannot be skipped over if you want to perform magic that shows your best abilities. Your magic is as powerful as your intention, and you are ironing your focus and your consistency in those intentions through these processes. Further on in this chapter, we will talk about them in more detail with some basic exercises that will help you as you begin.

Meditate

If you haven't meditated before, don't worry; it isn't that complicated. However, it may take a few attempts before you are really able to focus. Be patient, take your time, and try not to get frustrated.

You should choose the most comfortable sitting position. It can be on the ground or on your favorite chair. The point is that it needs to be a place where you won't get distracted. Put away your phone and silence it, and you should also turn off your TV. You can choose to meditate without music, or you can turn on some relaxing music that will help you focus. Music can be useful to help block other noise distractions at first. Later, when you become more skilled in meditating, you will be able to block the distractions without any help. Now, you should close your eyes and put all your attention to your breathing, which is the most important part of meditation in the beginning. Breathing is the key element for focus and connection to your inner self. The usual way to practice your breathing is to inhale on a count of five and then exhale on a count of five. When inhaling, you activate your diaphragm, the muscle beneath the rib cage, and feel the air filling your lungs. You should inhale as much air as you can while you count to five because it is important to activate both your diaphragm and your lungs. When you exhale, the important thing is to force the air out, which means that you have to empty the diaphragm and lungs again until you finish counting to five. It is necessary to repeat all of this, and after several minutes you will notice that you are calmer and that your body feels more relaxed. When you get used to this breathing, try focusing only on your breathing and prevent your mind from thinking about anything else. In case this is difficult for you when you start, there is another technique. Try focusing on only one image or word and don't think about anything else. This is the best way to focus your mind and relieve yourself from daily stress or worries.

Meditation is a great way to approach your consciousness. It enables you to put yourself into a state of tranquility while helping you exercise both your body and your mind. Additionally, it frees you from stress at the same time. In Wiccan tradition, meditation is considered to be a way to create a profound relationship with the Triple Goddess and the Horned God. Wiccans believe that meditation is a way of communicating with their deities and a way to cleanse yourself of negative energy and emotions before performing spells or rituals. Start with five minutes of meditation every day. When you feel comfortable enough, gradually prolong the time of your meditation. After some time, you will be able to enter a meditative state very quickly, which will be of great assistance to your Wiccan practices.

Visualize

Visualization is, like meditation, considered to be an important tool in order to create powerful and successful magical performances. If you are unable to visualize the impact of the spell you cast, it isn't possible for you to send the right amount of the energy required for that spell to materialize or have any effect.

To start exercising visualization, you need to have a set-up similar to what you had with meditation. This means that you need to find the most comfortable sitting position, whether it is a chair or a place on the ground. The next few minutes should be spent focusing only on your breathing and relaxation. When you calm your mind and close your eyes, you should start imagining a single object or symbol. It is best if you focus on something that you are familiar with. Try with something ordinary like your favorite glass or flower; it could be anything that you know well enough so you can focus on it without having trouble remembering the details. It can be useful to have that object close to you before you start your practice so you can observe it for a while and study its details.

When you start your visualization, you should concentrate on that object as much as you can and try to see it in as much detail as possible. The point is to create the feeling that the object is really in front of you without being able to touch it. It should look realistic in your thoughts. It is not unusual to only be able to concentrate on the basic shape of the object in the beginning. This is normal because it takes time to master the visualization. The problem could be that you can't focus on only one object, and that other things pop into your mind disturbing the picture. That is normal, too. In these cases, you should try to focus on blocking the distractions and keep thinking that the image will return when the distractions disappear. When you block the distractions, you bring your mind back and focus on the image from the beginning. This requires a lot of practice, and it will take some time before you are able to keep one image in your mind for five minutes. When you succeed in keeping one steady image of an object in your mind for five minutes, you should start visualizing things that you are not familiar with. Try to add as many details as possible.

The point is to create an image so realistic that it feels like you could touch that object if you reached out to it. The whole goal of the process of visualization and its training is to be able to perform high-class spells and rituals. The first step is to easily visualize objects with your eyes closed, and the next step is to do it even with your eyes opened. This other step requires much more practice and is more difficult to master.

Exercises

There are great exercises that include both meditation and visualization and can help you release negative energy. Practicing these techniques is a great way to relax, and it helps relieve stress, too. Here is a simple exercise, outlined in straightforward steps, that you can do whenever you feel the need to relieve negative energy, stress, and anxiety:

1. Find a comfortable position and close your eyes.

2. Dedicate a few minutes to your breathing and focus to center and relax the mind.

3. Visualize a glowing, white light that surrounds you. This light should emit tranquility.

4. Try to draw that light directly into the lungs while breathing in and let that light flow through the whole body. The glowing light that you inhaled should relax you and calm the tension in your muscles.

5. When you exhale, visualize all of your stress and anxiety going away with the air that you release from your lungs and your diaphragm.

6. Do this for about ten minutes, or until you feel that you have been released from your troubles.

7. Don't forget to release all negative energy into the ground once you finish the exercise.

It is important to maintain the speed of breathing and keep the same pace during the whole exercise. As your breathing continues, the light that you are imagining should flow through every part of your body, leaving no empty space for stress and tension. These negative emotions are driven away by your exhales.

Another type of exercise important for performing of magic is being able to raise energy. You can raise energy in numerous ways. You can use techniques like meditation, or you can simply achieve your energy goals through specific chants and physical activities, such as ritual dancing or singing.

This first exercise was provided to teach you how to manipulate the energy inside you. Practicing magic means that you know how to manipulate the energy inside you and the energy around you. That is why it is important to understand that all objects have their own energy. For magical performances, the most important energies are those from stones and plants because they have unique characteristics. To exercise how to connect to one of these energies you need to choose an object first. Preferably, it should be a stone or an herb in the beginning.

1. Try to enter the meditative state by closing your eyes and breathing deeply. You will know that you entered this state when your breathing is slow and steady.

2. Put your hand over the object you chose.

3. Focus in order to feel the energy coming from the stone or herb to your hand. There are different ways to sense that energy. It can be a tingling feeling or some kind of throbbing, or you can just feel warmer air touching your palm.

4. Concentrate and try to clarify what kind of feeling you get from this object and if you can connect it to an

image or a specific color.

5. Try to make a distinction between the energy you sense from it. Is it a feeling of protection, of peace, or of energy? Focus on opening all of your senses so you can be aware of the concrete energy that your stone or herb emits.

You should try to do this with different objects and try to feel their energies. Focus on sensing what images they could represent, or what colors you would tie them to. You also need to distinguish what kind of emotions they produce. The first group of objects should be natural ones, and when you feel like you've handled that, you can try to experiment and practice with other objects.

If the object is man-made it can have different kinds of energies. This can be energy from the materials used to make that object, or absorbed energy from the environment and the people around that object before you touched it. A good example of this is any piece of old jewelry. Jewelry is good because there is a good chance that at least a few people have worn it before, and they could have picked up different energies in the past. The exercise is the same: hold your hand on the object, close your eyes, and try to sense what kinds of feelings are there. The point is to get used to sensing other energies and tying them to different images, colors, and emotions.

One step further would be to learn how to put your own energy into the objects. We can use the herb as an example. When you harvest an herb, view it as a sacrifice. To honor that sacrifice, try to share your energy with the herb. The simplest way to do this is to take the herb, put your hand above it, and focus on sending energy from your hand into the herb. It is a kind of reversed process from sensing energies in objects. This is also a good way to learn how to create amulets or charms suitable for your needs. To empower the amulet, for example, you need to infuse your energy into the object in order to boost its magical abilities.

Chapter 6: Charms and Tools

Creating charms and amulets is an important way of practicing magic. As explained in the previous chapters, before you are able to create these kinds of objects, there is a path of mastering techniques like meditation, visualization, energy sensing, and finally, directing your own energy into the objects. When you master these steps, it should be easier for you to start making magical objects that will suit your needs. In order to make a charm or amulet, you must first determine its purpose. You need to decide whether that charm will be used to help you feel more comfortable at work, or you if need it to boost your confidence, for example. Charms and amulets can have different effects. They can be used for protection to fight against threats; they can be used as boosters, bringers of luck or sources of strength. Once you choose the purpose of your charm, the next step is to choose an object that will be fused with your energy. The most usual choices for charms and amulets are pieces of jewelry since you can wear them every day and on every occasion. However, you don't have to limit yourself to just jewelry; charms can be something that you can use as a home decoration or in the yard. It can be something that you put in your car or anywhere else that you like. You should just keep in mind that the object must fit the purpose of the charm, and you need to cleanse it before you direct your energy into it. Cleansing is important because it guarantees that there are no other traces of energy in the object used for the charm, and it is safe to direct your energy into it.

Create Your Charm

As discussed above, creating a magical charm requires a few things. The first is that you are already familiar with energy. The second is that you are able to manipulate the energy in you and around you. The third is that you know how to direct your energy into other objects. Next, you need to decide what kind of charm you want to create, what intent you have, and what the charm's purpose will be. Last, but not least, you need to choose an object that will be a basis for your charm.

Your charm can be useful to you in many ways. It can help you deal with negative emotions, or it can give you courage when you have a stressful situation and you lack confidence. Charms can lift your fears, boost your confidence, help you retain information, help you feel more comfortable when speaking in public, and so on. You can give your charm any purpose as long as it is concrete. Don't forget that the purpose is not the only important element of making a charm. Choosing an object is equally important. You need to find the object that fits all of the requirements; the charm will be as powerful as the object and its purpose combined and fused with your energy. If you decide to use a piece of jewelry, make sure that it is something that you can wear every day. If you need a charm for an energy boost during work, for example, you can make a charm out of your earrings or bracelet. If, however, you need the charm to protect your house, you can choose a decorative crystal or a stone so it can be at your house all the time. The point is that, if you need a charm for daily activities, you don't fuse your energy into that decorative stone; once when you leave your house, the charm won't have any effect. Charms need to be close to the subjects they are made for in order to work.

It is also important to purify your objects before you make

charms out of them. If there are other energies mixing with your own, the charms may not work the way you want them to, so don't forget to cleanse them. Once you have your object purified, it is prepared for the next step of creation.

The object should be put on a pentacle, or if you already have an altar, you can put your future charm on it. Then, you put your hands above the object and concentrate solely on the purpose of your future charm. This is where meditation and visualization practice come into play. You need to clearly visualize whatever this charm is supposed to do. You must be focused on it and block any other distractions. Your mind should be thinking and seeing only this one thing. While you do this, you should meditate and try to feel the energy of the object answering your call, which can be a short chant. Repeat this chant a few times and keep focusing on sensing the energy. The chant should be simple as you are just starting out. If you want a charm that makes you feel calm and relaxed, you can use a simple example such as: "Lord and Lady, I beseech thee; peace and relaxation bestow upon me." Once the energy of the object starts flowing through your body, you should focus to return all of it into your palms and then push it back into the object that you chose to be your charm. Don't forget that you must visualize that this energy is physically entering the charm from your body. The best way to see if the process of creating a charm worked is to try to feel the energy pulsating from the charm. If you feel the pulsation, the process was successful. As with meditation and visualization practices, you need to release any negative or excess energy into the earth after this. It is not unusual to feel tired or fatigued after you are done with the charm-making process. This kind of object empowerment takes a lot of energy out of a person, and you should consider replenishing your energy with food and rest.

Tools for Magic

Tools are a part of magical practices, but they are not a necessary element for those who want to start doing magic. If you don't have the power within you, tools can't help you; that is why it is more important to dedicate the time to master your inner abilities and gain the necessary knowledge. You need to train your mind to focus and to have the willpower to keep improving yourself even though it can be hard at first. If you have an iron will, the results will follow whether you choose to use these tools or not. However, it is important to be familiar with the basic elements that Wiccans use to improve or boost their rituals or spells.

Book of Shadows

The first basic tool that is also one of the most famous ones is the Book of Shadows. The Book of Shadows represents practitioners' personal lists of rituals, spells, lessons, herb attributes, correspondences, impressions, and so forth. Wiccan practitioners, generally speaking, consider this the go-to book for their next spells or rituals. It is recommended to keep a Book of Shadows because it gives you a good retrospective of everything that you've done as a practitioner, and it can be useful as a guide for your future work. Some practitioners use leather books as their Book of Shadows; others use regular notebooks of different sizes and designs. In this era of digitalization, there are many practitioners who choose to keep their Book of Shadows as a kind of electronic diary. It is up to your preference to choose what kind of book you would like to use and how you will organize it. Some Wiccans prefer to organize their Book of Shadows in sections such as chants, invocations, herbal work, stonework, and rituals for Sabbath. There could also be sections like evoking the Triple Goddess and the Horned God, protection spells, healing spells, cleansing rituals, and so on. Whenever you cast a spell or perform a ritual, you need to write down the whole process: what chant you uses, what objects you used, and how you felt during the ritual or the spell. You should write all of this down in your Book of Shadows even if the ritual or spell did not work. If it worked, explain the effects in detail and make notes if you think that something needs to be done differently or if you need to repeat some parts of the spell or the ritual more times. Write down the ingredients if you used any. The good thing about having a Book of Shadows, especially a well-organized one, is that if you need to repeat a certain spell or ritual, you immediately have all of the information you need. This way, you will save a lot of time and energy.

Candles

Another tool that we will discuss here is one of the most common items that any practitioner of magic uses. These tools are candles. Candles are used in almost every spell and every ritual, and this is why a lot of Wiccans usually have large supplies of candles in different colors and sizes. The colors of the candles vary depending on their purpose in the rituals, so it is best to have supplies of the ones you use the most since nearly every spell requires them. When it comes to size, candles are also different. They can be big pillars or just small birthday candles, but all of them are useful for spell work. For example, small candles are good if you need to wait for the whole candle to burn down during your ritual. It takes less time, and the effect is still the same. Another handy thing that you can add to your use of candles is a candle snuffer. Some argue that, if you blow out the candle, the magic blows away too and the spell or ritual won't be successful. That is why some practitioners recommend methods like snuffing the flame or even pinching it. According to them, this is the best way to put out the flame of the candle that was used in a spell or ritual. If you decide to pinch the flame out, be careful and try not to burn your fingers.

Still, if you still think that neither of these methods is useful to you, blowing the flame out isn't something that has been proven to take away the magical effect. Many Wiccans don't use the alternative techniques, and the only important thing is that you do what you feel is appropriate for your particular ritual or spell.

Besoms (Broomsticks)

Whenever you see a witch on TV, she is often portrayed as a lady that flies off on her broomstick into the night. This is a good introduction for another tool used by those who practice magic, even though they do not fly on it as portrayed in the media. This tool is called a besom. Besom is another name for a broomstick, which practitioners of magic use to sweep negative energy. Unfortunately, Wiccans can't fly around on their besoms. However, what they can do with them is to create a sacred space, free from all negative emotions and energies. The size and the kind of broom do not matter, you can choose the one that suits you the best. It can be a decorative broom, a regular broom that you use to clean your house, or just a broom made from branches that you collected in your yard. You can decorate the broom if you feel like it. If you are fond of flowers, you can wrap them around the handle or use ribbons made in different colors. Tools reflect our personality; that is why they are unique. You can use your imagination to adjust them so they feel like they are yours and yours only.

Cauldrons

When we say witch, people usually imagine a woman with two things, a broom and a cauldron. This is the stereotypical image of a witch portrayed in almost every movie, or any piece of popular literature that includes witches. However, just as the broom is not used for flying around, the cauldron is not used for nefarious means. A cauldron is a tool that represents the womb of the Triple Goddess. Wiccans believe that the cauldron is a symbol of creation and rebirth, and in the past, it was used for the preparation of different potions and for cooking. Nowadays, cauldrons are rarely used for making potions; they are more often used to burn ingredients for spells. For example, the cauldron is used by many Wiccans to burn pieces of leaves, paper, or herbs that are needed for a certain ritual or spell casting. Anyway, it isn't necessary to have a true cauldron. Any bowl will do the job. You can choose a steel or ceramic bowl, but just make sure that it is heat proof because you might need to burn something in it.

Wands

A tool that has always been connected to witches, and is used even now in many rituals and spell work, is a wand. Wands, of course, can't actually be used to turn you into a toad, but they are used to focus the practitioner's energy outside of their body when they cast a circle or do some spell. Wands are usually made from tree branches or wooden sticks. Every tree has different properties and magical impacts, so the best way to acquire a wand is to see the options and choose the one that fits you best.

We will name a few common trees and their properties. For starters, you could choose one of these types for your wand:

- **Apple Tree** - boosts healing spells, love, and the magic used in your garden.

- **Ash Tree** - helps your protection spells and rituals, and gives health and prosperity.

- **Maple Tree** - has attributes of longevity, and helps with love spells and money spells.

- **Oak Tree** - represents fertility and luck, and helps with protection, healing, and money spells.

- **Pine Tree** - boosts your energy for banishing danger and negativity, and is also used for healing and fertility spells.

- **Willow Tree** - represents divination and helps with protection, healing, and love spells.

Once you decide which tree is the most suitable for you, just cut a branch from it. The length of the wand can vary, but it is usually about 18 inches long. If the branch is cut from a live tree, you should consider it as the tree's sacrifice and give proper gratitude. Make sure to dry the branch; it is best to leave it for a few days. After you are done with that, you can use knives or other tools to smooth the surface of the branch and shape it. If you prefer, you can carve some decorations onto your wand. For example, you could choose to carve some runes or other symbols. You can even use colored stones or ribbons. On the other hand, you can leave it just the way it is.

It is up to you, as long as you feel happy and comfortable with it.

Athame (Ceremonial Blade)

An athame is another useful tool used during magic rituals. It is actually a dagger that serves pretty much the same purpose as the wand. This dagger is used to direct energy into objects or other things, and it is used in many Wiccan rituals. If you want to follow tradition, the athame should be a double-edged blade, and it should have a black handle. However, it is not necessary to use one, and if you don't mind breaking from tradition, it doesn't have to be a double-edged blade or have a black handle.

Censers

If you want to burn incense in your rituals or during your spell casting, it is important to have a safe place to do it. This is where a censer comes in handy. A censer is one of the tools that Wiccans use, and it is basically another name for an incense burner. Incense is not necessary for your magical practices, but if you want to have a pleasant scent during your work and if it can help you focus and raise your energy, you should think about getting a censer. Censers can be bought online, or you could simply use a seashell, which works excellent for this purpose because it absorbs the heat well.

Boline (Practical Blade)

We have already mentioned the athame, and there is another

knife that is used in magical practices. This knife is called a boline, and it usually has a white handle. Keep in mind that the athame is used to direct energy and is used for magical activities. On the other hand, the boline is used for practical things. Wiccans cut herbs with it or use it to carve symbols on their candles and wands, for example.

Pentacle

The last of the basic tools that Wiccans use is a pentacle, which is one of the most-used symbols in the Wiccan tradition. The pentacle is a symbol of a five-pointed star that is usually engraved onto some material. This could be a wooden or ceramic disk. You can even make one yourself. You can find a flat piece of wood and paint the pentacle on it. This star represents the element of earth and it is useful if you want to empower your charm or other tools.

Cleansing Your Tools

As we previously mentioned, every object has its own energy, and every object can absorb other energies, especially the ones around them. This is why every practitioner of magic will insist on cleansing every tool that they use for their spells and rituals. You can't be sure who used these tools before you, or if there is some bad energy left from the environment in which the tools were placed before. Any kind of unknown energy can affect your work and could be the reason why some of your spells or rituals don't work.

You can cleanse your tools with many different things. You can bury them in the ground, or use sunlight or moonlight to cleanse them. You can use fire, water, incense, or even salt. However, you should take note that tools like your knife or your dagger, which are made from metal, should not be in the water for a long time because they could start to corrode. Or, if you want to cleanse your stones, keep in mind that too much heat could damage them. If you want to cleanse something made out of leather, you should not use water because it will damage the material. You need to think carefully about how to cleanse your tool; the goal is to release foreign energy from them, not damage them.

Cleansing Ritual

A simple ritual that you can use for cleansing your tools requires a few things. These items are not difficult to find, yet they are still very effective. You will need a bowl full of water, a white candle, incense, a dish of salt, and either lavender or sage for this cleansing ritual. This ritual doesn't need circle casting, but if you'd feel more confident with it, you can cast one. After you collect all of these items, the ritual can begin. You should sit on the ground and make yourself comfortable. All the things previously mentioned should be in front of you. When you light the candles and incense, focus on your breathing. It should be steady and calm. Close your eyes. You should try to gently inhale and exhale as much air as possible. Focus on the energy that comes from the earth and rises up through your body. After that, you should visualize your blood as water going through your veins. Connect with the energy of the lighted candle that is heating the air around you. Inhale the scent of the incense and absorb its energy. When you collect all of these energies inside you and you feel like you can balance them, open your eyes. Put the tool that you want to cleanse into the incense smoke and say a simple chant. It could be something like: "I cleanse this tool [insert name of tool] in the name of the element of air." After you perform your chant, you should visualize the air blowing all of the negative energy away from the tool. This is a process that you need to repeat for all five elements if you decide to cast a circle to cleanse the tool. This means that you would need to perform five chants for each individual tool. Remember that you need to adapt the chants to the elements, and you should do the same with your visualization.

How to Cast a Simple Circle

Casting a circle means that you wish to create a sacred, pure space as the area for performing your magic. A circle is a form of barrier that holds your energy at a level required for your spell or ritual. The circle is not just a barrier to keep your energy in; it is also a barrier that keeps other energies out. This is especially important because it prevents disturbances or negative influences that can damage your work. Not all rituals and spells need a circle casting. However, if you wish to call upon the energies of the elements or to invoke spirits, it is recommended that you cast a circle because it will protect you from any negative energies lingering on you. Circles can be used to contain powerful energies, too. Sometimes, you need a lot of energy to perform a spell or ritual, and casting a circle is the best way to keep it in one place. Circle casting can be very simple, but it could also be rather complicated depending on the nature of your magic and its complexity. However, since you are a beginner, here is a simple ritual that will enable you to cast and complete your circle. Once you have successfully performed it, you can add your own changes; just keep them simple.

The first basic step is to set up an altar and draw a circle around you. Then, you should cast a circle by invoking the elements. You can do that by using the chants we discussed in previous chapters. After you have invoked all five elements, you should invoke your deities, the Horned God and the Triple Goddess. The next step is to perform the desired ritual or spell and to thank your God and your Goddess once you are done with your spell or ritual. Don't forget to thank the elements and release them, too. Once you are done, open the circle. This opening means that you have successfully completed the circle casting and the spell or ritual.

Chapter 7: Candle Magic

Throughout history, candle magic has been considered to be one of the oldest known forms of magic. In ancient times, every source of light was considered sacred since people didn't have any other source of illumination but the Sun before that. There aren't any records that can give us an exact year of the beginning of candle magic practices, but we can see that, in Pagan communities, for example, it was common to connect deities with candles and worship them through fire. They also used torches, flaming wheels, or even balefires to show their respect to the gods. This is just one reason why many of our ancestors believed that fire represents a sacred power.

Rituals Through Flame

In the modern world, we have electricity; therefore, light is no longer a problem. However, this doesn't mean that the cult of fire and its energy are not alive. In fact, there are numerous religions that use candles in their services. They use candles for different demonstrations, and to point out specific intentions. One of the simplest examples of a Pagan custom in the modern era is using candles on a birthday cake. It is believed, even today, that if you blow out all the candles in one breath and make a wish while blowing out the flame, your wish will come true. Sometimes, customs like this one are what makes people curious about its magical origins. Feeling comfortable around lit candles is a common thing whether you practice magic or not. They create a pleasant atmosphere and we feel peaceful and calm if we stare into the flame for a while.

If you want to explore this feeling on another level, you should keep in mind that lighting a candle and looking at its flame is considered to be the first step that connects you to the energies around you and shifts you from this reality. You don't even have to perform any spells or rituals for it.

If you are at the beginning of your magical journey, candle magic is considered to be the best starting point. Wiccans believe that candle magic is excellent for those who have just started to explore the possibilities of magic. Candle magic is great because it is very straightforward. It helps you focus your energy and establish correct relationships with elements, other energies, and yourself. Candle magic boosts your abilities and it is simple to use. Still, the strength of magic lies in the thoughts of the caster; that is the rule of all magic, whether you want to use a simple or more complex form of it.

It is important to understand the meaning of the word magic. Magic is defined as a form of art in which a caster sends a specific thought into the spiritual realm so that thought can be manifested and then sent back to our reality or the physical realm. In this context, we can say that the candles are messengers that help us send our particular message. When we perform a spell or a ritual, we actually send our message or our intention through the flame of the candle. The candle acts as our mediator, and as it burns, it sends our intention to the spiritual plane. This is good for a beginner because it is easier to understand the process of transformation and manifestation.

Elemental Representation

Candles are also considered to be a great representation of the elements. For example, the candle's base symbolizes Earth.

Earth keeps the flame lit and it grounds it. The wax represents the element of Water because it can change form and become liquid from its solid state, or it can just vaporize. Oxygen is needed to keep the flame burning and that is a symbol of Air in this comparison. It even becomes visible through the smoke of the candle. The fourth element has a very obvious representation. It is the flame of the candle that symbolizes the Fire itself. In the end, the fifth element, the Spirit, is actually the intention or message that you embed into the candle. This is how the candle is an amazing medium that is so small, yet represents everything that keeps the universe in balance.

Colors

Even though candles have valuable symbolic meaning, they are also very useful to practice the way we use colors and their magical properties. Many centuries ago, people started connecting colors to certain events, items, and attributes. Even today, with no knowledge of magic, we associate the color red with passion, or the color black color with power and death. We know that the color green is connected to the Earth because it symbolizes growth. Colors are associated with many other things; for example, green is associated with wealth, luck, envy, and so on. If you use colors in correspondence with candle magic, you can reinforce your intention and your spell. There are certain candles that are specifically designed for these purposes and they can be found in any color that you need.

Oils, Herbs, and Symbols

You can do other things to enhance the candle's magical

abilities. In addition to choosing the right color for your spells, you can put the candle into oil that is magically charged. Wiccans say that these kinds of oils often have scents that boost the magical power of the candle. Additionally, you can put your candles into herbal mixes that can also enhance its magical performance. You can also enhance the candle by carving specific symbols into it. You should analyze what kind of enhancement suits your spell the best; this is how you should decide whether you will use the herbal mix, symbols, or oils with your candles. Many practitioners watch the shape of the flame once they finish their chants and light their candles. According to them, the bigger the flame, the more potent the spell. Some other practitioners say that, if the flame is strong, the manifestation of the spell will be quick and powerful. However, if the flame isn't strong, this means that the caster hasn't invested enough energy, and the spell will not manifest. A sign of interference with your spells or rituals is seen as a cloud of black smoke coming from the flame. Interference can be caused by another practitioner or circumstances that the caster wasn't aware of.

Ceromancy

Some Wiccans tend to read the melted wax once the candle has burned down. The wax that has melted can have different shapes, and some believe that it is a kind of message or answer. This act of wax reading is called ceromancy. Ceromancy is usually performed by people who are clairvoyant. These people are able to stimulate visions by using crystal balls, bowls, or even clouds. When these people stare into the wax and read signs that they see in the shape of the wax, they can provide you with an answer about your intent. They read signs in the direction of the air that shaped the wax, the appearance of the wax, its general impression, and so forth. You shouldn't be burdened by this in the beginning because you will need to perform a number of spells before you can truly use the ceromancy properly.

Many spells and rituals used by Wiccan practitioners require that the candle burns all the way down without extinguishing the flame. Still, it is not a good idea to leave a burning candle in your house if you are not going to be around while it is burning. If, however, you are forced to be elsewhere, make sure that the candle is moved somewhere where it cannot affect anything else or accidentally ignite something. If you used oils to boost your candle, you need to be even more cautious because these oils are usually highly flammable. Be careful and take care of your environment. The first rule of Wiccan religion is still the same: harm no one, and that includes yourself.

Chapter 8: Crystal Magic

Crystals are some of the most mysterious natural objects that have been considered valuable throughout human history. They have almost always represented something valuable and have been used as a symbol of status in many societies. Crystals represent the power of the Earth, and they have energy that has been used in many cultures and religions. Different crystals have different properties, and they were often used as amulets or talismans for luck, health, and prosperity. Even today, crystals are utilized as sources of energy for different techniques in alternative medicine, for boosting energy in different spaces and, of course, for a large number of magical practices. In this chapter, we will describe the basics you need to know about crystals and their abilities since it is important for you to be familiar with one of the most used natural objects in the world of magic.

Crystals and Their Powers

Even though the most common word for crystal is gemstone, the Wiccan community, alongside other modern Pagan circles, uses the term mineral more often. According to them, there are minerals that are not crystals but still have magical abilities. However, crystal is an accepted expression, so we will use it equally. The definition of a mineral can be found anywhere; it usually states that minerals are substances formed through geological processes during the long existence of the Earth. These substances are inorganic and they represent naturally-formed firm materials that we can extract from the ground. Minerals have different chemical structures, and for many centuries, shamans, healers, and magic practitioners believed that, because of their different structures, minerals had specific abilities and energies. That belief is valid even today.

There are different patterns in minerals that enable them to form different geometric shapes. This is why we mainly call them crystals. Their structures vary and they can be found in different forms and sizes. The most commonly known mineral is called clear quartz. After this mineral, the most common ones are amethyst and rose quartz. These pure minerals are considered to be real crystals, while minerals such as jade, bloodstone, and lapis lazuli are considered to be a combination of several minerals, and not real crystals. On the other hand, some so-called crystals are not even a combination of minerals but, instead, fossilized organic substances.

Even though minerals are made of inorganic substances, Wiccans and other communities that use them believe that they have a life, or at least that they are alive because energy flows through them. In Wiccan practices, minerals are used as a part of many rituals, even those that include healing animals and people, and even rituals connected to the growth of plants.

The piezoelectric effect is a power that crystals like tourmaline and quartz produce. Scientists explain it this way: when we apply some kind of mechanical pressure on these minerals, they answer to the threat with an electrical charge. For example, if you try to smash quartz with a hammer, you will feel the electrical energy coming from the mineral. Other than the piezoelectric effect, some minerals, along with quartz, produce an effect called pyroelectricity; they release electrical power if we expose them to a dramatic difference in temperature.

These are just rare examples of crystals that have any scientific significance. In general, there is still no scientific proof to confirm the alternative healing techniques and effects of different crystals. Even though many alternative communities understand the essence of crystal work, conventional science has not found that undeniable proof. Still, many people around the globe, whether they practice magic or not, understand that crystals have their own energy and that they can affect everything around them with that energy.

Wiccan religion recognizes and nurtures the power of crystals and stones, and understands that this power is the same power that can be found in other natural occurrences like rivers, wind, and so on. Wiccans believe that everything in this universe, whether it is visible or not, is a form of energy, and all energy is connected in many different ways. This is why any thought or intent is also a form of energy; we can send it to any point in the universe if we have an adequate energy field that is made from the crystals we choose for our work. It is a Wiccan conviction that crystals conduct energy and that they can be mediums that can send and receive energy. We can bring healing energy from other objects or realms to us, and we can send our own energy to other people or objects, or to the spiritual realm in order to manifest a great change in our lives.

Wiccans use stones and crystals for many different things. The most common use of crystals is during the circle casting. Wiccans use different crystals to mark their sacred place where they plan to perform a ritual or cast a spell. Crystals are also used as a way to honor the Triple Goddess and the Horned God since they have their particular stones with attributes directly connected to them. As we already mentioned, many tools used for magic can be decorated with crystals. Many Wiccans put crystals on their wands or on their pentacles; they make their charms out of different crystals, put them in their jewelry, make amulets of them, and so on. Magic practices use crystals for many rituals and spells. Crystals are an essential part of a large number of healing spells and divination practices; they are even used to manifest someone's wealth and love.

Throughout the centuries, crystals have been used in the creation of good luck charms. That tradition is alive even today. They are considered especially powerful in protection spells, and they can be an important component or ingredient of complex spell work. The simplest example would be amethyst, which is usually used to boost the power of various spells. You can use crystals in other ways, too. You can charge them with energy and some specific intent and then put them into your house or into your office, or just carry the crystal with you. Some people wear red jasper to give them courage, or they wear a piece of citrine to attract money and wealth. Crystals have a unique ability to correspond with colors. They naturally resonate with vibrations of light which are colors by definition. Colors, in this context, can connect with multiple aspects of our lives; they can resonate with our feelings of love, with our health, or with our wealth when they pick up the right vibration. Take rose quartz as an example. The color of rose quartz, as its name suggests, is pink. Pink is a color that has the vibration of love; therefore, it can draw other love vibrations. This means that using rose quartz can draw you to love, or love to you. As another example, if you use a crystal that represents a green color, such as jade, it will help you attract prosperity.

If you want to acquire crystals, it is not difficult. They can be found in many shops, not only Wiccan ones, but in the shops of many other communities that believe in their power and use them for their practices. There are even some shops that specifically sell crystals, and there you can find a wide variety of different sizes and shapes of these natural objects. Still, there are those who practice magic and believe that crystals and stones choose you rather than you choosing them. According to this belief, even if someone gives you a nice and powerful stone or crystal, you can't tap into its full potential unless the crystal chooses you, too. These practitioners say that you could end up finding your chosen crystals in the most bizarre places. This can happen while you are on a hike or while you visit someone who has a big yard or a piece of land. If you prefer to order online, you need to be careful because the retailer should be someone that can be trusted. Don't forget to send the intent that the right crystals come to you.

If, however, you decide to visit a shop, you will probably be drawn to the stone without much effort. It is believed that the crystal will pull you to it with its color or shape. Make sure to do your homework and research before choosing your crystals. It is important that you understand your own physical and mental abilities, and that you choose your crystals according to those abilities. When you see the crystal, if you feel a positive vibration, that probably means that the crystal is right for you. If the feeling is different and more negative, you shouldn't take the crystal even though it should be suitable on paper. Your instincts are your best judgment when it comes to this matter. Last but not least, the important thing about choosing and using crystals is that you must always cleanse them! You need to repeat the process of cleansing every time you use the crystals, and especially before using them for the first time. After you do this, charge your crystals with some strong intentions and that will be a great basis for your spell work and exploration.

Crystal Uses

Crystals can be used for different purposes. We usually wear them as charms in the form of jewelry or amulets, but magical practitioners also place them on their altars in order to strengthen their magic. Here are some suggestions for crystals and their uses in spells:

- **Amplification** - Crystal Quartz, Opal

- **Beauty** - Jasper, Amber, Rose Quartz, Opal

- **Breaking Bad Habits** - Obsidian, Onyx, Moonstone

- **Childbirth** - Moonstone, Geode

- **Courage** - Carnelian, Amethyst, Bloodstone, Aquamarine, Diamond, Tiger's Eye, Lapis Lazuli, Turquoise

- **Dieting and Weight Loss** - Topaz, Moonstone

- **Divination** - Azurite, Amethyst, Moonstone, Hematite, Opal, Obsidian, Crystal Quartz, Tiger's Eye

- **Fertility** - Geode, Jade, Pearl, Green Agate, Moonstone

- **Friendship** - Pink Tourmaline, Rose Quartz, Turquoise

- **Grounding** - Obsidian, Salt, Moonstone, Hematite, Black Tourmaline

- **Happiness** - Amethyst, Blue Agate, Orange Calcite, Lapis Lazuli, Sunstone

- **Health and Healing** - Diamonds, Bloodstone, Aventurine, Amethyst, Green Agate, Peridot, Lapis

Lazuli, Smoky Quartz, Carnelian, Sapphire, Turquoise, Sunstone, Topaz

- **Love** - Jade, Moonstone, Lapis Lazuli, Emerald, Pearl, Amber, Amethyst, Pink Tourmaline, Sapphire, Turquoise, Pink Quartz, Topaz

- **Luck** - Tiger's Eye, Amber, Opal, Aventurine, Turquoise, Pearl

- **Lust** - Sunstone, Coral, Carnelian

- **Memory** - Emerald, Citrine, Aventurine, Crystal Quartz

- **Peace and Stress Reduction** - Aquamarine, Blue Agate, Aventurine, Coral, Diamond, Sapphire, Amethyst, Obsidian, Carnelian, Sodalite, Blue Tourmaline

- **Physical Strength** - Moss Agate, Tiger's Eye, Garnet, Banded Agate, Red Tourmaline

- **Prophetic Dreams** - Azurite, Moonstone, Amethyst

- **Prosperity** - Emerald, Opal, Jade, Ruby, Pearl, Aventurine, Bloodstone, Green Agate, Tiger's Eye, Green Tourmaline, Sapphire, Topaz

- **Protection** - Amber, Coral, Carnelian, Agate, Emeralds, Diamonds, Lapis Lazuli, Jade, Obsidian, Moonstone, Onyx, Peridot, Salt, Ruby, Topaz, Crystal Quartz, Sunstone, Tiger's Eye, Black and Red Tourmaline

- **Psychic Abilities** - Emerald, Crystal Quartz, Lapis Lazuli, Amethyst, Azurite, Amethyst

- **Purification** - Salt, Aquamarine

- **Sleep** - Moonstone, Blue Tourmaline, Peridot, Amethyst

Chapter 9: Herbal Magic

Herbal magic is considered to be a simple form of magic. Finding the right ingredients is what can make it complex. If you decide to practice herbal magic, you will soon realize that most of the herbs that you need are not that easy to find, and the best way to get them is to start growing them. You can do this in your garden or in your apartment. Still, there are herbs that are basic and easier to find and those are the herbs that you should use in the beginning. These herbs include rosemary, sage, and mint for example. In previous centuries, herbal medicine was very important since there was no other known way to heal people. Shamans and healers were very respected since they knew the properties of different herbs that could help with many health problems. In ancient times, it was believed that herbs connected them to their gods, and Wiccan tradition believes that as well. Ancient Romans and Greeks had considerable knowledge about herbs, and magical practitioners and healers known as druids had even more extensive knowledge of herb properties.

Herbal magic includes everything from herbal medicine to potent potions. The reason why many practitioners turn to herbal magic is because herbal magic always gives results. This magic doesn't rely on the caster's power; it has its own strength that is drawn from nature. With herbal magic, you can treat everything; you can help your friend with a sore throat or you can make your love life better. When modern medicine appeared, magic and medicine were no longer inseparable. Before that, they were always tightly connected. They were a combination of rituals and physical remedies made from herbs. With the advancement of modern medicine, more "rational" healing methods were offered, and herbal magic was relegated to an alternative method of healing. Now, it is even considered to be a superstition, and people are skeptical when practitioners offer them herbal cures.

Herbs for Beginners

There are many complex spells that require a lot of rare herbs. However, there are also basic herbs that are powerful, too, and if you know how to use them, they can be a valuable asset for your magical practices. These herbs are very easy to find, and you can grow them in your garden, or just find them in stores or online.

Lavender

The first and most common herb that you can use is lavender. Lavender is simple and easy to find, and it is durable so you can grow it in your yard or on your terrace, even if you don't have experience in growing plants. It has a specific aroma, and it can also be used as an additional flavor in cooking. However, it has magical uses, too, and it is simple yet quite efficient. Lavender has calming properties and you can often find it in bath oils, calming bags, or sleeping pillows. It is used in the preparation of many teas for anxiety and stress reduction since it helps keep you calm. Lavender is also used for alleviating depression.

One of the lesser known facts about lavender is that this herb belongs to the mint family. In ancient times, people used it when they had love problems or lack of passion. In many cultures, this herb was considered to be useful for protection, and it was an important ingredient for spells that were used to draw negative energy away from a place. Some cultures believed that bundles of lavender gave you strength and courage, so they gave them to women during childbirth. Women were supposed to hold onto these bundles so they could muster the strength to deliver the baby.

If you burn lavender and spread its ashes around your home, it will help promote peacefulness and it will drive away the negative energy. If you are feeling restless and you can't sleep well, you can use lavender to help you fall asleep. To clear your mind, you can take a purification bath using lavender oil. This bath will not just increase your concentration; it will also raise your magical abilities and strength. You may find that lavender is sometimes referred to by different names. It goes also by the names elf leaf, spike, and nardus. It is said that if you keep lavender in your closet or storage room, it will keep away fleas and moths. In astrology, lavender is associated with the planet Mercury and the signs of Virgo and Gemini. Lavender is connected to the element of air.

Nutmeg

Another versatile magic herb is nutmeg. This herb has several properties that make it an irreplaceable ingredient in many spells. Nutmeg is used for providing peace and clarity, encouraging restful sleep, and attracting love into your life. This herb is also used as a medication, and it can be a good booster for memory retention, divination, and any kind of healing. Additionally, it is considered to be a staple in love spells and people often used it for passion, or as a wedding blessing.

Nutmeg is considered to be a spice that is very useful, especially in baking. Nutmeg comes from Indonesia and is actually a seed of the evergreen tree. Nutmeg can be found in almost every store, even though its origin is from Indonesia, and it can be used as a whole or as powdered or ground; this entirely depends on the spell or medicine you will use. That is how you choose which one you need.

During the Middle Ages, nutmeg was worn as a charm for protection. It was believed that, if you made an amulet or charm that contained nutmeg, you would be protected from evil and danger. Still, not every part of nutmeg could be put in the charm. The only part of the herb that could be used for these purposes was its seed. Not only women thought that these charms would help them; men also wore them for different things. They thought that charms made of nutmeg would help them attract women or admirers in general. Charms were usually strengthened with ivory, wood, or silver because it was believed that these materials would enhance the strength of the seed.

If you ingest nutmeg, it will help you with your appetite and your digestion, and it will also help you to sleep better at night. Even though it is useful, nutmeg is also very potent so it is not recommended to ingest it in large amounts. More than one teaspoon of nutmeg can cause hallucinations for the person who ingested it, and it can also be toxic. There are more attributes for nutmeg when it comes to spells. This herb is commonly used for spells that involve prosperity and luck; it is also used for the purification of negative energy, protection, and attracting wealth.

If you spread nutmeg on a green candle that is placed on the ground, it will help you attract money, for example. Or, if you prefer, you can use oil for the same purpose. Just be careful and wear gloves because nutmeg oil is strong and can irritate your skin. If you want some help with your legal matters, the best thing is to carry nutmeg with you and wrap it in a purple cloth. To improve your divination abilities or your focus while meditating, nutmeg should be put in a hot drink, and you should drink it before you start meditating. When it comes to enhancing clarity, you could use nutmeg oil and put small amounts in the shape of a circle over your temples. Nutmeg is also referred to as myristica, which is the name used by Wiccans. Myristica is connected to the signs of Pisces and Sagittarius, and its planet is Jupiter. Nutmeg is associated with the element of air, as well.

Basil

Another herb that is used in cuisine, but has magic properties is basil. Basil is considered to be a basic herb for the kitchen, and it is used in many dishes, especially in Mediterranean and Thai meals. You can distinguish basil by its fragrant and large leaves, and you can use it both dried and fresh, whatever suits your needs whether those needs are magical or just for cooking. Basil is a durable herb and it is not difficult to grow it. This herb grows similarly to mint and it needs to be planted in small pots so it can flourish at its best.

Basil has many meanings, and it is an ingredient that is well-known in folk magic in England. This herb also represents a symbol of love in countries like Italy. This herb was considered to be a good protector against harmful curses or spells. Medically, basil is basically a kind of sedative, and it can help soothe your stomach if you ingest it through a tea. It can also help with digestion issues.

In spells, this herb has many attributes. It is used for spells that involve courage, wealth, fertility, or luck. As already mentioned, it also serves as an ingredient for protection spells, but some believe that it can also be used for exorcisms. If you want to utilize basil's primal function which is protection, you should just put the herb on the floor and let it dispel negative energy or even spirits. If, however, you seek prosperity and luck, you can spread this herb around your workplace or your home, or you can just simply put it in a charm satchel. Basil is associated with Aries and Scorpio. The planet of this herb is Mars, and it is connected to the element of fire.

Dandelion

Dandelion is an herb that many people consider to be a weed. However, the truth is that dandelion is a flower. Even though it can be used in cooking, dandelion's primal properties are medicinal. These herbs can be found anywhere in the world, and almost every part of this herb can be used for something. Dandelions can be eaten as a salad, but their flowers and roots can be used for many other purposes. In the kitchen, dandelion is used to make a few kinds of wine, and you can use their flowers if you want to make jams. When we consider the medical attributes of dandelions, we can see that these herbs are used to help kidney and liver issues because detoxifying tea made of dandelions releases the body from toxins and reinforces the endangered areas. Another benefit of dandelion tea is that it can even help with severe cases of acne issues, which are especially important for teenagers, and it can also assist with eczema and other skin problems.

When it comes to magical properties, dandelions are often used for divination. They are one of the main ingredients for unlocking inner wishes or desires, as tea from this herb helps enhance psychic power. Dandelion tea can be very helpful for spiritual interactions that you usually need in order to make a successful spell or ritual. If you have nightmares, this herb can help chase them away; you just need to put it under your pillow. If you want to attract good luck, you should bury a dandelion on the northwest side of your house. If you want your wishes granted, then the process is different. For your wishes to be granted you need to use dandelions in your bath, or use a more commonly-known tradition from when you were a child and blow on the dandelion. The only difference is that, before you blow on the dandelion in the Wiccan version, you need to say your wish out loud and focus all of your thoughts into it while you are blowing.

In Wiccan teachings, the dandelion has other names, too. You can find it by the names of cankerworm, blowball, wild endive, or even priest's crown. Zodiac signs that are associated with dandelions are Sagittarius and Pisces, and it is believed that its planet is the planet Jupiter. The element that is connected to dandelion as a Wiccan herb is the element of air.

Cinnamon

One of many people's favorite spices is cinnamon. However, it is little known that this herb has both medicinal and magical properties that can be very beneficial. Unlike the previous herbs, cinnamon isn't something that is easy to grow or collect out in nature. However, you can find it in almost any store so it is easy to obtain that way, whether you want it to be ground or in stick form. Cinnamon is actually an herb from an evergreen tree in Asia. This Asian tree has purple berries and its flowers are yellow. Its leaves, buds, and bark are also used for many things other than additional spices in dishes.

For example, cinnamon was used by the Ancient Egyptians as

one of the ingredients for mummification. Long after Ancient Egypt, this herb was brought to Europe, and Europeans used it for many issues, like problems with the digestive tract or stomach aches that they cured with cinnamon tea. Cinnamon is also used by women who are pregnant to ease their morning sickness.

When it comes to its magical attributes, cinnamon is used in spells for prosperity, luck, lust, or love. One of the common magical uses for this herb is spirituality, too, and you can use it if you want to enhance your chances for success or if you seek an overall power. In Wiccan teachings, cinnamon is given other names, including sweet wood. If you want to ward off negative energy, you should put cinnamon in your broom and sweep the energy away. You can use cinnamon sticks in combination with other herbs or objects to decorate your broom in order to strengthen it. If you have lust or love spells in mind, you can combine cinnamon with cardamom, nutmeg, cloves, or ginger, and make powerful spells and potent potions. This spice is connected to the signs of Aries and Gemini. It is said that cinnamon is associated with the Sun and the element of fire. If you decide to work with cinnamon, you need to be careful, because it can irritate your skin. You should wear gloves if you want to put cinnamon into your candle or something similar. If you don't like the idea of wearing gloves, you can just dilute the cinnamon with a carrier oil, and that will work, too.

Sage

Another herb that is easy to find is sage, and it also belongs to the mint family. Sage has been used since ancient times for healing, and you can find it as a garden sage or just a common sage. Be careful not to mix sage with white sage, since they are different herbs. Common sage can be easily found in any local store, and during the ancient times, sage was considered to be a sacred herb. Romans believed that sage could help boost your brainpower and your memory. If you boil sage leaves and make a sage tea with honey, for example, it can enhance your clarity and sharpen your mental acuity.

Many doctors from Arabia drink this tea before surgeries like a ritual to help them perform their best. This herb can also help with fevers. It is good at treating liver issues, and it is said that it can even help with epilepsy. Sage is usually used for smudging or cleansing negative energies from physical spaces around you. It is believed that sage helps people deal with losses and grief, and it can help a person release emotion faster to avoid suffering. Sage helps in protection spells, and it can help you with obtaining wisdom and fulfilling your wishes. There are beliefs that connect sage with spells for longevity, and people in England used to believe that sage could be used to make a health tonic that would prolong your life.

If you want your wish to come true, you should write it down on a sage leaf and put it under your bed. You should sleep with the sage leaf under your bed for three days, then bury that leaf outside your house. White sage is different; you can't ingest white sage. It is very difficult to find it and even more difficult to grow it because it is only typical in the Southwest region in America. Sage is good for many spells and it generally combines well with other things, while white sage has stronger and more potent protection properties. Zodiac signs that are connected to sage are the signs of Cancer, Taurus, and Sagittarius, and its planet is Jupiter. It is believed that sage is associated with the element of air.

Chamomile

One of the most common tea herbs that we use on a daily basis is chamomile. This herb is used in numerous remedies, teas, and medication. It is one of the most used ingredients for natural healing recipes and its basic effect is to calm. This is why chamomile is usually used in teas. In Egypt, during ancient times, the chamomile flower was used to help with fevers. The flower of this herb looks like a daisy, and it has a scent that reminds you of apples. Women use chamomile to help them with menstrual issues, and many people use it to help them reduce stress. It can be useful with digestive problems and healing in general.

When it comes to magical properties, chamomile can be used in spells for wealth and love, and it can be used to purify the body. If you burn chamomile, you can attract money, and if you put it into a satchel, you can make a prosperity bag. On the other hand, if you wash your hands with chamomile water, you can attract luck into your life. Chamomile is an herb that is used as a booster in many spells, and it is a well-known tranquilizer. If combined with other herbs, it can boost protection spells, too. Chamomile is connected to the signs of Scorpio and Leo. It is associated with the Sun and the element of water.

Lucky Tea Recipe

A simple way to practice herbal magic is to begin with simple teas. You can try making tea for luck since no one can have too much luck in their lives.

The simplest way is to buy a black tea bag and use it as a base for your tea. You should keep in mind that black tea has caffeine which is useful for boosting energy that can help you with attracting luck. You will need one bag of black tea, half of a teaspoon of ground cinnamon, and a quarter of a teaspoon of ground nutmeg. Wait until the black tea is fully brewed, then add the other ingredients and brew the tea again for one to three minutes. Wait until the tea and spices are completely stirred in, and then you can start chanting a simple incantation such as: "Luck, lucky me, luck; luck achieved with this tea." Repeat this a few times and take out the teabag. You can add honey if you like and that's it. Your lucky tea is prepared!

Spell to Attract Wealth

There is also a spell that you can use to attract wealth because there is no one who couldn't use extra money now and then. Even though money can't buy happiness, it can certainly make your life easier and open some opportunities. If you decide to use this kind of spell, keep in mind that if you think too hard about the source of the money, the spell can go wrong. You could end up with no success with your spell and you could make some bad decisions along the way.

The wealth should come to you; that's how it works. You can't decide where it comes from, and you can't use a spell to specify a certain amount. You should just focus your thoughts on wealth and the universe will provide. In order to make this spell work, you will need one green votive candle, one teaspoon of dried basil, half of a teaspoon of ground nutmeg, and half of a teaspoon of ground cinnamon. You will also need prosperity essential oil if you want your spell to work.

You need to take the green candle and put oil on it. The proper way to do that is to put a few drops on the base of the candle and rub the oil into the candle with your fingertips. Roll the oiled candle into the dried basil and place the candle into the holder. You should use a chant such as: "From the stream of abundance, allow money to flow to me." When you say this, you need to light the candle. After that, take a pinch of both cinnamon and nutmeg and mix them. Sprinkle the mixture above the lighted candle. Be careful because you must not put out the flame of the candle while sprinkling. In order for the spell to work, you must wait until the candle burns down entirely, and you need to use a combination of meditation and visualization of the wealth that will come to you while the candle burns down.

Chapter 10: Wicca and Ethics

Many of us started on the path of Wicca purely because we found the concepts interesting. Maybe the idea of magic intrigued you, or maybe you simply weren't satisfied with the modern-day monotheistic religions that dominate today's spirituality.

Regardless of that, chances are, you haven't given too much consideration to ethics in your pursuit of Wicca. After all, rarely does such a freeform religion need to police itself for morals.

With that being said, the power vested in magic can be quite tempting, and after all, who could blame you if you felt tempted to curse that girl who bullied you in high school? This is often done because of a lack of understanding of two main Wiccan principles: the Rede and the Threefold Law.

The Rede

It is highly unfortunate that many Wiccan authorities, especially many rising to fame online these days, don't give enough attention to morality in Wicca. Fundamentally, Wicca is about spirituality; it is a religion, and like all religions, it aims to do good.

While topics like tarot, crystals, or even fairies and mythical creatures are often explored in depth, topics like morality are often neglected and ignored.

To illustrate why this is important, an atheist could pray to

God, and it wouldn't make them Christian, because they don't follow Christianity. In that same way, anyone could do magic, or be interested in things that are beyond the scope of our own limited reality, but that alone doesn't make them Wiccan.

In order to truly be Wiccan, one needs to follow the principles of the religion itself. The core of Wicca is, in fact, in its morals. While anyone can worship Pagan gods and goddesses, that intrinsically does not make them Wiccan. On the other hand, if they do that and also follow the Wiccan principles, then they are.

The Wiccan Rede is a simple thing at first glance. It appears to be only a singular sentence; however, that sentence contains multitudes within it. The thing that sets Wiccans apart from other religions, and the thing that sets Wiccans apart from other Pagans is adherence to this simple, yet intricate sentence.

The Wiccan Rede reads as follows:

"An it harm none, do what you will."

Now, here raises a good question. Where did the Rede come from? After all, such a powerful and impactful sentence must have come from somewhere. It has shaped the Wiccan religion as we know it today on a very fundamental level, and yet many people misinterpret it, or are not aware of its origins.

Now then, let's do some digging, shall we?

In the year 1534, French novelist François Rabelais published the classic novel *Gargantua*. We can find within it a phrase that many believe became part of the Rede:

"Do as thou wilt, because men that are free, of gentle birth, well-bred and at home in civilized company possess a natural

instinct that inclines them to virtue and saves them from vice. This instinct they name their honor."

This appears slightly different than the Rede at first. After all, it is far wordier, and seems to posit an intrinsic value upon honor. Meanwhile, Wicca isn't really all that about honor. That is not to say it is impossible to include honor in your practices, or that you should have none, but the Rede itself doesn't argue for its cause. So, how did this turn into what we know today?

We go back to 1901 when another Frenchman by the name of Pierre Louÿs published his groundbreaking work *The Adventures of King Pausole.* While this work is often overlooked today, the main character of the book posits a statement that is quite similar to that of the Rede.

"Do no wrong to thy neighbor. Observing this, do as thou pleasest."

Now, this sounds pretty much like the Rede, doesn't it? Well, it does certainly seem like it at first glance. Upon a second look, however, we note that this doesn't include yourself. You are not your neighbor, after all.

A short three years after that, Aleister Crowley published *The Book of the Law,* another must-read of Wiccan literature. Due to Crowley being familiar with the two works mentioned above, he includes the following sentence within it:

"Do what thou wilt shall be the whole of the Law."

Now, it is important to note that this is in the context of Thelema. Because of that, the rest of the book goes on to say things like:

"Love is the law, love under will."

While we could stay here all day and debate interpretations of Thelema, I believe it is fair to say it has had a large hand in shaping Wicca as we know it today.

Fifty-three years later, Gardner published his book, *The Meaning of Witchcraft*. This book laid the foundations of Wicca almost single-handedly. Within it, we find the following sentence:

"They are inclined to the morality of the legendary Good King Pausole, 'Do what you like so long as you harm no one.'"

We will never know which of the two greats Gardner took inspiration from: Louÿs or Crowley.

Strangely, our journey doesn't end here. In 1964, Doreen Valiente, one of Gardner's past High Priestesses, who is also responsible for funding Wiccan liturgy together with him, gave a speech. In this speech we find the first usage of the Rede as we know it today:

"Eight words the Wiccan Rede fulfill, An' it harm none, do what ye will."

Now, let's take a good look at the language used in the Rede.

If you're confused, and not really sure what I'm talking about, keep in mind that the Rede is fairly old. In this chapter, we'll only be looking at the Rede in its original form. If you've done some independent reading, you might have run into extended versions of it. These are generally poems that evolved from the Rede. However, they are not considered to be part of it.

The fact that the Rede is so old is a double-edged sword. On one hand, it helped cement Wicca in the time it needed it the most. On the other hand, it can confuse younger people trying to get into it. This is because the words of the Rede can't simply be taken for what they mean in a modern context, and must instead be understood from the perspective of someone in the 20th century.

Let's analyze the Rede word by word, and determine what exactly makes it so complex:

An: I wasn't kidding when I said word by word! Many would think that this word stands for "an" or "and." However, that couldn't be further from the truth. In fact, due to its archaic usage, in this form, it means a variety of "if" implying a conditional. It can also be interpreted to mean "as long as" without changing the Rede's meaning.

It: Well at least this word retained its meaning! "It" just refers to whichever action you're currently in the process of doing.

Harm: Now, harm in Wicca is much more nuanced than it appears at first glance. In Wicca, telling someone off is the same level of harm that physical violence is. The "harm" here refers to any malicious deed, be it mental, emotional, spiritual, or physical. Wicca doesn't make a distinction here. Harm can also be further understood to refer to passive means as well. For example, manipulating or coercing someone into doing something can be regarded as harm.

None: Now, you'd think this refers to people, right? Well, not exactly, or at least, not exclusively. The "none" here refers to not just people, but also things and inanimate objects. For example, hurting the planet by littering would fall into this category.

Do: Commit an action. This implies that you have already considered and adhered to the caveat of "An it harm none," implying your action will be harmless.

What: This is also precisely what it looks like, the exact thing you're trying to do.

Ye: Here, ye is used not in its singular form, referring to you, the person, but rather the plural, referring to all Wiccans of the world.

Will: "Will" in this sense can be interpreted in a twofold manner. The first way that you can interpret the usage of this word in the Rede is "will" meaning want or desire. On the other hand, you can also interpret it the way Crowley did, and consider it the grand destiny of your life instead.

So, what would the Rede sound like in modern terms?

"If your action is not causing hurt to anyone, or anything, then proceed and commit the action that you desire to do."

Alternatively, if you ascribe to Crowley's definition of will:

"If your action is not causing hurt to anyone, or anything, then proceed and pursue the grand destiny of your life."

Forming a Proper Interpretation

Repeat after me: the Rede is not the same as the Ten Commandments.

Far too many Wiccans obsess over following the Rede as if it were a commandment. It might sound like a mandate to not cause harm in any way shape or form. This is where stances like supporting veganism and pacifism come from in Wicca.

Interpreting the Rede

There are many Wiccans who take this interpretation to extremes. Some see the Wiccan Rede as a commandment of sorts, a mandate to never, ever do harm. It has even been used in this context to support stances like veganism and pacifism. On the other hand, the Rede has also been used against Wiccans. In fact, it has been used to call Wiccans out on hypocrisy for failing to live up to the Rede's command.

The issue with taking the Rede literally is quite similar to the issue that arises when any religious document is taken to the extreme; it's impossible.

How are you supposed to live without doing any harm? Taking weeds out, or even just killing off a disease by taking your medication is technically causing harm. It is impossible to follow the Rede this literally, and it was never intended to be taken as such.

In fact, the word Rede itself is taken to mean "wise counsel," and said definition of it takes any kind of mandate out of it. It means that you should consult your own wisdom when applying it. It is most certainly not wise to let yourself die instead of killing off a flu virus.

The Rede is not a God-given commandment; rather, it was written by spiritual people like us. It is good advice, an excellent rule of thumb, and a guiding post for all aspiring Wiccans. However, it is still just advice, and should be applied with thought, rather than with haste.

The ideology proposed by the Rede is extremely simple: if what you want to do isn't causing hurt or bringing pain upon any person or object, just do it. Don't feel guilty about it or let anyone dissuade you; if you're not hurting anyone or anything else, then there is no reason to be dissuaded by anything. Keep in mind that this does include yourself, and the Rede frowns upon self-harm in every way, shape, or form.

Is Harm Really Inevitable?

Maybe you weren't convinced with our example before. Maybe you need some convincing that true harm, to people, rather than objects or viruses, is not unavoidable, and can only truly avoided if all people acted in the correct manner.

Now, think about it this way, would it be harmful to break up with someone that you love who is hurting you emotionally? Naturally, you would say yes, you are hurting them. But think of the converse; if you don't break up, you're hurting yourself.

Harm, in this case, is entirely inescapable. If a rat bit your child, of course you would lay down traps or call an exterminator. Just because you're Wiccan doesn't mean that you have to pretend to be a saint.

The Rede doesn't actually speak about what to do when harm is involved. If you read it carefully, it doesn't say "Don't do it if it harms someone;" it just says "Do it if you want to and it harms no one."

It doesn't really make sense to read into the Rede to the degree of making existing practically impossible. One of the most important aspects of Wicca is finding a good balance in all the things you do. Then, why would it also promote an extremely polarized philosophy that is literally impossible to uphold? This is usually proposed by Christians, who want to believe that Wicca is in line with their belief that man is sinful by nature. No, man harms by nature, but so do rats, bees, rocks, and quite literally everything that exists.

Wicca doesn't make arbitrary mandates; instead, it wants you to carefully consider your actions. It does not do this to limit you, but to help you grow, take responsibility, and see the world properly.

If you took the Rede as "never harm anything," then suddenly the Rede contradicts the rest of Wicca. In fact, it contradicts the whole realm of black magic. Take the advice to do what you wish when you're doing it with responsibility and considering the consequences at the same time.

Take note that Wicca only uses the Rede as a rule of thumb. It is not a god-invoked saying that should dominate your life, but rather a guideline to help you act.

Usually, when you hear someone talking about the Rede, it'll be in the context of using magic or casting spells. You can hardly find a Wiccan community online without seeing that some people are protesting the use of black magic, love spells, or hexes.

Now, sure, the Rede can apply here, but those same people rarely take the time to consider if they actually apply the Rede to their daily lives.

You may apply the Rede when thinking about whether you want to hex that teacher that was mean to you in middle school, but how about when going grocery shopping? Do most Wiccans think about the Rede when they're putting themselves and others in harm's way when they talk on the phone when they're driving? Do they get so arrogant to presume that in these cases they're above the very Rede that they preach about? Or maybe they consider themselves superior drivers for some reason, and believe themselves to be infallible?

Do we invoke the Rede when we intake chemicals that are found in our food, and we all know are harmful to us? How about when we smoke cigarettes? Do we think about the health impacts of these things before we buy them?

How about giving in to our hedonistic desires? We've all bought something on impulse, and we might know that it's a bad decision, but we still do it. Are we violating the Rede here?

It's worth keeping in mind that, while we Wiccans try to stay moral and ethical, we are only human. Humans naturally make mistakes, and cannot force themselves to consider everyone else with every decision they make.

Humans are not sinful; they are simply imperfect. They make mistakes, and they do things that they shouldn't. And you know what? That's perfectly fine.

Have you ever gotten irrationally mad at a grocery store clerk for not wanting to take a coupon that might have expired, even though it could lead to getting a mark against them, which in turn could even cost them their job? Quite possibly, but later you thought about it and understood that it wasn't their fault.

On the other hand, if a cashier gives you the wrong change, you have probably gone back and told them about it. After all, the extra $10-15 might be the difference between them keeping their job or losing it.

I'm not trying to play the moral judge here. All I want to show you is that Wicca, like all religions, is fallible because people are. I also want to point out that Wicca is not just a hobby; it isn't just something you do for fun whenever it's a full moon. Sometimes you have to make hard decisions, and sometimes the right choice won't even be clear. When those situations arise, we need ethics and morality to guide us. Because of that, while applying the Rede in every situation is pretty much impossible, we should strive for it as much as possible. Not only for our sake, but for everyone else's.

With that being said, the Rede is not all there is to Wiccan morality. The Rede is not the end of all moral tenets that you should be following. Rather, it is merely the start. There are quite a few others that are definitely worth a mention.

Now, we'll take another side of Wiccan morality, one that is possibly even more important than the Rede. We'll think about how it is applied, and analyze it just as closely as we just did the Rede.

The Threefold Law (Rule Of Three)

The Threefold Law is the best reason not to curse someone. It's one of the most fundamental laws in Wicca.

The Threefold Law can be put simply as:

"If you put energy into something, you shall reap the returns threefold."

The "threefold" here is highly debated. It is best taken metaphorically, rather than literally. Sure, you might not precisely get three times the energy, but you will get it back.

Essentially, what this means is that anything you do, whether good or bad, will come back to you three times over.

So, let's try to take a numerical approach here. Say you perform an act that can be qualified as good; let's number that with a 1.

The threefold law states that something will happen to you that is three times as good, or a 3. Alternatively, you might just get three things that are that good.

This might seem familiar to you because the concept is similar to karma. However, the threefold law is a lot more potent.

For example, when dealing with karmic laws, sometimes you might feel like something bad is deserved enough that, even if it returned to you it would be worth it.

For example, you might dislike someone enough that if you just do one bad thing to them then even if it comes back to you, you would feel like you have done the correct thing.

In the case of the threefold law, your returns would be threefold. This means that, in order for you to do something bad to someone and have it been "worth it" you have to endure three times the pain.

This is an extremely powerful thought, and should be put to mind not only in your spellcasting and magic, but also daily life.

The threefold law is part of many Wiccan traditions. However, there are some Wiccans who don't ascribe to it.

The "three" here descends from chaos magic. Many Wiccans have tried to perform experiments on the subject, and have concluded that the law operates in a symbolic twist.

There are two versions of the threefold law, one of which applies only to magical energy, suggesting that the law itself is of supernatural origin. On the other hand, the other version says that it descends from the fundamental laws of the world, and applies to anything we do.

There are two main ways of looking at the "three times" in the threefold law. The first is that the energy will be returned to you three times, regardless of intensity. For example, regardless of whether you killed someone, or just shouted at them angrily, you would experience misfortune thrice. This might be something as mundane as getting an annoying piece of popcorn stuck in your teeth, or as serious as a death in the family.

This version of the law is much more unforgiving because it means every time you harm someone, you might experience some serious misfortune. On the other hand, it is also less rewarding because good deeds aren't returned with the same intensity.

This is the less ascribed to version of the law, for the obvious reason that it is a lot more random.

The other version is the version we described above, where an input of 1 results in an output of 3 towards you.

The origins of this law are, well, fairly muddled. This is because the concept of threes, as well as the concept of karma are widely recognized in a variety of cultures. In general, most people believe it descends from the teachings of Gardner again, who put it up in his first work on Witchcraft. On the other hand, Gardner did not consider the Threefold Law to be intrinsic to his craft.

Later on, others began to pick it up. For example, Raymond Buckland is largely credited for making the Threefold Law more mainstream in Wicca circles. It is also referred to in most of the extended versions of the Rede that try to unite the whole of Wicca with some basic tenets and principles.

Regardless of that, there are many in the origins of Wicca that had never even seen or heard about the Threefold Law. There are also many who simply doubt that it involves the precise number 3, or even that it exists in the first place.

Many modern-day Wiccans regard the law as simply a product of wanting to include morality in Wicca. Instead of the Threefold Law, many think that the Laws of Cause and Effect or the Law of Return are much more accurate for the karmic events that occur in magic.

Both of these laws are simply variations of the Threefold Law, boiling down to a concept of "if you do bad things, bad things will happen to you," and vice versa.

Despite all of that, the Threefold Law is still an extremely important thing to include due to its importance in the rising of Wicca, as well as its general principle being followed in most of its denominations.

Conclusion – Wicca Book of Spells

We've come to the end of our journey. Finally, we've reached the finale of our story, at the very least, for your introduction.

The world of Wicca can be frightening; it can make you restless. It is not, nor will it ever be, cut-and-dried and simple. It is less of a religion, and more of a way of life. You cannot simply put a stamp on yourself that says "Wiccan" like many other religions are wont to do; you must live while upholding the teachings of Wicca.

Which teachings, you ask? Whichever ones you wish to follow! Wicca is not a religion that exists simply to be followed; you need to find your own path. Nobody else can define your craft.

For example, you might want to worship Pagan gods. In this case, the issue becomes which gods? After all, there are countless Pagan gods, ranging from the Egyptian pantheon to the wild and uncertain gods of the Slavic nations.

You do not need to pick just one, or even any at all. There are plenty of Wiccans who don't buy into the idea of a god. You could even call them atheist, not believing in anything but the magic of the Earth.

If you worship, say, Perun, you might feel a strong connection to thunder and lightning. You might even love saint Ilija, who is the Christian incarnation of this god. In these cases, you might feel like you need to bind your craft to that god. You might feel like you want to add lightning to your life. Maybe you simply want to leave water out while there's a thunderstorm to charge it with energy. Maybe you feel like your sigils do best whenever there's lightning.

In all of these cases, your god is your own, and your connection with them is unique. You might not even do anything special other than praying to them every now and again.

In this book, I hope I have managed to give you an objective and balanced view of Wicca. Naturally, some of my own beliefs and systems might have seeped into the book, but do not feel like you have to agree.

If you don't agree with the Rule of Three, then don't follow it; don't believe in it.

The biggest difficulty in this book was presenting the variety that Wicca offers. The five elements, what most would think are the main things about Wicca, aren't even the same in all denominations.

If you simply read this book as a skeptic, as someone that does not and will not believe, I hope I have given you a good view of Wicca. To you, first and foremost, I want to show Wicca not as Satanism, which is an absurd comparison bred from ignorance, but as a tightly-knit, free system of beliefs.

You should also have understood by now that there are no such things as black witches and white witches. There are those that practice primarily black or white magic, but generally, all of them will dabble in the opposite sometimes. Know that black magic isn't evil and white magic isn't good.

Meditation is also an important aspect of Wicca. While it isn't a necessary component of every Wiccan's daily life, it helps bring us closer to the spiritual ideals that have brought us to Wicca in the first place.

I also hope that the meditation techniques I've taught you will come in handy for you. The visualization techniques are also very important, so make sure you practice them often.

Charms and sigils are also very important to making magic. I've taught you one way of creating your own charms, though some people draw sigils on things, even their body parts, and find that this helps them.

I've also recommended some tools to you. Keep in mind this is what I have found most useful, personally. You might find that some of them are useless, or that there are too many for you. The only thing I'd strongly recommend is cleansing your tools before any use.

Even if you think that no one has tampered with them, who knows what kind of energies have been going around, or if a spirit has laid its hands on your tools.

Candle and herbal magics are two types of magic that are very close to my heart. It saddens me to know that many modern Wicca circles neglect them. Candle magic was the first kind of magic that my mentor taught me, so it holds a dear place in my heart, as well as in my craft.

Crystal magic is more in vogue, though it is also much more subjective. If you have ever looked at online resources for Wicca, then you have probably seen about a thousand contradictory meanings for a single crystal.

This is largely due to a lot of misinformation going around these days due to the Internet. Because of that, I tried to keep the portions regarding specific crystals relatively small, and instead focus on what crystals can do in principle, as well as how they work.

Herbal magic is another kind of magic that has slowly been

picking up steam. It is especially popular among younger Wiccans who don't want to "out" themselves to their families. There is a lot of stigma surrounding Wicca. Because of this, many young people prefer to stay private with their craft.

Herbal magic lets you do this easily because all you need is plants. You could easily tell the people around you that you're just really interested in botany. The luck and wealth recipe is also easy to follow, and can really provide a massive boost to your life.

Finally, we considered Wicca and ethics. The only two things I want you to take from that is to use your craft with care, and to beware when you are cursing or hexing, for it can end up rather badly for you.

Finally, a word of caution: beware of online forums.

There are many people on the Internet who have been putting their own thoughts online. For the uninitiated, these may appear as gospel coming from an authority. However, many of these people simply don't have the necessary credentials, or might just be talking without any knowledge of the topic.

This has become increasingly common with the phenomenon of "Witchblrs" which are Wicca-themed blogs on the popular social network Tumblr. These Witchblrs tend to be where people post Wicca-related stuff.

This Wicca-related stuff is quite often wrong, and can sometimes even be dangerous. You may see people talking about how mythical creatures are no big deal, and spirits are easy to deal with. This is an easy way to spot someone that's talking without experience.

Dealing with a malicious spirit is one of the most terrifying experiences a Wiccan can have. People that say that it happens to them daily tend to be those that are, for lack of a better phrase, doing it for attention.

After all, it is pretty much wrestling with forces of nature. There has also been a large upswing in the "chaos magic" movement, which, contrary to its name, focuses on treating magic as a science. If magic were that simple, it would already be a part of science. This does not mean that chaos magic is bad per se; some people just go too far and too deep with it.

Finally, stay independent. As a beginner, you might want to find a mentor to help you, or your learning might stem from books like these, but always keep your craft unique. Remember that nobody else can tell you what your craft is and is not. It is your own, and you can use it in the manner that you want. Although adhering to some basic morality is definitely a good idea.

As your experience grows, chances are you'll go far away from what most of us might consider Wicca. However, it is still your own craft, and it works for you. In the end, Wicca is both a religion and a lifestyle.

It is not only about facts; it is also about faith. You must have faith in your gods, in your abilities, and in your practices. If you do not truly believe that what you are doing will work, then, according to Wicca, it won't. That is why it is so vitally important to keep it in mind.

I hope this book has provided a good first step. You will find that there is a treasure trove of resources out there that can help you out with your learning. This book is not meant to replace, but to complement.

Never stand still, always keep learning, keep advancing your craft, and who knows, maybe in a few years you will be teaching me something new!

Witchcraft

A Book of Shadow to Practicing Wiccan Magic with Traditional and Contemporary Paths (Elemental Magic, Moon Magic, Wheel of the Year Magic)

Introduction - Witchcraft

On a daily basis, we are bombarded with news that leaves us alarmed and surprised: violence, hunger, prejudice, crimes, uncontrolled exploitation of natural resources, and global overheating to name a few. There are so many problems that sometimes it seems that some divine force has abandoned us, leaving us at the mercy of the mess we've made and the problems we've created ourselves. If the Earth is under the rule of what some call God, that god has proven extremely inefficient and unable to successfully manage it. Our planet now resembles the home of a family whose mother has gone on vacation and everything has been left to the father, who is trying to manage the home and the children at the same time. Everything had become chaos.

Our world is like this: chaotic! People without direction, lives without goals, and a stunning lack of ethics. This is the astonishing vision of contemporary society. The father does not seem to have been able to educate his children well. The values that are usually transmitted to us through the maternal figure seem to be missing. The reason for this is obvious: the world has grown for thousands of years without its mother, the Goddess. It's time to return it to your former ruler!

Wicca is one of the few religions today, if not the only one, which again proposes to celebrate a feminine deity as Creator of all life. At a time when we are suffering from the marks that the androcroscopic and heteronormative religions have left us, it is understandable that Wicca is one of the fastest growing religions in the West.

People are no longer satisfied with corrupt and political religions with outdated visions of the world, with the same empty speeches that have long failed to inspire us. Wicca is a response to this lack of spiritual significance provided over time by religions that have done nothing but exploit the world and human beings. Because it is a highly individualized and cell-like religion, Wicca has demonstrated itself to be a perfect religion for modern humans. There is no room for manipulation, political play, or inadequacy in the contemporary world. Wicca is different for each person and group. It has been so since its inception and will continue to be for much longer.

Even so, it does not escape the vices of human nature. In it, there are those who, still contaminated by centuries of patriarchy, insist on upholding the discourse of truth that is unique and irrefutable. Daily we come across practitioners who in their orthodoxy do not spare energy in spouting at those who think differently and defy their false authority. Those who are accustomed to frequenting mailing lists, chats, and communities on the Internet are more than accustomed to seeing this in an endless repetitive pattern.

The saddest thing is to see those who began their journey in the Art with sincerity, precisely because it offers a liberating spiritual vision different from those found in conventional religions, be contaminated by such people and become exactly the opposite of what they sought at the beginning of their search for Wicca. A phrase more than appropriate to these people rests in the wise words of Victor Anderson, the founder of the Tradition Feri of Witchcraft: "Do not become what you reject!"

In his last address, Doreen Valiente, one of Gerald Gardner's first initiates and considered the Mother of Wicca, uttered the following words:

"To the initiates of the ancient Pagan Mysteries I was taught to say, 'I am the son of the earth and the starry sky, and there is no part of me that is not of the Gods.'"

From the days of the old Witchcraft Study Association in the 60s, we have made great progress in my opinion. We've spread ourselves throughout the world. We are a creative and fertile movement. We inspire art, literature, television, music, and historical research. We live under slander and abuse. And we survived treachery. So it seems to me that the 'Powers That Are' must have a purpose for us in the Age of Aquarius that enters. So be it.

Doreen, like many around the world, has made her invaluable contribution to Art to help it become what it is today: a religion without frontiers, seeking to stay aloof from the vices of the dominant religions. Her wise words should inspire all those who at the top of their illusion are the owners of Wicca or the only true Wiccanians.

Many people around the world are being manipulated today, and this book is an acknowledgement of that struggle. This book was written with the intention of ensuring that you do not let yourself be manipulated. I hope it will inspire you to continue to do your part in this struggle.

Experts claimed that a new mythologem was emerging through our dreams, asking to be integrated into our lives: the myth of the ancient Goddess who ruled the earth and the sky before the advent of patriarchal religions. Denied and suppressed for thousands of years of male domination, she reappears in a moment of intense need.

Our mind is bringing back the image of the Goddess through dreams and insights that for years have been ignored by us. Although not literal objects, these symbolic representations are real, powerful, and now emerge as energetic configurations from very deep levels of our inner world to proclaim the Return of the Goddess!

What we were saying 10 years ago is today a reality: The Goddess is not coming back, She is already here among us. My experience of over a decade in the field of Wicca will certainly help you understand how witchcraft works and what you can expect   from   its   practice.

Chapter 1 - What Is Wicca?

Wicca is a religion of Mysteries and veneration of nature with its beliefs, practices, and profound philosophy centered on Paganism.

Paganism is a broad and general term given to pantheistic, animistic, totemic, shamanistic, and most often polytheistic forms of spirituality centered on the forces of nature. Paganism cannot be considered a religion, but rather the central pillar that encompasses the way of life, the spiritual, and philosophical concepts in which all religious expressions focused on nature are based. Thus, we could say that any religion centered on the Earth that does not face the Holy in a transcendent way and is not monotheistic is Pagan.

Scholars have classified Paganism into three subdivisions: Paleo Paganism, Meso Paganism, and Neopaganism.

Paleo Paganism is the general term used for the intact, nature-centered tribal faiths found in ancient Europe, Africa, Asia, and polytheistic Americas. Paleo Paganism is practically non-existent in modern urban societies and is only found, perhaps, in regions distant and untouched by the presence of contemporary man's influence.

Meso Paganism is used to refer to a series of organized and unorganized movements that arose in order to recreate and/or revive what would be Paleo Paganism. It can be considered an intermediate paganism, which includes the pagan elements that remained alive until the Middle Ages and influenced Freemasonry, Rosicrucianism, and Theosophy, for example. However, such attempts cannot be considered Paganism per se, for they were strongly influenced by the concepts, values, and practices of many Judeo-Christian monotheistic religions.

Neopaganism is the current modern terminology used for a variety of movements, usually unorganized, initiated since the 1960s, with ancient roots or not. In this classification of Paganism are included all those who tried to create, recreate, revive or continue the practices of Paganism of different cultures. This category of Paganism includes ideas and attempts to eliminate inappropriate concepts, as well as attitudes and practices, of monotheistic, dualistic, and atheistic religions and worldviews. It can be considered a movement initiated by contemporary society to reestablish the worship of nature. This definition may include any attempt, ranging from reconstructionist movements to non-reconstructionist groups such as Neodymium Ism and Wicca.

Thus, Wicca is a Neopagan religion, an alternative name given to Modern Witchcraft, which is inspired by the Paganism of the Ancient Peoples of Europe and which proposes to re-celebrate the Mother Goddess and the Ancient Gods of nature, creating and recreating the rituals of ancient cultures where these deities were once celebrated. Wicca is the revival and modern survival of this ancient religion based on Earth and its manifestations. Its spiritual roots lie in the Neolithic and Paleolithic Europe, at a time when primitive peoples worshiped the Mother Goddess as the great creator, nurturer, and sustainer of life.

For thousands of years, the ancient European peoples continued to revere the Great Mother as their main divinity, until a new religion would arise to take the place of worshiping the Goddess and implanting her faith in European soil.

Christianity

Christianity arrived in Europe in the mid-400s, first entering Rome some time before, at a time when the Empire was expanding and conquering several countries of the world. Gradually, the Christian faith spread, came together and gained adherents all while conquering the political boundaries.

Crying for a unique faith and God, Christianity gradually went on to persecute the Pagan Gods and festivities and to syncretize some of the most important feasts of the Pagan calendar, turning some ancient gods into saints so that Goddess worshipers would gradually assimilate the new faith. Others were given more sinister roles. The Horned God, for example, was transformed into the figure of the Devil by European Christians. Paganism had seen the Horned God as the son and Consort of the Goddess, who was represented with horns on her head in allusion to the animals she protected, and was once celebrated as the principle of good, plenty, and abundance.

With this, the Pagans had to go underground and were forced to participate in the new faith. Gradually the practice of Old Religion in the cities became impossible, so that those who remained faithful to it had to move to rural areas. From there came the name "Pagan," from the Latin "Paganus," meaning "country people," a term often used to diminish and depreciate those who kept alive the flame of Paganism and the many expressions of the Goddess Religion. Over time, the term "Pagan" became an insult used by Christians to refer to all who had not converted to the new faith. Gradually the terminology "Pagan" came to gain new connotations, as a follower of a false religion and anything that expressed a mixture of atheist, agnostic, hedonist, and practitioner or worshiper of evil.

From 1231 CE (Common Era), Paganism was brutally persecuted and countless of its followers were tried and executed through the Inquisition. This led to Pagan practices entering a steady decline. The ancient myths of the Goddess were gradually turned into fairy tales, their rituals into folk beliefs, and for centuries it seemed that the ancient Pagan religion had definitely disappeared.

The Renaissance Of Witchcraft

In 1951, when the last law against witchcraft was revoked in England, Gerald Gardner, considered the father of Modern Witchcraft, decided to reveal that the practices of witchcraft of ancient Europe had not died, but were still alive and were still practiced in the interior of the covens and by many families of witches under a new name: Wicca!

Gardner published some works that revealed a little of the practice of his Coven, among which included the famous book *Witchcraft Today*, and thus shed new light on the practices of Witchcraft, giving rise to a great Neopagan movement of revival and recreation of practices and rites of the Old Religion.

Since then, the Pagan movement has grown substantially and many witches, who claimed to have been instructed by their families for decades, decided to leave the mists and became visible, revealing the teachings of the Old Religion to the world. And so, in full bloom of the twentieth century, there arose a religion that sought to celebrate nature again by finding inspiration for its rites in the ancient religiosity of Europe and in worshiping the Goddess, considered the Earth itself. Wicca is then the modern reconstruction of the ancient religion of the peoples of Europe, since many of the mysteries, rituals and practices have been lost since the time when Paganism was persecuted. Precisely for this reason, Modern Witchcraft in its construction was largely influenced by the spirituality of different European cultures, ranging from Celtic to Greek or Roman. However, much of its philosophy and liturgy is based on the ancient calendar and religiosity of the Celtic people, who spread throughout Europe about 1200 years BCE and who were probably the culture that most preserved the worship of the Goddess and her rituals.

Origin Of The Word Wicca

The word Wicca comes from archaic English Wicce meaning to rotate, bend, and shape. We find other words in the same root, always linking it to something magical or sacred. Some researchers say that the term Wicca originates from the Indo-European "weik," meaning something like magic. Others claim that it originates from the Anglo-Saxon "wic" meaning wise.
Some scholars, however, claim that this word comes from the Germanic root "wit," which means "to know." We deduce from this that the word Wicca means "the wisdom of turning, bending, and shaping the forces of nature to our advantage," one of the goals of witchcraft.

Most scholars, however, emphatically affirm that witchcraft has not survived to the point of becoming hereditary and that many who claim to belong to witch families are actually lying. So, be aware when someone tells you that they belong to a family of witches, whose origin goes back to the Inquisition period. We cannot say that such claims are false, but most of the time they have been proven to be pure deception.

Wicca is often called the Art of the Wise or the Art of Shaping. Some of the meanings can refer to the Wiccanians who seek to attain wisdom, molding themselves in resonance with the fluxes of nature.

Wicca Today

As Wicca emerged from the mists and swept the world, innumerable people began to identify with this religious manifestation because it was the only one up to that time that had a female central deity as Creator. This was in the mid-1950s and lasted until the 1970s and early 80s.

In the 70's the forerunners of the feminist movements discovered Wicca and were enchanted to find a religion that proposed to worship the Mother Goddess again. From this encounter, the first Feminist Traditions of Witchcraft were born, which would forever change the face of Wicca.

From its emergence in 1951, Wicca acquired new expectations and underwent significant transformations. Being embraced by the feminist and environmental movements meant it gained a new face, became much more matrifocal and oriented to the Goddess than at the beginning of its history, and relegated the God to a secondary position. This is understandable, since the Sacred Male was revered by thousands of years, while the Goddess was mutilated and forgotten.

It was in 1970 that the feminist movement embraced Wicca as its "official" religion, finding in the Goddess a strong figure capable of bringing about profound changes in the thinking of society and its way of facing the world. Many feminist traditions came of this and contributed substantial creative and quality material that would change Wicca forever.

Women who fought for gender equality rights found in this religion a safe haven for them to feel strong, alive, and active. It was in Wicca that they found a religion capable of rescuing their dignity, both social and religious. From the search for a new religion where women were not excluded in the United States, through the efforts of countless women engaged in feminist causes, a Wicca emerged with a new identity more focused on the figure of the Goddess. From this growing movement there arose various traditions of this religion, from the Goddess and God having the same importance to others where God is less visible and the Goddess exerts supremacy and preponderance.

Along with the growth and spread of Wicca in the mid-80s came several other pagan movements. Druidism, Kemetism, Hellenism, Asatrú and countless other Neopagan world movements began to be visible thanks to the efforts of Wiccanians who sought to revive a religion more centered on the Earth and in the Sacred Feminine in search of connection with nature. This rose together with the banner of the struggle for religious freedom in heavily monotheistic countries, showing that each one can revere the Divine in his own way, rescuing rituals almost forgotten in time.

As Wicca had in its structure Celtic, Nordic, Greek, Sumerian and any other influences that seemed correct, with the passage of time many groups separated in search of the spiritual and cultural identity of the gods with whom they felt most connected. Thus arose the reconstructionist movements, which try to reconstruct the cult of the ancient Gods in exactly the same way as it was in the past. Many people who came to belong to these movements then began to criticize the flexibility of Wicca, saying that it was not the true heir of the European religion, that Wicca was not Celtic, that Wicca was Gardner's invention, etc.

Despite all of this, Wicca continued its escalation and with that underwent a revolution in its own way. This revolution led to congresses, meetings, and seminars held to discuss the practice of this religion in the USA. Because of the various attacks on Wicca, even a Council, whose members included the most renowned Wiccan of the time, was created to write the 13 principles of Witchcraft, which was published in the form of a public notice. The 11th Principle says, "As American Witches, we do not feel threatened by debates about the history of art, the origins of various terms, the legitimacy of various aspects of different traditions. We are concerned about our present and our future."

Along with this new identity that Wicca was beginning to assume, the Goddess as the center of worship of this religion was emphasized more and more. It came to be invoked in the rites as "The Goddess of the Ten Thousand Names" (as well as Isis, who was all the Goddesses in one) and the claim that all Goddesses are the same.

The highest visibility of Wicca is still in the United States and Europe, where it is considered an authentic religion, with the right to Chaplaincy in the army and marriages recognized by the State.

In several countries, Wicca has been growing substantially. We see more and more literary works being proposed to clarify their religious and philosophical aspects, and we are constantly faced with people embellishing our sacred symbols, such as the Pentagram or Triluna, on the subway, busses, bank queues and streets.

Today, there are a lot more people practicing the Art of Witchcraft alone than in groups which are called covens. Wicca has been transformed from a secret religion into a modern alternative religiosity.

Groups of different ethnicities have incorporated much of their culture into Wicca, making it more flexible and consequently eclectic. The saying "All Goddesses Are Goddess" has become a Wiccan axiom since the last decade and so Hindu, Native American, African, Hawaiian, Chinese, and many other cultures have been assimilated by Wicca and have come to be recognized as different faces of the Goddess.

Most of humanity's current religions are based on divine male figures and principles, with Gods and Priests rather than Goddesses and Priestesses. For millennia, feminine values were placed in the background and in many cultures women were subjugated and came to occupy a lower position than men, whether on the social or spiritual level. Wicca seeks to recover the Sacred Feminine and the role of women in religion as Priestesses of the Great Mother, as well as the complementarity and balance between man and woman, symbolized through the Goddess and God, who complement each other. Wicca gives the Goddess a preponderant role, both in her practices and in her myths, being thus the main divinity worshiped and invoked in the sacred rites.

Wicca & Witchcraft

During the process of the Christianization of Europe, the word witchcraft was often used to describe other forms of native religion that existed before Christianity. When the Inquisitors came to a place and found a religion they did not know how to name, they gave it the name of Witchcraft. Jews, Gypsies, and even scientists were called warlocks or witches and condemned to the bonfire. This has generated a confusion that persists into the present times about when and where the word witchcraft should be applied.

Wicca as a religion is based on the folklore, spirituality, and folk wisdom of ancient Europe, and for this reason Wiccans call themselves Witches. Many believe that the time has come to rescue the dignity of this word as a way to honor those who died in the Inquisition after being accused of practicing witchcraft. This act is seen as a way of undoing the misrepresentations by shedding light to construct a new reality so that the words Witchcraft, Witches and Wizards will finally be viewed positively by society.

The Structure Of Wicca

Wicca does not have a central authority. Many witches are solitary while others practice in covens, which are small groups of up to 13 people who often meet to worship the Gods. Wicca is not a sect or just a philosophy or way of life, as many claim. It has all the characteristics of a religion.

According to Sociology:

"Religion can be defined as a set of beliefs related to what humanity regards as supernatural, divine, sacred and transcendental."

Here we have the Goddess as the source and origin of all

things. From her we come and to her we will return. It is the first cause of all existence. It manifests itself in nature and in all things that exist, which means that it is also beyond time and space as well as "the set of rituals."

Wicca has a liturgical calendar with 8 Sabbats (Seasonal Rituals) and 13 Esbats (Full Moon Rituals). In addition, there is a whole body of knowledge about how these rituals are performed, with themes and symbolism common to most Wicca practitioners. All rituals begin with the launching of the circle, invoking the quadrants, the Gods, and ending with the unlocking of the Circle. It does not matter if you're in the United States, England, Japan, or Tibet. If there is a Wiccan there, they will initiate their rituals using the same procedure, or something very similar, that any other Wiccan anywhere in the world would use. It is this cohesion that characterizes a religion. A sect has no cohesion in its symbolism, philosophy, and ritual and moral codes that derive from these beliefs.

In Wicca, there are two simple moral codes that are observed: The Wiccan Rede and the Threefold Law.

The Wiccan Rede is a simple moral code that says "Do what you wish, without anyone harming." It is followed by all Wicca practitioners, or at least it should be, just as the 10 commandments should be followed by all Christians.

The Triple Law is another accepted Wiccan foundation and it states that "Whatever we do for good or for evil comes back to us in triplicate and in this incarnation." It is a foundation, derived from the Wiccan Rede, which is commonly accepted by all.

Since we're talking about morals, it is necessary to relate a short list with answers to the various misrepresentations attributed to Witchcraft:

- Witches do not believe in or worship the deity known as Satan, Devil, or Demon

- Witches do not sacrifice animals or humans

- Witches do not use aborted fetuses in their rituals

- Witches do not formally renounce the Christian God, they just believe in other divine aspects

- Witches do not hate Christians, the Bible, or Jesus, nor are they antichrists; they are not Christians in any way

- Witches are not sexually unconventional

- In Sabbats and Esbats, no drugs are used or sexual orgies performed

- Witches do not necessarily practice Black Magic

- Witches do not force anyone to do something against their will

- Witches are not trying to subvert Christianity

- Witches do not profane Christian Churches, hosts, and bibles

- Witches do not make a pact with the Devil

- Witches do not commit crimes in the name of their religion

Witchcraft has its own philosophy about reincarnation and life after death, as any religion, as well as codes of ethics and conduct that everyone should respect and follow to guide their lives. Certainly, there are many variations of beliefs and concepts among the various branches of Wicca. Although rites, symbols, and customs may be different, all traditions rely on common points:

- Conviction in reincarnation

- Belief in the feminine and masculine aspects of the Divine

- Respect in the same proportion not only to humans, but to Earth, animals, and plants

- Observation of the change of the seasons, with 8 Solar Sabbats and 13 Lunar Esbats, making 21 annual rites

- Rejection of proselytism

- Equality for women and men. Although women are more often the focus, both genders are considered to be complementary and important to life.

- Performing rituals inside a Magic Circle because the Circle is a sacred space used for worship

- Importance to "3 Rs": Reduce, Reuse, Recycle

- The sense of bondage to the Earth

- Respect for all religions and religious freedom

- The rejection of any form of prejudice

- Conscience in relation to citizenship

Witches never compromise their children with their particular faith because they believe that each one must go their own way. Children are always taught to honor their family, friends, to have integrity, honesty, to treat the Earth as sacred, and to love and respect all forms of life.

Wiccan Principles And Beliefs

Many consider Wicca a Polytheistic religion since we revere various deities as faces of the Goddess and God. Even though it can be considered Polytheistic, to revere several Gods, and even Monotheist, since it believes in a single source of energy (the Goddess), Wicca is in fact a Henotheist religion, observing the existence of several deities, but attributing the creation of all to a supreme deity: The Goddess. It is also Pantheistic in its worldview, which means the recognition of the Sacred in all things, seeing Gods and nature as being united. Thus, the world becomes divine and sacred in its essence.

For Wiccans, the Divine is not something transcendent and not separate from humanity. It is inside, outside, and around us. They believe that all things that exist are different manifestations of the Goddess, because they were created by Her. This develops the idea that everything is interconnected, like threads of the same web that form the great whole. If one of your wires is damaged, the whole web will also be damaged. Thus, individual damages are viewed collectively and the harm of one is detrimental to the whole. This is what we call immanence. This concept is very old, and we can find references to it in many cultures centered around the Earth.

There is a theory called the "Butterfly Effect," which states that everything that exists is intertwined. In terms of climate, for example, this translates into the notion that a butterfly that flutters in the air with its wings today in Australia can influence storms next month in Texas. This demonstrates that small actions bring about gigantic consequences, and the principles of Wiccan beliefs are grounded in exactly this. This is the starting point for understanding the conduct and ethics of a Witch.

Ethics consists of standards of conduct that include a judgment and moral philosophy. There is no set of ethics that can be applied to all people in all times and religions. Ethics is usually based on local and social patterns from where we live.

Wicca does not have large lists of rules and laws to follow, but there are certain behaviors with which many Wiccans guide their lives. All of them are based on common sense and core values, which are strong guidelines for human ethics, including Wiccan.

Wicca is a libertarian religion, where there are no different rules that tell us what we should do or how we should live. As mentioned earlier, there are only two "codes" that guide Wiccan principles, and these are explained in detail below.

The Wiccan Rede

"Do whatever you want, as long as you do not hurt anything or anyone."

This is essentially the main Wiccan guideline and is taken into account every time we perform a magical act as well as in our daily behavior. As in many religions, Wicca practices magick. Witches believe that the mind and the human body have the power to create changes and events in ways not yet understood by science.

In their rituals, where they honor their Gods, they perform various spells for innumerable purposes such as healing and overcoming problems. However, magick is always practiced according to a code of ethics that states that we can only help others or ourselves, respecting the free will of the people involved and never harming anyone.

Doing no harm to anything or anybody means not harming nature, the people around us, or ourselves. This involves observing our way of life, including eating and behavioral habits, and especially living in harmony with nature, taking into account the 3rs: Reduce, Recycle, and Reuse.

The Wiccan Rede encourages respect for and celebration of diversity, honoring existing differences, and repudiating all forms of prejudice rather than enacting intolerance.

This attitude is the essence of Wicca.

The Triple Law

"Whatever we do, for good or evil, will return to us in triplicate and in this incarnation."

This is the Threefold Law which is grounded in the power of immanence. If we desire good we will reap the good, and if we do evil it will also return invariably. We believe that the energies we create influence what happens to us. It is perfectly compatible with the law of cause and effect, action and reaction.

The Triple Law is centered on the Law of Immanence and is easily explained by the theory of the web of life and the butterfly effect. It is triplicate because all actions, magical or not, have an effect on the lives of those who practice the act (1), in the lives of those who suffer the actions of this act (2), and indirectly in the lives of those who are connected with the victim of this action and in the world around us (3). It is logical and natural that these actions return to their issuer in an intensified degree. This can easily be explained by a simple and physical allegory: "If you plant peppers, you will not harvest strawberries. You will harvest pepper in a much larger amount than you have planted. Plant just one pepper seed and you'll have whole pepper plant."

This does not mean that doing evil is a sin or anything like that. The concept of sin does not exist in Wicca. The triple law is called a law because of the way it works. We are all free and can transgress any law, but we will invariably suffer the consequences of our actions.

Witches are wise people who know that what they want represents a vibrating energy. Thus, they strive to vibrate on a positive energy level, channeling good for everything and everyone. If everyone wished others exactly what they would wish for themselves, soon the world would be full of blessings and positivity.

Wicca, The Religion Of Nature

Most of the most visible religions today talk about the relationship of the human being with other people, but Wicca goes much further. It speaks not only about our human relations, but also about animals, nature, and ourselves.

Wiccans celebrate the changing seasons and lunar phases through rituals that are able to connect us with the fluxes and ebbs brought back to Earth and, consequently, to our lives as a result of these natural changes.

Nature is the heart and soul of the Wicca religion which teaches that all beings, animate and inanimate, have life and deserve our respect and consideration. Therefore, we see nature as different faces of the Goddess capable of supporting us, protecting us, nourishing and keeping us alive. For this reason, Wiccans express a great reverence for nature and seek in their daily lives ways to integrate with it, seeking to live in harmony with natural laws, taking into consideration ways of living ecologically, recycling, reusing, and reducing exploitation of natural resources.

The Pagan position of reverence and preservation of nature is completely different from that encouraged by the patriarchal religions, where man was commanded to dominate and exploit natural resources and the environment. Nowadays, many witches are ecologists, environmentalists, community leaders, and are always concerned with the current ecological and social situations in the world.

Wicca is a very plural religion, meaning different witches will express their respect for the Earth in various ways. Some are vegetarians, other conscious recyclers, and many still become environmental activists engaged in the struggle and preservation of the Earth. Each one has their own calling.

The main characteristics of Wicca as a religion of nature are based on:

- The belief that there are sleeping rituals and powers within us that need to be awoken to transform and heal life.

- The conviction that we must search through nature for ways to contact it and seek to reconnect with its natural flows that invariably bring about inner changes in each being.

- Affirming life and the sacredness of the Earth as a symbol of perfection, totality, unity, completeness, and healing of all evils.

- The forces of nature as the sustaining energy of life, seeing in it the Goddess herself manifested.

- The preservation and care of nature, considered to be the temple and dwelling of the Gods that we believe in.

Wicca is not an anthropocentric religion, and for this very reason does not place human needs above those found in nature. The philosophy preaches a better relationship between man and nature.

Traditions Of Wicca

Every Wiccan is a Pagan, which means that their way of life, spirituality, and worldview are centered on Paganism. This simple definition determines the set of ethics, values, and moral conduct by which the individual rules and lives their life. While monotheistic religions understand the Divine as transcendent, Paganism is Pantheistic, which means that the Divine is present in all things.

Of course, defining yourself as a Monotheist or Pantheist is something that is not very comprehensive. Such nomenclatures can give you a general idea of what you believe and how you lead your life, but they are not enough to define your beliefs, specifically speaking. For this we need to be even more specific, subdividing the many forms of religion. Thus, the term Pagan includes various forms of religion, and Wicca is only one of them.

Wicca is a spiritual path with several subgroups that have a specific structure, philosophy, and practice. These subgroups are called Traditions. We could say that the traditions characterize the type and the system of Wicca that is practiced. There are many traditions and every day there are many others created. The term tradition applies both to the version of Wicca that is practiced and the group of covens that practice a certain system of witchcraft. Such groups are united by principles, ethics, rituals, magical practices, and ancestral lineage in common.

Each tradition is formed by several covens. Each coven is authorized to act, to teach, and to speak in the name of the Tradition. We could compare this to a network system. A coven would be a local branch of a Tradition, in the same way that bank agencies or chain stores are a branch of a large corporation.

Initiation is the way through which people are officially accepted as part of a Tradition. That is to say, that the fact that a witch practices a particular Tradition does not make them a practitioner of it. To be an official member of a Tradition, one must be formally initiated by someone already initiated on that path. This means that solitary or self-initiated witches have no Tradition whatsoever. Only by joining a coven will it be possible to receive a Traditional Initiation and become a member of a Tradition of Witchcraft.

The Main Traditions of Witchcraft

1734

Typically British, it is based on the ideas of the poet Robert Cochrane, a self-titled hereditary witch who became prominent at the same time as Gardner. 1734 is used as a cryptogram for the name of the Goddess honored in this Tradition. It is not considered by its members because it does not follow the Wiccan Rede and it is run by its own set of guidelines.

Dedication

This is the name of the ritual performed to mark the beginning of a person's learning process in Wicca. Those who undergo the ritual of Dedication receive the name of Dedicant or Dedicated and remains the minimum term of 1 year and 1 day studying the fundamentals of the Art to receive its Initiation.

Alexandrina

A popular Tradition that began around England in 1960 and was founded by Alex Sanders, the Alexandrian Tradition is very similar to the Gardnerian, with some minor changes and amendments. This Tradition works in the manner of Alex and Maxine Sanders. Alex Sanders claimed to have been initiated by his grandmother in 1933 when he was still a child. Most of the rituals of this Tradition are very formal and based on ceremonial magic.

Algard

An American initiated in the Gardnerian and Alexandrian Traditions, named Mary Nesnick, founded this "new" Wicca path that brings together the teachings of both Traditions, Gardneriana and Alexandrina, under a single insignia.

Dianic

The term "Dianic" refers to a witchcraft branch that emphasizes the feminism in nature, life, and spirituality above the masculine, and this includes many, if not most, of the Wicca Traditions currently in existence. Some Dianic witches only focus their worship on the Goddess, others on the Goddess and God while giving supremacy to the Sacred Feminine, whether in the rituals or philosophy of Tradition.

Georgina

This Tradition was created by George Patterson, who called himself "High Priest Georgino." The Georgina Tradition brings a composite of Celtic, Alexandrian, Gardnerian, and Traditionalist rituals. Even though most of the material provided to students is Alexandrian, it has never been imperative to blindly follow its content.

Ecletica

An eclectic witch is one who fuses ideas from many Traditions or sources. As in the witch's cauldron, where elements are added to complete the potion that is prepared, so too is various information from a range of Traditions fused to create a magical and eclectic way of working. This "Tradition," which is not really a specific kind of Tradition, is flexible but sometimes unfounded. Usually solitary and self-initiated witches work eclectically by creating free-form rituals.

Feri

There are several factions of the Feri Tradition, founded by Victor Anderson in Oregon in the 1920's. Its structure, despite being different from Wicca in some respects, is similar in many ways and surely Victor Anderson was inspired very much by Wicca for the construction of his Tradition. The Star Goddess is at the center of Feri philosophy and the Tradition is polytheistic, with different Gods recognized and worshiped. The concept of the Three Selves, which express the different stages of our consciousness, is one of the foundations of the Feri Tradition. Most of the Feri practitioners work alone or in very small groups and the Tradition has no degrees of initiation.

Gardneriana

Founded by Gerald Gardner in the 1950s in England, this Tradition has contributed so much to Wicca as it is today. The structure of many rituals in numerous Traditions originates from Gardner's works. However, this Tradition is supported many modern witches. Gerald B. Gardner said that he was initiated into a Coven of Newforest in England in 1939. In 1951, the last of the English laws against witchcraft was banned (primarily due to the pressure of spiritualists), and Gardner published the famous book *Witchcraft Today*, bringing to light a version of the rituals and traditions of the coven that supposedly started it, and this gave birth to Wicca as it is practiced today. This Tradition is extremely hierarchical. The Priestess and Priest rule the coven, the principles of love and trust preside over the groups, and the practitioners of this Tradition work "Dresses of Heaven." In the USA and England, the Gardnerians are called "Snobs of the Craft," and many believe they are the only direct descendants of purist Paganism.

Hereditary

Hereditary, or Genetic Witches, are people who assume they have pagan ancestry (mother, aunt, and grandmother are the most often cited pagan ancestors). Many claims of magical ancestry are highly questionable and have often been seen as pure fraud and fantasy. According to historians, it is impossible to have hereditary witches, since witchcraft as we know it is a modern religious phenomenon. If someone tells you they are hereditary witch, have a healthy dose of skepticism. It is almost certain you are being deceived.

This short list of Traditions, of course, is not complete. There are many other ways of Wicca that have not been mentioned here and other new Traditions are created and founded daily. Each Tradition has its own structure, rituals, liturgies, and myths that are passed from practitioner to practitioner. But they all follow the same philosophical principles:

1. The celebration of the Goddess and the God through seasonal rituals linked to the Moon and the Sun, the Sabbats and Esbats

2. Respect for the Earth, which is seen as a manifestation of the Goddess herself.

3. Magick is seen as a natural part of religion and is used for constructive purposes, never destructive

4. Proselytism is considered as inadmissible

If you are drawn to a Tradition, explore it. Try to learn as much as you can about it, and then look for a legitimate coven of this Tradition to be initiated into.

Covens and Solitary Witches

Witches practice art in small communities of up to 13 members, called covens. Covens gather to celebrate the ancient Gods, perform rituals during the lunar and seasonal changes, and practice magick. There are also those who practice alone, without belonging to any group. These people are called solitary witches.

Choosing to practice alone or in a coven of a particular tradition can be a difficult decision. This decision involves several factors, ranging from the willingness to share your religion with others, to the imprisoned nature of each person that may be a determining factor in the choice of solitary practice. You should make some reflections for yourself in order to find out which way is best for you:

- What kind of witch do you want to be?

- Are you easy to get along with in a group and community?

- Do you have a more extroverted or introspective nature?

- Do you feel comfortable in groups?

- Are covens available in the area where you live?

- Is there a Tradition you are attracted to?

- Do you have the time and availability to join a community?

- Is there family and financial independence on your part to participate in a coven without relying on the permission of others?

All of these issues are important to consider when deciding whether the best course for you is a coven or solitary practice.

In a coven, you will have strong support in your learning process, while in solitary practice there will be more freedom to do things at your own pace. Covens are usually formed by people with vast experience in Wicca with whom you can learn directly. In a coven you can also achieve a high degree experience through magick training, but much training will be required. Covens will invariably have expectations of their members, some of which you may not feel comfortable with or are unable to meet.

On the other hand, a solitary can learn by themselves in their own time. There will be no pressure to meet deadlines in the proposed studies, and you can follow your own schedule which matches your own expectations. If on the one hand this sounds beneficial, it can become a problem when doubts arise and you have no one to turn to. Properly trained witches will not be as available as they are when you are part of a coven, and you will need to understand things or solve problems alone, without the help of anyone. The lonely road, most of the time, is limited. Since most of the solitary magick training is done through books, and the information out there is not always accurate, there is a risk of remaining restricted by what one finds, thus advancing very slowly in the studies and practices of witchcraft.

Once you are part of a coven, there will probably be a program of studies that you must follow. In addition, there will be a number of requirements that should be observed by you as a Dedicant, which include: attending rituals, observing the Coven Laws, writing reports accompanying your studies, reading works designed to improve your studies, etc. Commitment is the key word for all who wish to be members of a coven.

It does not matter which path you choose to follow, either within a Tradition or alone. Surely the Gods will be with you whatever your decision. Participating or not in a Tradition is a personal matter. That will not make you a more or less powerful witch. The important thing is to follow your path with all your heart and honor the Gods in the best way you can, whether you are in a group or not.

Rite Of Passage

Like any other religion, Wicca also has Rites of Passage that celebrate the different phases in a person's life. Each Rite of Passage can be considered a different "initiation," since it plays an extremely important role in the life of the religious because such rituals always involve an ontological change and provides a mystical element to the individual that passes through them.

Rites of Passage are much more than sacred rituals that mark the life of a Witch. For Wicca, they are seen as a magical and social process that will prepare people to live in community and respect life in all its manifestations. There are innumerable Rites of Passage, but they are usually associated with the three phases of human life:

- Birth

- Life

- Death

The most well-known and practiced Rites of Passage include the following:

Rite Of Anointing

Occurs in the first days of the birth of a child. In this ritual, the witches anoint the child with sacred oils and give them magick gifts.

Wiccaning

This is a ritual that takes place shortly after the Rite of Anointing, usually on the next Full Moon. In it, the child is presented to the Goddess and God. This ritual is only to ask for the protection of the Gods for the child and never to compromise it with the Wiccan religion itself. Any such commitment can only occur when the child reaches an age where he or she has the ability to decide what is the best spiritual path for them. In Wiccaning, the child gains two godparents who will help them in times of need in their life.

Rites Of Puberty

Many primitive cultures, including Celtic and Native American, had rituals to mark a person's passage into adulthood. For girls, this occurs after their first menstruation in the Rite of Menarche, which is celebrated through a ritual exclusively for women. For boys, the ceremony marking their introduction into adulthood is the Transition Rite, which occurs around the age of 13 or 14 and is celebrated only by men.

Handfasting

This is the pagan tradition of marriage, which occurs when two people decide to unite to live together as a couple. The Handfasting, or Union of Hands, is officiated by a Wiccan Priest, and the bride and groom vow fidelity and love for one another. In the end their hands are joined with a bow. The ceremony can take place at any time, except between Samhain and Imbolc, whose energies of death and transformation do not harmonize with the purposes of Handfasting. Some Traditions claim that Beltane is not a good time for weddings either, while others claim it to be the best date.

Croning

In ancestral cultures, older women were respected for their knowledge and wisdom. They were revered as the living memory of the world and were the keepers of the ancestral wisdom of their culture. The Croning marks the entrance of women into menopause and the way of the Elder Goddess, when they become one of the Wise.

Saging

In Wicca, the ritual that honors the wisdom of a man acquired through age is called Saging and occurs traditionally around 65 years of age. Like any part of a person's life, the third age must be respected and observed, since our elders have much wisdom and experience to share with us if we allow ourselves to listen.

Requiem

The Requiem is a Pagan ceremony that occurs when a witch dies. In this ceremony it is requested that the Summer Country Portals be opened so that the soul of the person can pass. Three distinct ceremonies mark the Requiem. One occurs on the day of the burial of the person, the other a lunation after death, and the third a year and a day after the date of death.

Through the Rites of Passage, we can find the answers to the questions that are asked of the soul, so that the spirit shines and shows us the correct way. In this way, we can nourish the spirit of truth in each of us so that it flourishes and bears good fruit. Through this, Wicca shapes individuals and prepares them for life.

Your First Steps into Wicca

If you have come to this book, it is because you want to know a little more about witchcraft and most likely practice it. This work will introduce you to the basic aspects of Wicca that will inspire you to know more, starting a search that will never end. There are few people who are lucky enough to find an experienced and honest witch to train them and teach what they know about Wicca.

With the overexposure of witchcraft in recent times, many are the courses, teachers, and initiators who have appeared and who most often wish to make money instead of convey reliable and quality information. Trainers and sources of serious information are rare. For this reason, most Wiccans today drive their own learning, and there is no reason why you should not do that, too. If you choose to be solitary, or you never find a reliable instructor, you can receive valuable insight from many sources.

Today, books on the subject abound in the market as well as websites and mailing lists on the Internet. Nature is also a valuable resource, and you can learn from it without having to spend a penny. The Goddess and God also make available to us their teachings through insights, dreams, reflections, and messages conveyed in daily meditations.

Read as much as you can. Even if each author has divergent opinions, sometimes completely opposite ones, something of value will be taken from a book, most of the time. Many authors present their theories and thoughts as unequivocal truths, as if they were true for all witches and Traditions. Therefore, adapt the teachings of the books to your way of living, according to your beliefs.

Be open to learning from anyone and everything. The nature around you is full of teachings waiting to be conveyed to you, and the Goddess is reflected in every living thing. Open your senses when you are in nature. Take frequent walks in a park, on the beach, or in the forest. This will lead you to realize how many different things you can feel, see, smell, and taste. This shows us the diversity of the Goddess world, and such experiences will affect you substantially at different levels of life.

While walking in nature, collect objects to make an altar. A stone for the land, a feather for air, a stick for fire, and a ladle of some sort for water are just a few suggestions of what you can find on your walks that can be used in the creation of an altar. Arrange all of this nicely on some surface, light incense and candles frequently at this location, and reflect for peace, harmony, and centering. The altar is the place where we can contact the divine.

Live what you believe!

Wicca celebrates life and teaches that everything that exists is sacred. How would you translate this into your way of living? Where would it begin?

If you wish to practice Wicca, open yourself to the sacred and let it communicate with you. You could follow a few of these suggestions to start your walk into Wicca:

- We are co-creators of reality together with the Gods. Open yourself to the sacred and let it act through you.

- The sacred is in and out of us. Identify the interconnectedness of energies, realizing that we are all connected to one another.

- Wicca is a religion of transformation achieved through practice and not theory. Reading is good, but often you must put your books aside and practice what you know in theory. Only this can open the way for the Gods to communicate with you.

- Wiccans live in a sacred way, because life is magic. Respect everything that exists and you will also be respected.

- Magick comes from our relationship with nature and the harmony and balance of our being. Always seek to be centered, sensible, honest, and true. Where there is truth, there is power.

- Magick is unpredictable and follows our inner flow. If you are in balance, your magick will be balanced.

- Witches do not perform manipulative magic. Respect the free will of others, starting with your own.

- Nature is our bridge of communication with the Gods. If you are in harmony with nature, you will be in harmony with the sacred.

- Have the Goddess as your main source of inspiration and information. She resides within you and is ready to awaken and make your light shine deep within you, enlightening your life and everything around you.

Wicca has many paths. They are varied and very different from each other, except that they are bound by the same energy: love, friendship, and celebration of nature.
Welcome to Wicca's fantastic and enchanting universe!

Chapter 2 - The Goddess And The God

"In the infinite moment the Goddess rose from chaos and created all that is, was and will be." - Excerpt from the Wiccan Myth of Creation

Religion In Prehistory

The human mind, 30,000 years ago, had begun its process of seeking explanations about the mysteries of life, just as we do today. The art associated with the human revolution of that time is indispensable to support the theory that Homo sapiens possessed certain spiritual beliefs. Art and religion have always had an inextricable relationship with each other.

The common thread that unites all modern faiths is best explained through the definition of the term religion. It is the Shaman who is able to intercede and interpret relationships with the spiritual realm, as Joseph Campbell explains: "The shaman is a particular type of healing man, whose powers can cause healing or illness, can communicate with the world beyond, predict the future, and can both influence the time and movements of animals whose pregnancy is believed to be derived from their sexual relations with glimpsed spirits."

Despite the fact that Shamanism enjoyed neither the popularity nor the high number of followers of the world's major religions, Shamans continued to practice an art that has remained relatively unchanged since time immemorial. The roots of pre-Shamanism date back to all the world's current religions. Although Shamanism is found primarily in simple hunting societies around the world, its influence may well be found in practically all hierarchically more complex cultures and religions. To evidence such a hypothesis, it is necessary to follow the progress of the archaic Homo Sapiens as they developed into modern Homo Sapiens. The artists and shamans were probably only one person in the Paleolithic period. Through their magical powers of recreating animals on the walls of the temple caves, they—the shaman-artists—connected with the source of life that animated both humans and animals, becoming vehicles of that source, creators of form alive, as well as the source of it.

Art was a form of communication of early Homo Sapiens. Modern Homo Sapien paintings found on cave walls such as Trois Freres and Lascaux in France represent more than mere representations of animals as seen in their daily lives by artists. As experts explain, "A word or image is symbolic when it encloses something more than its obvious immediate meaning. Since there are innumerable things beyond the reach of understanding of the human being, we constantly use symbolic terms to represent concepts that we cannot define or fully understand. This is the reason why all religions employ symbolic images or language."

The artwork found within these caves were hand painted by people with a greater purpose in mind than just portraying the everyday animal life. In fact, most of the artwork found in the bottom of these caves was not easily accessible. The work of art was done to say something beyond the world of the simplistic. It has been said that the art found on the walls of these caves represents some form of magic or religious ceremony.

Within the deep recesses of these caves, in indistinct light or total darkness, the shaman-artist practiced his art, and his magic, with the hope of communicating with the spirits of animals. Perhaps these caves served as centers for fertility rites, initiation rituals, and maturity rites, with "The Sorcerer of Trois Freres" conducting the ceremonies. What is clear is that Paleolithic caves such as Trois Freres and Lascaux were probably centers of some spiritual importance. The work of art reflected more than just a representation of the natural world. It reflected a form of symbolism known only to the shaman-artist and the society in which he worked.

The rites of these early peoples were mostly of the socioeconomic type (hunting, fishing, war rites), with the absence of a specific cult to some named divine figure. In short, we can say that the first human groups did not come to a clear concept of divinity, much less worship a single deity.

The wandering life to which they were compelled by the adverse conditions of the climate and by the continuous fights between groups prevented the more refined elaboration of their beliefs and the development of a specific cult.

However, in this historical past are numerous vestiges of religiosity in prehistory. Among the Men of Cro-Magnon, we find signs of religious rituals like the burial of the dead. Religiousness manifested itself in the main concerns of daily life and in the level of development of peoples. In the Paleolithic period (100,000 to 30,000 BCE), there was a belief in a superior power, and this power was offered treats so that, in return, they would multiply their offspring. In the Neolithic period (from 10,000 to 5,000 BCE), urban civilization began, and with settled life came problems of social and administrative hierarchy, thus religion became more complex. The idea of a supreme being, which was outlined in the Paleolithic, begins at this period to be covered up by a series of divine entities, closer to man, representing the atmospheric forces (the wind and the rain for example, which were so important in agriculture).

For the man of archaic societies, everything was liable to become sacred. Human life unfolded parallel to a sacralized life, the cosmos, or the Gods. Rituals were not reserved only for specific occasions or activities, but involved routine activities such as: meals, sexual acts, greetings, waking, and falling asleep.

Religiousness was a way, perhaps the first way, through which a knowledge about the rhythms, cycles, and functioning of the universe was constructed. Primitive men had complex symbolic systems with micro-macrocosmic correspondences such as: the association of the belly to the grotto, veins and arteries to the Sun and Moon, etc.

The Goddess And God: The Interaction That Creates The World, The Seasons, and All Reality Manifest

From the primitive origins of the Neolithic and Paleolithic, all forms of magic and religion emerged and became the inspiration to recreate many other forms of spirituality that came later, including Wicca. This is exactly why we honor the Sacred Feminine in all its manifold manifestations. In Wiccan belief, the universe and all that exists was created by the Goddess, who is considered the first deity of humanity since the beginning of time, according to archaeological evidence.

The worship of the Mother Goddess predates the Age of Taurus (4000 BCE to 2000 BCE), when men lived on hunting and fishing, and women were the great Priestesses, Shamans, and holders of religious power. At this time respect for the feminine and the mysteries of procreation were at their peak. Men had not yet associated the sexual act with conception and saw pregnancy and birth as something sacred, received directly from the Gods. The ancestral men believed that women became pregnant in the moonlight through the Great Goddess personified as the Moon itself.

It was from there that the concept of the Sacred Feminine came into existence and prevailed for millennia. Our ancestors believed that the power that conspired for the Universe to exist was feminine, and so they worshiped the Goddess as the Creator of the world and all that exists in it. According to primitive Pagan beliefs, this Goddess generally symbolized by the Earth and/or the Moon would have created everything and everyone, even her own complement, the God, who was personified through the Sun.

From the involvement of women with religion came many advances such as knowledge of the power of herbs, which healed the sick and alleviated the pain of childbirth. The first calendar, the lunar calendar, may have started with women observing their menstrual cycles and comparing them with the Moon cycles. In addition to early forms of astronomy, women also developed languages, agriculture, cooking, pottery, and more. The contributions of women to human cultures are numerous and have never had due credit and value.

The Goddess is the Divine Feminine principle, the supreme Divinity worshiped in Wicca. She continued to be revered around the world for thousands of years until she was silenced through patriarchal religions. In recent years, the Goddess and her associated religions have had a resurgence, and today there is a great popularity among feminists who seek a spiritual dimension for their political causes, those who are interested in the ancient religions encompassing here all the pagan manifestations, and among common women and men who feel that something is being lost in the prominent organized religions of today.

It is difficult to define the Goddess in a few paragraphs, but versatility is one of the most interesting characteristics. To some she is the only existing Divinity. The Goddess is not necessarily seen as a person, but a multifaceted force of energy that expresses itself in a variety of forms and can have many different names. Many symbols were attributed to her, such as serpents, birds, the Moon, and the Earth.

The Goddess is the Creator of all things and at the same time the Destroyer. Everything comes from her and everything will return to her. The Goddess is contained in everything and lives on Earth, in the sky, in the sea, in every flower, in each drop of water, and in each grain of sand. She is not a distant and untouchable being, but a Divinity that is here with us, living and manifested in each of us. She is Maiden, the Mother, and the Elder. She is you, she is me, she is everything, and everyone.

In pagan practices, the Goddess has three distinct aspects. The Triplicity of the Goddess traces back much earlier than Christianity, and it is not difficult for her to give rise to the thought of the Christian Trinity. But in Wicca, triplicity refers to three distinct states of the same deity.

Each of these aspects has its own particular characteristics, distinct from the others, and each of them has the possibility of being related to internal aspects of our psyche. The three faces are the Maiden, Mother, and Elder, and all aspects have been revered by all humanity since time immemorial. The Maiden represents impulses, the beginning, and is related to Crescent Moon. The Mother is the Giver of Life, the Great Nurse, and is associated with the Full Moon. The Elder Is the Keeper of Wisdom, The Great Knowing and Transformative, and is associated with the Waning Moon.

As a community, growth and transformation go through intimate interactions. The law of the Goddess is Love: Unconditional Love. There is no order to be followed except love, in all its manifestations and forms. The Goddess had great popularity and prominence until patriarchal religions such as Judaism, Christianity, and Islam silenced her. The shift to patriarchy was gradual and proceeded from a reformulation in kinship systems that went from matrilineal to patrilineal. The emphasis on fatherhood and man is clear and evident in the major religions practiced to this day. The father/son relationship and God/Jesus is the key to Christianity, although the mother figure has managed to persist and appear in Catholicism as Mary, who curiously is called "The Mother of God."

Other factors relating to the rise of patriarchal religions was the emphasis of military dictatorship, which increased the worship of warrior gods. Esther Harding wrote in *Women's Mysteries*, "The rise of male power and patriarchal society probably began when man began to accumulate goods which is not community property, and he felt that his personal strength and courage was able to increase his possessions." This shift in secular power coincided with the increase in sun worship under a male priesthood that began to replace the many moon-worship services that had been held. Thus, as men gained power over women and the masculine became the Great Divinity, the Sacred Feminine came to be recognized less and less. The absence of Goddess worship brought war, crime, rules, and tyranny.

Most of humanity's current religions are based on divine male figures and principles, with Gods and Priests rather than Goddesses and Priestesses. For millennia, feminine values were placed in the background and in many cultures women were subjugated and came to occupy a lower position than men, whether on the social or spiritual level. Wicca seeks to recover the Sacred Feminine and the role of women in religion as Priestesses of the Great Mother, as well as the complementarity and balance between man and woman, symbolized through the Goddess and God, who complement one another.

It must be made clear that the vision of God for Wicca is nothing like the patriarchal God expressed by the Judeo-Christian religions. The God of Wicca is alive, strong, sexual, connected with animals, being in no way similar to the asexual and transcendental God as monotheistic. It represents all that is good and pleasurable like life, love, light, sex, and fertilization. With the arrival of Christianity in Europe with all its sets of sins, prohibitions, and sexual taboos, the Conifer God was transformed into the figure of the Devil and evil by the early Christians. Until then, the Devil had never been represented with horns on his head, and this only happened to denigrate the image of the Witch God.

The Horned God has horns in his head not because he is the Devil, for witches do not even believe in a devil, but because of his connection with animals and hunting. He is by no means the Devil, much less any kind of Christian deity. He is the Pagan God of nature and of life.

The Horned God is generally depicted with deer antlers. In ancient cultures, deer were important symbolic animals. It seems that in the art of caves deer would have constituted, along with a bull, horse, and the wild ox, a dualistic mythical-cosmological system, according to historians. Because their horns resemble trees and renew themselves periodically, the deer was considered a symbol of life that continually rejuvenates, as well as a symbol of rebirth and the passage of time. In ancient Norse mythology, 4 deer would have fed on the branches of the world tree, Yggdrasil, eating their fruits (hours), flowers (days) and branches (seasons). In antiquity deer were considered an enemy of poisonous serpents, their skin was an amulet against snake bites, and the post of the horn defended seeds of sorcery.

The deer is an appropriate messenger for the great change that is to happen after the Winter Solstice. Although the Earth remains dark and unfruitful, the nights are much longer than the days, and the light has begun to grow but is still unnoticeable. We are still engaged in the darkness of time, but a spark begins to burn before us, reminding us to stay in touch with the vital energy, for soon we will be in the light. The "deer of seven branches," which has been strong through many cycles of growth and waning and has always fought for a triumphant life, is a guide on which we can rely.

A deer is flexible, tense, indifferent and incredibly strong. It embodies the wild spirit and is the ancient emblem not only of God but of the Goddess as giver of birth. On the other hand, its branching horns are connected to the rays of the Sun. The Sun has always been linked to God. Because it is symbolized by the sun, God shows its different faces through the journey of the star through the four seasons. This reflects the changes of the seasonal cycles. He is born in the winter Solstice as a young baby, grows in the spring, and become a young man. In the summer he attains maturity and in the autumn becomes the wise Elder, preparing to return to the womb of the Goddess and be reborn on the first day of winter.

The union of the Goddess and God brings life and light to the Earth and is therefore sacred. They are considered part of us and are alive in all things and everywhere.

Wiccans worship their Gods to ask for health, peace, harmony, success, and prosperity in the same way that practitioners of any other religions do. In our daily life we have developed a constant practice of meditations, rituals, and invocations that enable the development of our relationship with the sacred. Anyone can and should explore the energy and power of the Goddess and God in their life. Their law is love in its many forms.

If you are able to love, you will be able to reach them. They are within us all, waiting for our call so that we may become a reflection of love.

Calling the Presence Of the Goddess and God Into Your Life

To train our minds, souls and hearts to hear the voice of the Gods is one of the most enriching experiences. Our minds have been trained to believe that the Divine is separate from us, therefore we must reprogram it to remove this separative thought. In Wicca we perceive the presence of the Goddess and God in all things, in what is inside and outside of us.

To invoke means to make something become present. So become accustomed to calling the Holy to be part of your life and your actions. Here is an invocation that can be made daily to the Goddess and God. You can utter it by looking at the Sun, Moon, heavens, and stars as you contemplate the creation of the Goddess or by simply lighting a candle and incense on your altar as an offering to the Gods:

Goddess and God,

I ask for your blessings on this day so that I may know your love. As the leaves change and fall, help me to transform and release all that no longer serves me. I beg you to be on my mind so that my thoughts be clear and free from judgments.

Be in my eyes so that I may recognize them in all things.
Be in my mouth so that I speak only the truth.
Be in my hands, that I may build a world of high purposes.
Stand at my feet, that I may walk gently on your sacred ground.
May your presence surround me and may I never be alone. So be it!

Chapter 3 - Establishing An Altar

In Wicca, we use an altar as a focus place for honoring the Gods and also to establish a sacred space. This altar holds magical instruments, a set of ritual objects with which we work and that are used during ceremonies, when we perform a spell, consecrate a talisman, etc. The altar is our portal of communication with the Gods and is seen as a physical and spiritual offering to the Divine beyond representing our subconscious mind.

Thus, the altar is always treated with reverence because it not only supports symbols that represent the sacred, but also the essence of the elements of nature that are inside and outside of us, reminding us that everything that is done on the altar is done in honor of them.

Obviously, Wiccans know that the Gods do not live on the altar. They simply use an altar as a means of communication with them. The word altar comes from the Greek "altum" which means "high place." In this way, the altar becomes a place where we raise our consciousness to the Divine.

Most Wiccans reserve a small space in their houses where they have their altar, leaving it permanently mounted. This serves as a reminder, turning our thinking to the Holy every time we look toward it.

The Wiccan altar always faces north, which in addition to being the magnetic axis of the Earth is linked to the feminine energy and consequently to the Mother Goddess, the Mysteries, and growth. As there are always objects on the altar that bring us back to the elements, turning it north connects it directly to the Earth where all the other elements are sustained.

When we assemble an altar, we must keep in mind that it is divided into two sides, the left representing the Goddess and the right God. Therefore, when we have on the altar statues or symbols that represent the Sacred Feminine and Masculine, we must take this into account.

Usually, the altar is arranged with a statue of the Goddess on the left side and the God on the right side. Feminine symbols such as a chalice and flowers are placed on the side of the Goddess, and the masculine athame and stick are placed on the right side, which symbolizes the God.

Each corner of the altar is connected to an element of nature. The north, as mentioned earlier, represents the element earth, the east is connected to the air, the south to fire, and the west symbolizes water. A bell, rung to mark the beginning and end of rituals, is placed to the east. The bell is also touched to mark important moments of rituals.

Photos and objects that are of significant importance to the witch can also be part of the altar so that their thoughts are sent to the moments and people who bring them a sense of happiness and security. Candles to represent the Goddess and God are also arranged on the surface of the altar. The most used candle colors are black to represent the Goddess and white for God, placed on the left and right side respectively. Many place a red candle in the center of the altar, representing the Art and face of the Goddess. Other colors such as blue, silver, and violet are also widely used to symbolize the Goddess and green, brown, and gold for God.

Usually, the altar is arranged on a wooden table, since it is a great conduit of energy in addition to being a connection directly to nature. However, any flat space can be used to mount an altar. Many Wiccans establish their altar on the ground, believing that this puts them in direct contact with telluric forces. Magic oils, incense, and stones are also often found on Wiccan altars.

If you are not sure where to establish your altar, think of the following questions when deciding to create it:

- For what will your altar be used? As a focus to establish

contact with the Gods, or as a place of meditation and contemplation?

- Will it be used to perform enchantments and spells or will it be an exclusively devotional space?

- How big does it have to be to serve these purposes?

- Can it be available to curious eyes or should it be mounted in a reserved and private place?

- Will it have candles burning frequently on the surface? If yes, what preventive measures should you take to avoid accidents?

- What should you put on it to look pleasing to your eyes?

You can reflect on many other criteria, such as height and shape of the altar, which will be a good starting point for your establishment. The important thing is that all the things placed on the altar make sense to you so that you know why you are putting such items on it.

Everything you put on your altar should serve some purpose and represent something. Never place a chalice on the left side of your altar just because you read it somewhere if it has no meaning to you. Proceed in the same way with everything else. Remember, the altar represents your essence and therefore must vibrate in resonance with your being.

Instruments, Objects, and Magic Utensils

In Wicca, there is a set of objects used to contact the sacred. These utensils are used not only to establish an altar but also to practice the Wiccan Art. Many say that magical instruments are useful early in our training as witches and can be discarded over time. Others say that a person who is starting now on the path should use only their mind and body to do magic and to leave instruments and magical objects for advanced practice.

It must be made clear that the instruments are not magical in and of themselves. The magical characteristics of an instrument actually reside in its bearer. It is we who create, elevate, and channel energy to be directed by an instrument. Many people turning to Wicca want to buy as many instruments as possible, as they believe that only in this way is it possible to practice the Goddess Religion.

Is this really necessary? The answer is no!

The only thing we really need to do magic is our body and mind. We say that our bodies are sacred and carry within them the four elements. Our body mass and bones are the earth, our body's temperature fire, our breath air, our blood and saliva water, and our mind is the sacred quintessence, the dwelling of the spirit, and the potentiality of change and transformation.

It is only this, and nothing else, that we need to effectively practice our religion.

I particularly believe that new witches should first leave magic instruments aside and learn to work with the energy of the manifestations of the body like breathing, contemplating, feeling, etc.

This helps us a lot to grow in our magical path, free from artifacts that often limit us. There are some objects that are extremely detrimental in the way of the art. Instruments are great aids but should be used only when necessary or to facilitate the work of those who have minimally developed their psychic gifts and the powers inherent to their body and mind.

Magic tools is another name widely used to refer to instruments, and they do exactly what any tool would do: they make the work of the user easier. However, it is necessary to remember that the strength and ability of the tools will be useful to those who use them. Still, it is likely that you will want to acquire some ritual utensils to begin your practice in Wicca.

For this, it is important to spend some time looking for the right object. Many believe that in reality it is the object that seeks its owner and not the other way around. Be that as it may, the important thing is that the magical utensils that will be part of your altar reflect your personality. So do not buy a cauldron you do not like just because it's the only one you could find, for example. Look for something that satisfies you and if you do not find it, let time create the way for the appropriate instrument to reach you.

Here are the most common instruments and magical utensils found on Wiccan altars and used by most witches, along with their symbolism:

You

You are the greatest magic tool of all. It is your intentions and energies that determine the results of any magical work. Many witches never use any type of instrument but their own personal energy during magical rituals. Some of the most powerful rituals can be done without leaving the armchair in your living room. The focus, concentration, intentions, and desires reside within, and these are the true tools of a witch.

Pentacle

It has the size and shape of a coffee saucer with a Pentagram (5-pointed star). The pentacle is used to consecrate herbs, stones, and all things to be used in a ritual. The pentacle is a reservoir of energy. At each ritual, a little of the created power is automatically drawn to the pentacle, which can later be used to sacralize magically an amulet, talisman, or other object with energy. Some use the pentacle to store salt that is used in rituals and serves to purify, clean, and banish. The pentacle is connected to the earth and the altar, and so is positioned at the north cardinal point.

Athame

It is used to direct and manipulate energies in a ritual. It is with this that we draw the Magic Circle, consecrate the foods that are shared at the end of the ceremonies, etc. The athame is nothing less than a double-bladed dagger with a black handle. However, today many witches have athames with different shapes and colors of handles. Sometimes the blade or handle is engraved with magic symbols or the name of the witch written in some ancient alphabet as the runic. It is never used for physical cuts or to harm someone. The athame is connected to the element air, and on the altar it is positioned in the cardinal point east.

Stick/Wand

The use of the stick, or wand, is similar to that of the athame and can be used for the same functions. The wand is made with a tree branch or with a copper or bronze barrel with a crystal tip at one end. Usually it has the same measure that goes from our elbow to the tip of the middle finger of the hand with which we write, called the hand of power. The most common wood to use to make a magic wand are willow, oak, and birch. If you cannot find any of these trees in the area where you live, you can make your stick with a branch of any other that has special meaning for you.

The staff is attached to the fire element and its place on the altar is positioned at the south cardinal point.

Cup

The chalice is used to contain wine, water, and other sacred drinks to be ingested during a ritual. Most Wiccan chalices are made of silver, but you can have one of any other material such as soapstone, crystal, or ordinary glass. The chalice represents the Goddess and fertility of life and is used in the ceremony of the Great Rite, a ceremony that represents the union of the Goddess and God, when the blade of the athame is immersed in the liquid contained within.

The chalice is connected to the element water and on the altar, it is in the cardinal point west.

Cauldron

This is perhaps the best-known witch's magic instrument. Contrary to popular belief, it is not used to cook small children or perform curses, but to make beneficial potions and spells to heal and inspire peace and happiness. The cauldron represents the power of transformation and is usually made of iron, possessing a tripod representing the three faces of the Goddess.

The cauldron is in the center of the altar, representing the quintessence, the spirit element, and the union of the four elements.

Broom

The broom has also long been associated with witchcraft. It is often used to prepare the sacred space, serve as a portal, and also represents the union of the Goddess (bristles) and God (phallic shape of the broom). Precisely for this reason, it was used among peasants in rites of magic where witches hopped on their brooms, believing that the higher they hopped, the higher the seeds would grow and the more plentiful the crops would be. The broom is used to energetically sweep a space that will be used for performing a ritual. The sweep does not have to be performed physically, and we often simply sweep the air as we visualize the site being cleared of negative influences.

The traditional trees for making your broom are birch, willow, and ash.

The Stake

The stake is made of the branch of a tree that divides into 2 branches, like a sling, and must have the same measure of its owner. It is a secondary instrument, but of a very deep symbolism for several kinds of witchcraft. Some Traditions make use of it, while others do not even mention its existence. The stake represents the Horned God and therefore its owner is symbolically represented as the direct descendant of God.

When performing rituals alone, the stake is placed on the floor behind the altar or in the center of the Magic Circle, with the altar in front of it. A candle, representing the theme of the ritual, is usually lit in the middle of the fork. When working in a group, it is placed outside the Magic Circle, in the north position. For a group, it represents the Guardian of the Circle and the link that will be established between the two worlds under its protection.

The tree chosen to make the stake from is usually ash or laurel, and its owner must cut the branch with their own hands in the period of the full moon, with a knife purified and consecrated by the four elements.

Bell

It is used to mark the beginning and end of the ceremony. It can also be used for cleaning a place or our auric field. It can be used to invoke positive energies, Gods, and spirits of the elements.

The Cauldron

It is used to burn herbs as incense. It is believed that the smoke released by the herbs elevates our requests to the Gods. Smoke is also used as a visual resource to focus our intentions and desires.

Bolline

It is a white curved knife used to cut herbs, engrave symbols in candles, make talismans, etc. The first bollines were made in the form of a small sickle, similar to that of the old Druids. Today knives of any size and shape, used only for magic purposes, can be considered a bolline.

The Spoon

The spoon is the symbol of union and life, for it is with it that we feed and mix the spices with the food that is prepared, thus making the great alchemy of the day to day. Many witches use the spoon as a power rod with which to banish negative energies, blessed food, and trace the Magic Circle around the stove while preparing potions and even daily food.

Shadow Book

It is not considered a magical instrument proper, but a very important artifact. The Book of Shadows is our magical diary, where we record our incantations, spells, rituals, and experiences. In it we transcribe all the sorcery that we find interesting, myths of Goddesses and Gods, our thoughts, invocations, and everything else that is relevant.

The Magic Oil

Magic oil is not a magical instrument in itself but is used in rituals to potentiate the objects that will be used. It is based on olive oil, symbol of wisdom. It purifies in a simple way everything that will be used in magical rites. Below is a simple recipe of an effective magic oil you can use:

- 2 tbsp of olive oil

- 15 drops of essential oil of roses

- 5 drops of essential oil of basil

- 5 drops of essential oil of jasmine

There are many other recipes for magic oils available. However, the one provided here is perfect to be used for multiple purposes such as cleaning, purifying, blessing, or magically loading an object or magic instrument. Before beginning a ritual or sorcery, a few drops of oil are placed in the hands and scattered to purify. The instruments and utensils that will be used in the ritual are also anointed with the same oil.

To Finish

When you are choosing your magic instruments, remember that they can often be replaced by things that we find in nature itself. Using stones, shells, crystals, feathers, and other objects directly from nature puts us in more direct contact with the elements than many expensive and imported athames. Using what nature can give us is extremely important and gives very satisfactory results.

Knowing to alternate the use of instruments with objects from nature can form a witch with an unimaginable ritualistic and ceremonial plurality. I usually switch my altar with instruments and things I can find in nature itself.

In this way, all magick is done!

Consecrating The Magical Instruments

When we acquire our magical instruments, they come to us with different energies absorbed from other places and people with whom they have had contact. Therefore, before making an altar with them, it is necessary to consecrate them so that all the negative influences impregnated in them are neutralized.

For this you will need incense in your favorite aroma, a candle, a glass with water and salt, and a small dish with a little fresh earth. Arrange these elements on a small table placing the earth to the north, the incense to the east, the candle to the south, and the glass with water to the west. They represent the four elements of nature and link us directly to them.

Before you begin your ritual of consecration, take a shower, wear clean clothes, and relax for a few moments. If desired, anoint your wrists with your favorite essential oil. This will be putting you in an altered state of consciousness gradually, preparing you to practice magic.

Place the instruments you wish to consecrate in the middle of the altar. Light the candle south of the altar. Take a deep breath a few times and see a circle of light forming around you. Ask for the presence of the Goddess, God, and the spirits of the elements to be with you.

Then begin the sacralization of one of the chosen instruments.

Pass it through the earth and introduce it to this element with words such as the following: *"I cleanse, consecrate, and bless you with the strength of this element so that you become an instrument full of light and power. May it be so, and so be it."*

Pass the instrument in the smoke of the incense and repeat the same words. Then proceed in the same manner by passing the instrument in the candle flame and then afterwards splashing a few drops of salt water on it. Present it to the Goddess and God with words similar to these:

"Goddess and God, I present mine today (say the name of the

Instrument). May it be blessed and consecrated with power. Let it be a bridge between us. Let it so be, and let it be so!"

Proceed in the same way with all other instruments, then arrange them on your altar according to the element they represent. When you are done, thank the Goddess, God, and the elements, and visualize the circle of light around you undoing itself.

This little ritual of consecration can be used not only to bless a magic instrument, but any object such as pendants, bracelets, chains, amulets, etc.

Chapter 4 - The Magic Circle

Pagan ritual practices were always performed alongside sacred nature, considered to be the abode of the Gods and divine by itself. When witchcraft came to be persecuted and the witches had to move their rituals from the forests and woods to the interiors of their houses, the rites were then carried out inside a Magic Circle. Rituals took place in areas that were far from natural places of power, such as stone circles or sacred groves, and the act of launching the Magic Circle began to establish not only a sacred space, a vortex of power where the spirits of nature were attracted, but also a portal of communication with the sacred.

We continue to do this today, drawing a circle around us to invoke the energies we revere so that they will work with us in perfect harmony. Plotting a Magic Circle precedes any Wiccan ritual. The circle helps to contain the energy and magical power created and elevated in the rituals. It also serves to keep out unwanted energies from the outside along with containing what is desired within.

The Magic Circle does not necessarily have to be delimited on the floor with chalk, rope, or any physical marking, although many witches use this as a visual reminder. What is important is the energetic creation of the circle, mentally visualizing a circle of light around it that becomes a sphere as the sacred space is created and released, while walking or circulating the whole place where we perform the ritual clockwise. After that, the elements are invoked as we return to the four quadrants, and then the Goddess and God are summoned to witness the ritual.

After the Magic Circle is cast, all movements while in it must be clockwise (movement called deosil) except when it is being pulled back, where we move the space counterclockwise (movement called widdershins).

Creating A Magic Circle

Before casting a Magic Circle, pay attention to your surroundings and see how big your circle would be if you had to physically delimit it. If you have already established a real dimension with chalk, stones, shells, ropes, or other artifacts, this will be easier. If not, simply estimate the proportions.

If your space is significantly small and you are unable to establish a wider circle, no problem. What matters is its symbolic meaning in this creation. Make the same suggested gestures and movements to follow without leaving the place, just moving around yourself and mentally declaring that you are sacralizing the space in which you will perform your ritual.

Light the incense and candles that are on your altar. Take your athame and head to the north quadrant, approaching the perimeter of the circle. Hold the athame in your power hand (the one with which you write), point to the perimeter of the circle, and begin to walk around the imagined or bounded area clockwise, going north to east, south to west, viewing a circle of light being drawn around while saying:

"I cast this Circle of power to be my shield and my bridge between the worlds of men and Gods, I consecrate and bless you in the name of the Goddess and God."

Walk around the circle two more times, repeating the same words and proceeding in the same way. When you have circled the third time, say:

"The Circle is drawn, so be it!"

Now it is time to invoke the help of the 4 elements residing at the cardinal points. As you invoke each element, turn your thinking to the forces of nature. When invoking earth, think of this element by visualizing trees, rocks, and mountains. To invoke air, see the wind, leaves traveling on the wind, and so on. This will direct your mind to what is most sacred to us Wiccans: nature. Still in the north, raise your athame and invoke the powers of the Earth and say:

"Earth, which bears fruit and begets,

I invoke its strength in this ritual.
Earth powers
are welcome!"

Now head east and, raising your athame again, invoke the powers of the air saying:
"Air that blows the inspiration
I invoke your strength in this ritual
Powers of the Air
Welcome!"

Now go to the south and proceed as before to invoke the element fire:
"Fire that brings warmth and light to Earth
I invoke your strength in this ritual
Powers of fire
Welcome!"

Lastly, head west, raise your athame and say:
"Water that washes and purifies
I invoke your strength in this ritual
Powers of water
Welcome!"

Go to the altar, place your athame on it, and raise your arms to your sides. Invoke the presence of the Gods by saying:
"Goddess and God,
I invoke your presence in this ritual,
be here and unite with me through my actions and thoughts, pour your blessings on this Sacred Circle,
Lady and Lord,
Welcome!"

Proceed in this way, and your circle will be traced and blessed. Now you can perform whatever ritual you like or use this sacred space to talk to the Gods, offer poetry, sing, dance, or meditate.

When you have finished your magical work, consecrate food and drink if it is part of your ritual. Make a libation to the Gods and deposit some of the food on the altar in a dish specially prepared for this purpose, and then unlock the Magic Circle.

Unlocking The Circle

Every time a Magic Circle is drawn at the beginning of a ritual, it must be drawn back at the end. This is not only a way of dispensing with the energies that have been invoked for your ritual, but also a symbolic way of returning to your habitual and worldly consciousness.

To do this you should thank the presence of the elements, the Goddess, and the God with words that spontaneously come to you or something similar to the following:

"Goddess and God

I thank you for your presence and help in this ritual.

Blessed be and follow in peace!"

Chapter 5 - The Sabbats

The main Wiccan rituals are the Sabbats, which celebrate the changes of the seasons and the path of the God, symbolized by the Sun, through the seasonal cycles. For us, the year is a great wheel with no beginning or end, and so the eight Sabbats are jointly called Wheel of the Year. They have great significance for Wiccans and are some of the keys to understanding the religion.

Wicca sees a deep relationship between human beings and the environment in which we live. We believe that nature is the very manifestation of the Goddess and in this way, we celebrate the changes of seasons. The Wheel of the Year is seen as an uninterrupted cycle of life, death, and rebirth. Thus, it reflects the passage of the seasons, as well as the inner and outer changes brought about by them and our own connection with the world. For us, everything that lives and breathes is divine, and by celebrating life through the changes of the seasons we establish contact with the world of the Gods, attracting the energies of the natural world into us, thus achieving unity with the divine world.

A witch always seeks to connect with nature in all its manifestations, not only by observing but also feeling the flow of it in us and the changes brought about in everyday life through it. The Mysteries of Goddess and God and their different aspects are contained in each season. The Wheel of the Year symbolizes the ancestral history of the Goddess and the cycle of death and rebirth of God, her Son and Consort.

The Wiccan Wheel of the Year has two meanings:

1. Nature Celebration Wheel: all covens and Wiccans gather on the Sabbat days to celebrate the Goddess and the blessings that she bestows to the Earth through the changing seasons.

2. Wheel of Initiation: expressing the teachings of the ancients through the seasons, for the Gods and nature are one.

The Sabbats are celebrated with bonfires, candles, songs, and sacred foods where Wiccans are grateful for the blessings and abundance in our lives.

Some archaeological sites dating to the Neolithic period, such as Stonehenge, were used as natural calendars to mark the change and cycles of seasons, indicating that such dates were considered important moments for ancient civilizations.

Know The Traditions And Symbols Of The Wheel Of The Year

The Wheel of the Year is divided among four larger Sabbats called Samhain, Imbolc, Beltane, and Lammas, which celebrate the Earth's agricultural cycle, marking sowing, planting, and harvesting. The names and origins of the main Sabbats are Celtic, and there are also four smaller Sabbats named Yule, Ostara, Litha, and Mabon, which mark the equinoxes and solstices and the trajectory of the Sun through the sky. We will be listing out the materials used in Sabbat rituals, themes, and the procedure for some of them. If you find that you like the rituals and would like to perform all of them, you can find out how to do the others, keeping in mind the essence of the rituals described below:

Samhain

It is celebrated on May 1 in the Southern Hemisphere and October 31 in the Northern Hemisphere. Samhain is the most important Pagan date and marks the Wiccan New Year. For the ancient peoples, this was considered not only a moment of power, but also the time when the veil separating the world was thinner and the Gods and ancestors could meet the living. As it is a celebration of ancestors, this Sabbat also speaks of the death that for pagans is seen as part of life, always opening the way for the new. On this Sabbat, all those who died are remembered and their spirits are invited to be part of the rituals as guests of honor.

As death reminds us of the ending, on this Sabbat we reflect on the end of relationships, work, and periods of life that must pass and also what we must let go of. One of the traditions of this Sabbat consists of leaving a plate and place at the table for the ancestors as well as lighting an orange candle at midnight to guide the spirits on their journey back to Earth.

It is the festival in which we honor our ancestors and those who have already left for Summer Country. This is the night when the veil separating the material world from the spiritual world is very tenuous and contact with our ancestors is facilitated. The Sun is at its lowest point on the horizon and so the Old King dies and the Elder Goddess regrets his absence in the next six weeks. Samhain was the day on which the Celtic New Year and the winter began, so it was an ideal time for beginnings.

Sabbat Theme

This is the night the Old God dies and returns to Summer Country to await his rebirth on Yule. The Goddess in her aspect of the Elder regrets the loss of her Consort, leaving people in temporary darkness. Pagans believe that the veil between the living world and the spirit world gets thinner tonight, and spirits roam the Earth to visit their family and friends and take part in ritual celebrations.

Summer country is the Pagan Outworld, a place of rest and joy where souls rescue their energies between one incarnation and another.

The Ritual Of Samhain

Material needed to perform the Sabbat:

- 1 gourd cut in half

- 7 different colored candles

- 1 cauldron with water

- Several apples

- 6 black candles

- 6 orange candles

- Sage incense

- Athame

- Goblet with wine

Procedure:

Place the cauldron with water and some apples inside and around it in the middle of the place where the Sabbat will be held. Make a big circle around the cauldron with the black and orange candles, interspersing them so that when you launch the Circle you stay inside it. Light the incense and then the black and orange candles. Draw the Magic Circle and then say:

"Tonight, the doors of the material and spiritual planes are open. On this night so holy and powerful, all magic is possible. May the summer country brothers join me in this Circle of strength and power.

Oh, Great Old Gods, today all Elves, Spirits, and ghosts roam the world. That through his powers the good spirits and energies be present in this place for me to bless us."

Fill the gourd with some water from the cauldron and surround it with the 7 colored candles, light them, raise your hands to the heavens and say:

"The Wheel of the Year continues to spin. Today God returns to the womb of the Great Mother. When she is reborn again, life will be crowned with peace and fertility. The Earth awaits the rebirth of Life. May He come once more to bless us."

Begin to circulate the cauldron, saying:

"May those who have gone before me return today to bless me. May the ancestral Witches be present. They know everything, they can do everything. They have light, strength, power and magic. They have brilliance, charms, and wisdom. May they transmit good energies and help me in this sacred rite of witchcraft."

While saying these words imagine several women dressed in long black robes dancing around you. They are the ancient witches who came to bless the Sabbat rite. While viewing this scene, lift the athame and say:

"That through the power of the 4 Elements this Magical Instrument be blessed."

Continuing with the athame in your hands, take one of the apples that is inside the cauldron, divide it, and eat it. When you finish eating the apple say:

"May the fruit of life invigorate my body and my soul so that all my dreams, desires, hopes, and goals can be fulfilled. By the power of 3 times 3, so be it and so be it!"

Take the cup with the wine, take a sip, and pour a little on the ground saying:

"In the name of the Goddess and her Son and consort the beloved God, I make this libation in honor of all those who went before me."

After performing the libation in honor of the ancestral spirits, thank the Gods with the following words:

"Once again the Wheel of the Year turns and will always continue to spin. May the Goddess, the mighty Hornet, and all the Ancient Gods of the North Hill protect me with health, joy, and prosperity. So be it and so be it!"

Unlock the Magic Circle, thanking and dispensing all the Gods and energies that were present.

Yule

It is celebrated on the Winter Solstice that occurs around June 20 in the Southern Hemisphere and around December 20 in the Northern Hemisphere. This is the time to celebrate the return of the Sun. After the long winter nights, from this moment the Sun will shine again and the days will be longer than the nights.

To the ancient people, the climate was something extremely important, since they spent most of the time outdoors. Because of this, the Winter Solstice was a date revered because it heralded the promise of the return of the Sun, the light, and the fertilization of life. God, as the Child of Promise (the rising and setting sun), was celebrated to bring warmth and light.

Yule signals the hope of a new time, paving the way for innumerable possibilities.

It was celebrated with lights, fire, and the traditional Yule tree with ornaments and oak acorns, which was later assimilated by Christianity and became the Christmas tree.

The tradition of this Sabbat is to make a yule log where a white candle, a black candle, and a red candle (representing the three faces of the Goddess) are placed in the middle of a small halved trunk lying on its side and lit while we make our requests. The yule log is stored until the following year, when it should be burned.

Yule represents the return of light, when on the coldest and longest night of the year, the Goddess gives birth to the Sun God, the Child of Promise. With that, hopes are reborn and fertility and heat are brought back to the Earth.

Sabbat Theme

Yule is one of the oldest and most widely observed Sabbat, celebrate the rebirth of God, symbolized by the Sun, which begins to return again after this night of darkness. It is a time when the King of Holly (representing the aspects of God's death) is overcome by the King of Oak (representing the rebirth of God). The Christmas Tree and the gifts exchanged between beloved people are derived from pagan traditions, because in the Northern Hemisphere this Sabbat is celebrated near Christmas.

Yule Ritual

Material needed to perform the Sabbat:

- Several red candles

- Rosemary incense

- Goblet with wine

- 1 small tree, like pine

- Paper with requests/wishes written in pencil

- Cauldron with 1 red candle in its interior

- Bay leaves

- Bell

- 1 black candle, 1 white candle, and 1 red candle

Procedure:

Spread some red candles and incense in every place where the ceremony will be held. Light them. Put the cauldron in the middle of the area, fill it with the bay leaves, and put a red candle inside it. Make a triangle with the black, red, and white candles so that the cauldron is inside this triangle. Place the chalice with the wine and the small tree on the altar.

Launch the Magic Circle, ring the bell, and then say:

"May the power of the Sun and the Spirit of Light be awakened!

May the power of the Sun and the Spirit of Light come back. May they come back from Summer Country. May the extinguished light be reborn now."

Then light the triangle formed by the red, black, and white candles and the candle that is inside the cauldron, saying:

"From now on, the light will increase and the strength of winter will gradually weaken. O Great Goddess and Ancient Gods, may the sun be reborn through your help and love."

Begin to walk around the cauldron, with the papers of your requests in hand, saying uninterruptedly:

"Love will be reborn and light will return."

Say this statement several times, walking around the cauldron, until you feel your consciousness is in an altered state. When you feel you can stop the chant, blow the paper with your requests three times in a row and then say:

"Sun of the valleys, rivers, and waterfalls. Sun of fountains, seas, and mountains, the Wheel of the Year continues to spin. That during the same year, my requests may bear fruit. So be it, and so be it!"

Distribute the papers with the requests in the tree, asking the Gods for them to take place.

Take the cup, raise it, and say:

"For You and for You, God of Light, Luminosity, Lord of Dawn."

Take a sip of the wine and also pour a little on the root of the request tree.

Unlock the Magic Circle.

Note: Leave the papers in the tree until the next day. Then burn them and blow their ashes into the wind.

Imbolc

It is celebrated on August 1 in the Southern Hemisphere and February 2 in the Northern Hemisphere. The Imbolc word means "in the milk" and marked the lactation period of the sheep and cattle in Europe.

It was the coldest time of the year, when there was no more wood available for the bonfires that were so common in celebrations of the greater Sabbats.

This was also the day dedicated to Brigit, the Celtic goddess of fire, home, and family. She was also a Goddess of healing and fertility. The many candles represented the power and the light of the Sun that approached with the arrival of spring. A traditional custom of this Sabbat is to harvest a green branch and leave it hanging somewhere in the house to bless it with new energies.

Imbolc is the festival that celebrates light in the dark. It is the ideal time to banish our remorse and guilt, and plan for the future. The Goddess is taking care of her baby, the Child of the Sun (the God). She and her son turn away the winter and the God grows strong and powerful. At this celebration, Goddess Brigit, Lady of Fire, life, and knowledge was honored, and everyone was grateful that she had kept the fire burning during the dark and cold nights of winter.

Sabbat Theme

This is the Sabbat that honors the Goddess as the bride waiting for the return of the Sun God. In Ireland, it is a special day to honor the Goddess Brigit in her bridal aspect. The Celts clothed little rag dolls with grains and fixed them in a place of honor inside the houses, for example, on their altars or on the fireplace. Usually, they were placed in cots called Bride's Beds, symbols of fertility.

Imbolc Ritual

Material needed to perform the Sabbat:

- 1 straw broom

- 1 cauldron

- Alcohol

- Red candles

- 1 Jar of salt

- Incense of myrrh

- 1 black candle, 1 white, 1 red

- Stick/wand that has been anointed

- 1 Small fabric doll stuffed with basil

- 1 Goblet of wine

- 1 Wooden stake

Procedure:
Separate out some red candles, then spread the incense and the rest of the candles wherever the Sabbat will be held. Light the candles and the incense. Place the cauldron in the middle of the circle and pour the alcohol into it. Light the cauldron carefully with one of the candles. Then arrange the black, red, and white candles on the altar in a triangular pattern. Place the doll in the middle of the triangle of candles and the wine glass under the doll. Light the three candles.

Draw the Magic Circle in the usual way. Then begin to sweep the circle energetically, without the broom touching the ground. In reality you will sweep the air, because the broom should stay a little above the ground. Say this:

"Great Goddess, in your name I cleanse and sweep this circle so that all evil energies are removed. May the sorrow, hatred, rancor, dissatisfaction, obstacles, and difficulties of my life be swept away from this circle. In his name I open my way and I bless this place. So be it and so be it."

Take the salt and start pouring it around the circle, saying:

"With the salt I consecrate, with the salt I purify, with the salt I bless this circle."

Hold the wand with your power hand (the hand you write with) and start walking around the circle clockwise, raising the wand above your head, then say:

"*Brigit, Lady of Fire, come and witness this ceremony. Oh, Goddess of poetry and inspiration, enchanted Druid of the Full Moon. Lady who heals and wars, Great Mother of the beauty of all things on earth, Mistress of spring fire, blessed be you Triple Goddess, Lady of love and wisdom.*"

Place the wand again on the altar. Take the stake and go to the cauldron, tap the stake base firmly on the ground three times, and then say:

"*Let him come from the mountains, valleys, woods and meadows. Oh, Lord of all animals, come great fecundator of the universe. God who enlightens and brings life, ruler of the heavens and the stars, ruler of the forests, Lord of all that exists and of what is to come. Come and enlighten the world. May the path be open and spring may pass. Without spring there will be no birth of light, without light there will be no fertility on earth. Blessed be you, Lord of plenty and prosperity.*"

Place the stake behind the altar. Raise the doll to the heavens and say:

"*May this day the light of the Goddess and her benevolence reach all.*"

Place the doll on the stake, saying:

"*Brigit has come, welcome. Brigit is here, be blessed. Brigit arrived, be well loved.*"

Start walking around the cauldron, saying nonstop:

"*The light of inspiration will grow, for Brigit brings life to every dawn.*"

Head to the altar, stare at the doll, raise your hands to the heavens and say,

"*May the union of Brigit and God bring prosperity to the earth.*"

Take the red candles that were not lit and were set aside at the beginning of the Sabbat and blow three times in succession on them and say:

"*That by the power of this magical breath, the energy of the Ancient Gods be transmitted to these symbols of enlightenment. May these candles help all those who make use of them.*"

Take the glass of wine and head for the cauldron. Drink three sips of wine and say:

"By the power of 3 times the 3 I drink this magic liquid in the name of all the Ancient Gods."
Pour some of the wine into the cauldron, saying:
"May the earth be strengthened, O Lady of the Silver Moon and God of the Paths. This drink offering is made by you and in your names. So be it and so be it."
Unlock the Magic Circle.
These candles should be given as gifts to loved ones.
Such rituals have been the cornerstone of the Wiccan religion, and they should be performed with incredible dedication, utmost care, and full commitment. Let the magic flow!

Celebrating A Sabbat

Each of us can and should celebrate the Wheel of the Year because it reflects not only the change of nature, but also our inner and outer cycles. When we integrate the Sabbat celebrations in our lives we attach ourselves directly and integrally to nature. Consequently this brings us peace, tranquility, harmony, and balance because we seek in our ancestral memory to reconnect with the same forces once invoked by those who preceded us.

To celebrate a Sabbat, you do not need to follow the rituals discussed above in a strict way or have great theoretical knowledge about the myths, historical contexts, and traditions of these dates, because this information is within you. It just needs to be awakened.

To access this knowledge, simply observe the nature around you and remove from it elements that are symbolic for you and can be part of a small ceremony held to mark the change of a season or celebration of a cycle.

For example, by observing spring, you can identify that at this time the sky becomes intensely blue, and the red, yellow, and white flowers open up, bringing a multitude of colors and aromas that surround them.

All of these elements can be part of a ritual to celebrate the arrival of the season using the colors of the sky and the flowers in the candles, clothes, or cloth used to cover your altar. The abundant aromas can take the form of incense or oils to anoint and purify the body and so on.

After lighting the candles and incense, you can anoint your body with the oil and try to connect with the nature that thrives in your surroundings, visualizing the changes that take place in it and in you at that time, meditating deeply on it.

What internal transformations arising from this change of cycle occur within it? How did you see the world a few months ago and how do you perceive it now? How do people around you behave this season? Does this affect you in any way? After meditating, you can read a poem written by you and offer it to the Goddess and God. You can sing, dance, or simply be silent, listening to your inner voice and ending by thanking the Gods for another spin on the Wheel and for all the blessings bestowed. By observing the nature that surrounds you, you can celebrate the eight Sabbats by performing beautiful rituals.

In Wicca, rituals created by yourself have much more power and value than those read, memorized, and copied from books.

The more you exercise the art of creating rituals, the more beautiful and elaborate they will become.

Each of us is a source of inspiration and creation, and therefore we must put our abilities at the disposal of the Gods, building rituals and ceremonies to celebrate the change of life that happens inside and outside of us.

Chapter 6 - The Esbats

In addition to the celebration of the Sabbats, Wiccans revere other important changes occurring in nature, including the change of the lunar phases.

The most important lunar phase is the full moon, which is when the moon is at its maximum power, the apex of its force. The full moon represents the Goddess in her Mother face, her primordial aspect. Full moon rituals are called Esbats, a term that has been popularly used since the early 20th century. The word Esbat comes from the archaic French "Esbatre" which means "to have fun."

At Full Moon Rituals, Wiccans gather in their covens or perform private ceremonies to worship their Goddess and God and practice magick, make talismans, consecrate objects and magical implements, or simply worship the ancient Gods. Esbats are moments where witches not only perform their celebrations in honor of the Goddess, but also share news, opinions, and information about their different experiences and practices in witchcraft. Usually, chants and dances are an integral part of the Esbats.

Thirteen lunations are celebrated in the course of a year. This is because Wiccans follow the ancient lunar calendars of the Celtic peoples, based on thirteen months and twenty-eight days. Among the ancient peoples, when practicing witchcraft was forbidden, Esbat rituals were performed in the dead of night, within a forest or other private location, away from curious eyes and where few dared to enter.

During the Esbat, we honor our Gods and thank them for their blessings and presence in our lives. In this period we also cast spells according to the lunar influences or moment of the year in which we are. If there is a need, we can also perform divinatory practices and healing rituals. A Full Moon Ritual may also consist, solely and exclusively, of simply feeling the flow of energy or a meditative practice.

A common practice in Esbat rituals is the pulling down of the Moon, where moon and Goddess powers are drawn to a Priestess or witch. This can be done in a coven or even by the solitary practitioner. When we pull the Moon, we summon the lunar magical powers to enter into us and illuminate our soul. This energy can be used later to perform a spell, consecration, or be issued to someone who needs healing.

In an Esbat held in a coven, the Moon-Down ritual is one of the most beautiful and transformative experiences, where the Priest invokes the spirit of the Goddess to become one with the Priestess. At this time, the Priestess may declare the Charge of the Goddess or inspired spontaneous words, representing the power of the Goddess on Earth.

Among the solitary practitioners, the act of pulling the Moon down can be done simply by visualizing the energy and lunar light illuminating our being.

Today, with growing interest in pagan practices, people of all ages and conditions meet on Full Moon evenings to revere the Goddess and life. As with the Sabbats, celebrating the Esbats puts us in harmony with all of nature because if the changes in the lunar phases exert influence on the tides and planting of the seeds, they surely influence our daily emotions and events.

Each of the lunations receives a specific name that reflects the moment of the Wheel of the Year in which it finds itself, expressing one of the many themes of human life. These names may vary from witch to witch or depending on Tradition. The names that follow are the most common and widely used among the Pagan community:

January

Hay moon
It is the moment where we see nature in its full maturity.

At this time in the past, the seeds germinated and it was time to think about what would be saved for the winter and remember the grains (dreams) that were planted in September in the Moon of the Plow. Now is the time to prepare for the materialization of the fruits of our actions.

Plant: Honeysuckle
Color: White, brown, silver and gray
Ideal time to: prepare for success, meditate on goals, and plan for the future.

February

Corn Moon
This lunation marks the period of the first harvest and the retribution of the benefits of our actions. It's a time to feed ourselves internally and externally, as well as fight for our dreams.

Plant: Sorrel "blonde de lyon"
Color: Orange, gold and yellow
Ideal time for: meetings, strengthening friendships, and fighting for dreams

March

Harvest Moon
This lunation marks the period of the second harvest. It is a time to give thanks for abundance and meditate on the balance of life. It is the ideal time to organize our spiritual and emotional lives.

Plant: Hazelnut
Color: Brown and yellow
Ideal time to: give thanks for achievements, meditate, organize, and strengthen the different aspects of life.

April

Blood Moon
This lunation marked the seasonal period of hunting and stockpiling of food for the winter. It's time to celebrate the ancestors and meditate on the theme of death and rebirth, as the Sabbat Samhain approaches. Time to put aside harmful habits and get rid of things that no longer serve us, inside and outside us.
Plant: Cypress
Color: Orange, black, purple
Ideal moment to: get rid of addictions, purify and seek harmony

May

Dark Moon
It is the lunation of transformation and preparation for the arrival of winter. Ideal moment to make peace with oneself and with those around you.
Plant: Cedar
Color: Black, gray, dark green
Ideal time to: seek understanding, strengthen communication with Goddess and with God, find peace.

June

The Sun Moon
Lunation of spiritual rebirth. After the solstice that occurs this month marking the longest night of the year, the days will be greater than the nights. Exactly for this reason, this lunation is ideal to lead us to meet our soul. As the sunlight grows, your energy will light up in your life, showing you the path to be traveled.

Plant: Holly
Color: Red, white, green
Ideal moment to: seek for rebirth, help friends and family, ask for guidance from the Gods

July

Wolf Moon

Ideal lunation to work on inner feelings. The period of seclusion in the cold and long nights of winter is over and it is time to wake up to the spring and summer blooms.
Plant: Birch
Color: White and violet
Ideal moment for: gestation, conception, protection, study the projects that we wish to see realized.

August

Storm Moon

This lunation is associated with the Sabbat Imbolc and is therefore ideal for purification, cleaning, and discarding what no longer serves us. The Sun begins to give its first signs of strength and light and the darkness is dispelled.
Plant: Sorveira
Color: Red, green, orange, sky blue
Ideal moment to: channel the energy needed for the realization of desires, purification, healing, home, and family.

September

Moon Of The Plow

It is the lunation that marks the moment of plowing and sowing. The Earth has awakened from its deep sleep and now it is time to have hope and let the winds of transformation bring new energy into your life.

Plant: Alder

Color: Blue, yellow, white

Ideal time to: grow, thrive, believe, start over something that has been left behind in the past

October

Moon of the Grains

Earth is filled with light and what has been planted now begins to slowly germinate. The union of the Goddess and God brings the necessary fertilizing energy so that the future harvest will be abundant.

Plant: Pine

Color: Green and red

Ideal moment to: produce or develop something, seize opportunities and luck, work on your temperament

November

Hare's Moon

It's time to celebrate love and life. This lunation marks the period following the union of the Goddess and God. Earth is full of power ready to be used. It is time to embrace the various parts of ourselves and recognize that they are all part of our nature and need to be balanced

Plant: Roses

Color: Pink, green, red

Ideal moment to: use our creative energy, strengthen our connection with nature.

December

Moon of the Meadows

This lunation indicates the moment to honor the Goddess and to give thanks for the learning she has gained over the course of the year. Summer now begins in the southern hemisphere by bringing the power of the solar God to Earth. The old man will die to make space for the new one, and so we are now able to strengthen ourselves.

Plant: Field flower

Color: Light blue, pink, and orange

Ideal time to: make decisions, take responsibility, strengthen love relationships, win a new love

Celebrating An Esbat

If you have watched the blossoming of nature around you and celebrated the change of the seasonal cycles, you will already have several elements that can be used in your Esbat ritual. The Esbats as exemplified in this chapter are a reaffirmation of the Wheel of the Year changes and how much they have to offer us for the understanding of the Wicca religion.

Include the colors and aromas already identified by you on the occasion of the Sabbat as well on your Esbat. Also, use the information provided for each lunation when composing a Full Moon ritual. You may want to include launching a Magic Circle to perform your full moon ritual inside a sacred space.

If you wish, you can perform the formal launch of the circle as shown beforehand or simply sit for a few moments, breathe, and imagine a circle of light around you in the color you like the most. As you imagine it forming around you, utter phrases like "I draw this circle to protect myself and make this sacred space" or "I cast a circle of light around me. Let no evil come into it, and let no evil escape from it. " You can choose to change the phrases exemplified to fit your needs and even create others spontaneously at the time. After that, it is common to summon the strength of the four elements of nature: Earth, Air, Fire, and Water, as well as Goddess and God, to witness the ritual.

It is also common to perform the full moon rituals in honor of the face of the Goddess. Therefore, identify the one that most corresponds to your needs at the time and compose poetry, song, or dance in celebration of her.

Meditate on the subject of the Esbat you are carrying out and find answers to your questions. Ask for peace, light, love, healing, and unity. Consecrate some object like a chain, pendant, or ring with the aromatic oil you like best, asking for the blessings of the Goddess and God and use it daily to protect you or to help you achieve your dreams.

Contemplate the Moon, feel your energy entering within you, and keep within yourself the power generated by it. This force will be your fuel and will help you reach the next lunation in harmony and fullness. Sing to the Moon, raise your arms to it, and let your magic promote your reunion with the Great Mother.

Chapter 7 - Rituals

The definition of the word ritual is a religious ceremony with an order of predefined events.

In Wicca, contact with the Gods happens through rituals. It is also ritualistically that we formulate our desires, construct a talisman, or consecrate an object to protect us or attract positive energies.

In Wicca, a ritual does not always begin with the launching of the circle and end with the extinguishing of the candles, and not all are formal or idealized only for magical works. Most of the time, they are devotional in character only to honor our Gods as occurs when we celebrate a Sabbat or Esbat.

A ritual is a way of connecting with the energies of nature, with the Sun, Moon or ancestors. Rituals are our bridge of communication with the Otherworld, and we practice rituals to ensure that we do not lose contact with these forces.

According to the philosophy of Wicca, a ritual can present itself in many different ways. Anything can become a ritual. Even conventional tasks such as reading, writing, eating, waking, or sleeping can be ritualized to give them spiritual meaning. Raising thoughts to the Goddess, thanking her for the plentiful gifts in our lives before we feed, or greeting the Sun in the morning are simple ritual practices that put us in direct contact with the sacred, calling it to be a part of our lives so that all moments become magical.

Most often a ritual involves communicating with a deity. Through it, a psychic bond is established, bringing the consciousness of the sacred closer to us, inviting it to be part of the devotional ceremony so that it extends its blessings and presence in our daily life. Know that not all Wiccans ritualize in the same way. Rituals vary greatly from one witch to another and between the covens. This is because, for the rituals to really work, they need to reflect the personality of their operator, and this is only possible by giving a personal touch and adapting them according to our vision and understanding of the Divine. There are basically two classifications of rituals in Wicca:

Devotional rituals: To honor a Goddess, God, a particular deity, or celebrate a Sabbat or Esbat.

Magic Rituals: To direct the magical energy to the achievement of personal desires through spells, sorcery, talismans, etc. In many cases, as in the rituals of Esbat, a ritual can be magical and/or devotional, revering the Goddess in her Mother face at the same time as an enchantment or sorcery is made and cast.

Ritualizing

Now it's time to learn a little of the magick that Wiccans use and understand their essence so that you can practice bringing rituals into your own life.

What is described is only a guideline for you to begin performing your rituals. The suggestions given reflect what is done by most witches. However, feel free to give your personal touch and develop your own particular way of performing rituals that reflect your personality and personal beliefs. The best way to learn to ritualize is by practicing.

A ritual follows some guidelines to be created and realized. It is important that you know these bases, as they are essential for the success of any operation in magick:

1- Preparation Of The Objects And The Ritual Area

It is important to clear the objects and the space that will be used to do your ritual. Clean the instruments of the altar, sweep the floor of the room chosen for the ritual, and decorate the are with flowers, candles, and incense. Leave the environment pleasant to your eyes.

You need to ensure that everything you need is on hand by the time the ritual begins. So, double check that you have the herbs that will be used, the candles, instruments, etc.

2 - Personal Preparation

Personal preparation is also important because it puts us in a receptive state to the energy of the Gods and centers us inwardly. When we do a ritual, we carry our own energy into the Magic Circle. So, we need to be clean of mind, body, and heart.

Take a shower of cleansing herbs such as rosemary, cloves, or sage before performing a ritual. Wipe off with a freshly washed towel and dress yourself in clean clothing. If you want to anoint yourself with your favorite aroma of oil and purify yourself in the smoke of incense, feel free to. As you do so, reflect on the purpose of your ritual and ask the Gods to purify your being.

The act of purification is a practice that puts us in an altered state of consciousness, preparing us for magick.

3 - Creation Of The Sacred Space

The creation of the sacred space can be divided into three different stages: purify, cast, and bless. A room can be used for a ritual. But as they are also used for other functions, many residual energies end up staying in these places. The purpose of purifying the sacred space is to remove from the area all energies incompatible with your practice.

Put some salt in a bowl of water and splash it on the floor while visualizing all the negative energies being destroyed and nullified. You can also use incense and even the flame of a candle to purify the area that will be used. Circle the environment counterclockwise, the movement used to ban. While doing this, say something like:

"I purify this place of all negative energy
May evil come out and good enter
Through all power, three times three
So be it and so be done!"

After purification, the next step is to launch the Magic Circle, which will consecrate the area used. As you'll remember, launching a circle basically consists of circling the ritual area clockwise three times with the athame as you visualize a light coming out of its tip going toward the ground and forming a bubble of light around you.

4 - Give Welcome To The Elements And Gods

Soon after the Magic Circle is released, the elements of nature and the Gods are invoked. The invocation of these powers is nothing less than a personal request for them to be present and to bless the ritual.

The first to be called are the elements. The invocations to the elements of nature are always made in order starting from the north, then east, south, and west invoking respectively the elements earth, air, fire, and water. Then the Goddess, the God, and all other deities that you wish to invoke are also summoned for the ritual.

When we invoke the presence of an energy in our rituals we expect an answer, but you will not always perceive a strong presence in ritual practices, especially in the first experiences. With time and practice, the energies invoked will become more and more noticeable and their presence will be strongly felt.

5 - Aligning A Ritual With Sabbat, Esbat, Or For A Purpose

If you are performing a ritual to celebrate the arrival of a season or a full moon night, rituals on this date should be associated with its theme. When your ritual also includes a magick practice, this is the time to make a talisman or to perform the chosen spell, for example. Many are the magick practices that can be used in a ritual, ranging from rituals with candles to magick ropes/cords.

6 - The Banquette

The Banquette marks the end of the ritual and is used to return your consciousness to the normal state, since eating is one of the most human acts and can easily return our mind to daily activities.

The foods and drinks that are part of a banquet vary a lot from witch to witch, but the most common are fruit, wine, and bread. Many Wiccans use cakes, seeds, and many other food sources as part of the banquet. Dishes with food are usually on the altar or at their feet, and before being ingested they are consecrated with the touch of the staff while saying something like:

"In the sacred name of the Goddess and the God I consecrate and bless you, that by ingesting this food I may be reinvigorated internally and spiritually, and may they bring me health, harmony, and prosperity. Let it be done!"

This is also the time to realize the Great Rite, a moment where wine, water, or any other liquid present in the chalice of the altar is consecrated. The Great Rite represents the Union of the Goddess and God, who bring the blessings of abundance to the Earth. To accomplish it, take your athame in your right hand and the chalice in your left. Slowly dip the blade of the athame into the goblet of liquid, see it shine through the mind's eye, and then say:

"The union of the Goddess and God is represented here. May this wine (or any other liquid) *bring me health, success, prosperity, and harmony. In the sacred name of the Goddess and God, so be it and so be done!"*

7 - Finalize The Ritual

It's time to thank the elements, Gods, and all the energies that were present in your ritual.

At this time, the Magic Circle is pulled back. This is when you thank the elements, the Goddess, the God, and all invoked energies, and then traverse the ritual area three times counterclockwise while visualizing the sphere of light dissipating.

The completion of the ritual is an important part and should never be forgotten, because it is going to make us return to our daily, mundane state of consciousness necessary to perform the tasks of the day to day.

After completion, incense and candles should be erased without blowing through a damper or other artifact, or they may also be left on the altar to burn out on their own. Everything that was used in the ritual is collected and saved.

The Effectiveness Of The Ritual

A ritual is an important part of the religious life of people around the world. The first purpose of a ritual is to invoke or connect with the Great Mystery: a Goddess or a God, a force of nature, the different spiritual worlds, or even the simple rhythms of the seasons. Thus, ritual is invocation in action.

In Wicca and other pagan religions, every ritual is a moment of transformation, a magic moment where a portal between the worlds is opened and everything becomes possible. It is through the rituals that we connect with our Old Deities for physical and spiritual changes to take place. The call to these Divinities occurs through invocations, prayers, and sacred texts that are recited or read during ritualistic practices as an invitation for the Divine to manifest. Such invocations call specific aspects and divine forces so that they become perceptible in our rites. The perception of these forces can be felt in many ways: through emotional, mental, and even synesthetic connection.

Rituals help us in this connection with the Great Mysteries of existence. Remember that they are portals of access to other realities of power, and we could make a simple analogy with television being a portal to connect with the world. The world will always exist; news programs, soap operas, and documentaries will be going on in many people's homes if we turn on the TV or not. But the television is a channel that encodes the signals that are sent by the antennas and helps us to see them in an understandable way to our mind and eyes. This also occurs in magick: Gods are always present around us, but rituals and invocations are the focus for us to connect with them.

Following a few simple guidelines, a ritual for the invocation of a Deity or force can be created for any kind of need in a satisfactory way.

13 Steps To An Effective Invocation Ritual

There are 13 basic steps that must be followed to perform a successful invocatory ritual. They are essential for a rite to be designed in a cohesive manner:

1.   Defining the goal
2.   Choosing and preparing the symbols
3.   Purifying and consecrating objects
4.   Using symbols
5.   Identifying the right moment
6.   Strength of the word
7.   Invocation of the Gods
8.   Preparing the Sacred Space
9.   Creating a state of relaxation
10.   Using the 5 senses
11.   Statement of desire
12.   Power generation
13.   Releasing the magic

We will analyze each of these steps, all of which are so important in the art of invocation, in detail, beginning with the definition of the goal.

1. Defining The Goal

When we perform a ritual, we need to have specific plans, and therefore the goal is very important. We must take care that our purpose is not misinterpreted if it is incorrectly expressed through invocations. The desire for an invocation must be built in very precise terms. Meditation can be a good thing when choosing terms, phrases, and words that will be used in your invocations during a ritual.

When preparing a ritual or sketching a spontaneous invocation to be used in a ceremony and/or your daily devotional practice, use the following exercise to assist you:

Breathe deeply and try not to let your mind wander. Focus your attention only on your desire.

Write extensively your wish on a piece of paper. Let your ideas flow freely. Then look it over and refine it. Reduce the least meaningful words, leaving only those that have the greatest emotional and visual impact, but be careful that your formula does not lose its meaning.

The resulting phrase can be recited during an invocation in the form of a song, litany, enchantment, etc.

Wishing:

When invoking, formulate the desire clearly and as you see fit. Repeat the desire daily and do whatever it takes to make it materialize.

When the invocation is pronounced, focus on it and direct all your personal energy so that your practical efforts are directed toward realization.

Invocations are always mechanisms that drive the will. So, they are very important in any magical process. Repeating the invocation and desire several times emits waves of energy to help the desire be realized, since it is our will that awakens, directs, and manifests the magical energy.

Desiring With Responsibility:

Responsibility for your desires is entirely yours, and you should reflect a lot before making an invocation. The realization of the desires expressed in an invocation may have consequences you never imagined. Therefore, always perform this exercise before invoking:

Write down the purpose of your ritual by answering a number of questions about how you are doing in the world.

Answer the questions while thinking about the positive and negative sides, the good and bad things that can happen. Think seriously about your ritual, what it means to you, and how it might affect others.

Write, taking into account all of the above, a very accurate verbal formula expressing your desire. With this, create an invocation or additional words that will be directed to a Deity or force of nature to be used in your ritual.

The Words:

Man has always used sound to communicate with this and other planes of existence. Magically speaking, a ritual is a verbal and mental projection, that is, it is composed of image and sound. Without these two factors, there is no magick.

We need to learn to use language correctly, both its energy and wisdom. Expressions and positive phrases related to our desires help to reinforce invocations and rituals.

Think for a moment about your desire and choose a short expression that describes it. Let the phrase echo in your mind and visualize a light shining above you. After a few moments, visualize the words of your sentence shining in the light, moving toward an image of the Deity formed on your mental screen. This means that you should visualize the Goddess or God invoked by you shining in this light. Slowly see the words being sent back to you, being poured over your head. Notice that they become compelled to come out of your mouth. Shout the phrase or sing it, visualizing the fulfillment of your desire as you perceive the image of the Godhead above you blessing it.

2. Choosing And Preparing The Symbols

Here we refer to the symbols related to the deity that will be invoked or the representation of your desire or goal in magical terms, which further amplifies the power of your ritual. You can use traditional symbols, long used to represent what you want, or a symbol that speaks especially to your mind and subconscious. Remember that symbols are also a form of invocation because they awaken memories, feelings, and energies that are asleep in each one of us.

To choose which symbols to use in your invocations during a ritual, look for their meanings in correlation tables and analogies to identify the representation that catches your attention. You can use objects, plants, stones, pictures, figures, etc.

Here is a short list to reference according to the themes pertinent to the ritual:

Love: roses, hearts, rose quartz, basil, verbena, bows, ribbons, colors pink and red, honey, sweets, perfumes, pigeon

Prosperity: coins, pyrite, citrus, horns, earth, clay, laurel, rosemary, seeds, colors orange/green/navy blue

Health: birch, tobacco, cotton, rosemary, lemon incense, photo of the person who is sick, circle on a paper, green quartz, agate, the color yellow

Protection: cord, obsidian, black tourmaline, onyx, garnet, black and red colors, ginger, annatto, garlic, algiz rune

With the symbols described above, create a small ritual invocation that represents your desire using words, symbols, and gestures related to your goal. Another exercise that could be done is the following:

Think of the ritual you want to perform or the divinity that will be invoked. What first comes to mind? Can you identify a symbol in this scene? If so, which one? If not, what is the first symbol that comes to your mind regarding your ritual?

Think of other symbols, at least three and at most nine. How would you join all the symbols (such as incense, candles, amulets, or visualization) to be part of your ritual?

3. Purifying And Consecrating Objects

The consecration and purification of the symbols and objects used in a ritual are essential, as this eliminates all past memory and influences on the materials that will be used in your ritual so that they are properly programmed to work exclusively for you.

Try to find the symbols that you identified in the previous exercise in physical form.

It will take you a few moments to consecrate them and carry them with you. This will be a simple way to remove any negative energy acquired by the object, as well as give it a specific function.

Ritual purifications can be done in numerous ways. Here are some examples:

- Pass the symbol through salt while visualizing what you want and the symbol fulfilling your mission

- Leave the object buried outside for a 24-hour cycle.

- Rub some leaves or seeds on the object, particularly those related to your desire

- Pass the symbol through the smoke of incense while visualizing what you want. This smoke can be generated by herbs associated with your desire, related to purification like blackheads, cedar, sage, or something sacred to the divinity that will be invoked by you.

- Blow on the symbol a few times while visualizing your breath in the color of your desire (red for love, orange and green for prosperity, black and red for protection, yellow and brown for health, etc.) or in the sacred color related to God invoked

- Submerge the symbol in water with salt, or water from the ocean, a river, waterfall, etc.

- Make an anointing on the symbol with an essential oil related to your desire

- Pass the symbol through a candle flame in the sacred color of the deity that will be invoked

Choosing How to Purify the Symbol
Take the symbol for a moment and let it communicate with you. Approach it three times from your front chakra and notice what it communicates to you. What kind of cleaning does it want you to do? Any of the types listed above, or another that's completely different? Let the symbol interact with you and let it tell you the best form of purification. Raise your mind to the divinity that will be invoked by you in your ritual and ask it to give you insight into which purification is most suitable for the object and to accomplish it.
Programming the Symbol

After you have cleansed, you begin the actual programming or consecration. This involves the invocation of a Goddess or a God, elemental spirits, or any energy you will invoke. This can simply be done with a brief invocation of the specific energy describing the intended use.

You can place your hands as a blessing on the object and make the invocation, lift it to the heavens, present it in the four directions, or bring it to your lips while pronouncing what you want. The forms of programming are many, and you can develop the one that best suits the nature of the ritual in question. What is important is that the symbolism of this act works for you.

Another additional form of purification:

Run your hands a few times over the chosen symbol and try to feel the psychic impressions contained within it. Visualize the deity for which symbol will be consecrated and ask it to assist you in this task. In a few minutes, the best way to consecrate your magick symbol will appear in your mind. Feel what the object wants to communicate to you. It can even tell you what is the best way to use it during the ritual, where, how, when, and in what situations. Be open to magick.

4. Using Symbols

After being prepared, the symbol should be used. It is believed that what is done with the symbol in the sacred space must be according to its function. If you want to attract something, slowly bring something that represents your desire closer to something that represents you, while making an invocation and expressing your desire. If you want to find a loved one, for example, unite two hearts while verbalizing your desire to a divinity of love. If you want to banish something from your life, destroy the symbol, turn it into powder, tear out that which represents evil, and dispose of it by invoking an appropriate divinity. And so on.

Take the symbol in your hands and for a few moments leave your mind empty, free of thoughts or images. Think now about the function of the symbol and without rationalizing much, feel what you should do with it, at that moment of the ritual. Then verify your desire while using the object.

5. Identifying the Right Moment

Any time can be used to make a ritual, but there are days, moons, and traditional times favorable for the formulation of desires.

You can use dates that inspire some special meaning to perform the ritual. Is there a special date that relates to your wish? A date of birth symbolizes longevity and new beginnings. Wedding anniversaries are great for renewing your relationship and love.

Can the seasons of the year interfere with your ritual? For example conception, births, and fertility strongly relate to spring. The opposite of these themes would be the winter period, and so on. What is the best season to add even more power to your ritual? Are you performing the ritual at the most appropriate time?

Are there lunar signs and phases that interfere with your desire? If so, which ones? Can your ritual wait for the most appropriate time to be made, or is it important that it be done now to harness your willpower?

Make a list of major times to formulate your requests and make your invocations and rituals by theme.

Here are some ideas and times of the year you can use:

Waxing Moon: makes desire grow, gives greater force to invocation

Full Moon: moment of great power, ideal for any invocation

Waning Moon: banish, restrict, diminish

New Moon: banish evil, break spells

Dawn: New beginnings, hope, magnification

Noon Time: elimination of negativity, strength, courage, power
Spring: Awaken, renew
Summer: Abundance, socialization, energy
Autumn: Harvest what was planted, seclusion
Winter: consummate

6. The Strength Of The Word

The words, the act of prophesying and proclaiming, have existed since time immemorial. Words have power. They can build, destroy, change the course of something, and more. They express feelings and communicate events. With them, we can create problems or solutions, offend or support. We can then see how the power of words transforms and weaves the events of life. Speaking properly and expressing yourself clearly, safely, and correctly when performing an invocation or ritual is imperative for success in magical processes.

It is important that you get to know the traditional chants and invocations as well as compose your own songs and incantations to be used in your invocative rituals.

Gestures, images, and symbols can be added as you work the power of your words to further strengthen your intention during rituals.

Verbalizing the Desire:

Create a phrase that represents your desire and then repeat this phrase uninterruptedly, transforming it into a melody.

Let the cone of power rise, projecting the scenes in your mind to the realization of your desires or toward the image of the invoked deity created on your mental screen.

You can also choose a single word associated with your invocation. Make this word vibrate in your vocal chords. Feel the word resounding within you until you realize the power it carries. When this happens, you are ready to make your invocation.

If you prefer, after relaxing for a few minutes, feel a spontaneous sound coming out of you. This sound must be associated with the nature of its invocation. It can be an expression of emotional background like a grunt, a letter or syllable sung continuously, etc. Then make your prayers or invocations, knowing that your intention has been amplified through this act.

Relaxing is important, as well. Relax for a few moments and then let a verbal expression come out of you spontaneously. Feel the power of this expression and slowly begin to perform gestures that are associated with the God you are invoking. For Artemis, throw an imaginary arrow; reproduce martial movements to Mars or Athena; imagine a lyre in your hands and touch it while invoking Apollo or Lugh, and so on. Do this until you feel that the intention was well fixed in your mind.

7. Invocation To The Gods

Using the power of words and our voice can be an unlimited magical act. Everything in nature and in life carries power: the stars, the winds, the Sun, the Moon. Words and names bring with them dormant powers that can be awakened from their deep sleep through our clear intent.

Simply invoking the name of a Goddess or a God can be of great help. We need to be attentive to the divinities invoked or called into our circles. However, invoking a Goddess or God may consist solely and exclusively in calling them by their names or titles.

It is important that you learn to meditate at least with a Goddess whose stories and powers are particularly appealing to you. Some myths of the Goddess include a God, who is the son and consort of her as in the legends of Isis and Osiris, Freya and Odin, Morgana and Arthur, and Inanna and Dumuzi. Other myths like those of Diana, the virgin hunter, do not involve a male God. Only you are the correct authority to establish your personal relationship with the Gods and if you are starting now in witchcraft, feel free to experiment. Be curious, open-minded, and persistent. In time, you will learn to feel the presence of the Godhead at your altar and in your life as you invoke them.

The beginning of this quest may be through the investigation of the Gods who were important to your ancestors. Or, many times, you will be attracted to Gods and Goddesses whose qualities resemble your personality and personal characteristics.

A woman in trouble and feeling weak can turn to Artemis, the Goddess who is untamed, wild, free, and self-possessed. Someone who needs to make a decision can call for Hecate, who stretches at the crossroads where three paths converge. A person who wishes to develop their artistic abilities can turn to Apollo, the God of the thousand arts. When you find out what inspiration and wisdom you need, you are ready to invoke a specific Goddess or God.

Calling the Divinities:

Open your heart, your ears, and your vision. Listen. Where is the Goddess? Call her name. Feel her approaching. Call on her to tell her legend. She is approaching. Move, recite poetry, present gifts and offerings. Now she's here, inside of you, everywhere. Say to yourself, "She is here, welcome!" Look at a mirror and admire the creation of the Goddess, yourself. Sing the name of the Goddess. You do not need to use any specific names of the most famous pantheons. She may simply be called "The One Who Hears," "The One Who Smiles," "She Who Shines," "Mistress of Inspiration," or whatever other name seems appropriate. Feel her presence and let her communicate with you.

Choose a Goddess with Whom You Can Work:
Write the names of several Goddesses on various pieces of paper, fold them, and put them in a small bag. Then reach in and choose one. This is the Goddess with whom you must work during a period of your life, for there is something she can teach you at that moment.

Meditate with the Goddess So She Can be Part of Your Life:
Breathe deeply for a few moments and enter into an altered state of consciousness. Go mentally to some place in nature that you enjoy, and find the Goddess there. Imagine the space with a wealth of detail. If necessary, look for her appearance in books and other sources beforehand to serve as a reference. Speak with her and ask her to tell some of her legends and myths to you. After you have reached out to her, thank her and return to your normal state of consciousness. Open your eyes and say a prayer to her in front of your altar. Be aware in the coming days as you feel the synchronicities that will confirm to you that your connection to the Goddess was effective.

Sing the Name of the Divinity:
To the sound of a drum or rattle, sing the name of the Goddess that you are invoking. Explore some possibilities of unfolding the name of the chosen deity. In this way, you will be invoking all aspects of this divinity.

8. Preparing The Sacred Space

The purification of the sacred space before the ritual begins is very important.

Every ritual is an invocation to our higher self to do magick and bring about change. When we perform an energetic cleansing in the sacred space before the ritual begins, we are sending a warning, through symbols, to our subconscious, saying that something important is about to happen, and that it is time to set aside anything that might undermine good performance of our ritual practice.

The forms of energy cleansing are varied, and it is important that with the passage of time you develop your own techniques.

Purification with the Four Elements:

You will need salt, 1 stick of incense, 1 candle, and 1 goblet filled with water.

Once the Magic Circle is released, circle the perimeter of the sacred space once more with each of the items listed above.

Bring the salt to the direction of earth, then the incense to the air, then the candle to the fire, and last the chalice to the water.

As the elements are placed in their respective positions, use words that inspire cleanliness and protection. Examples:

"By the earth which is the body of it, the air which is its breath, the fire which is the spirit of it, the water which is its living womb, this sacred space is clean and prepared."

"In the sacred name of the Goddess and the God and the four elements, I purify this soil so that it becomes sacred and appropriate to receive the Old Powers."

"With the 4 elements I purify this magical space for the beginning of this ritual."

These are just some examples. It is important that over time you create your own forms of invocation. Use your creativity.

Purification with Water and Salt:

You will need salt and 1 bowl or goblet filled with water.

Place the bowl of water in the center of the circle and place salt next to it.

Take a few deep breaths and let your mind drift for a moment. Let go of all the thoughts that are unrelated to your ritual. Pay attention to some for a moment and then let them go.

Take the bowl with water, place your hands on it, and say:

"Blessed be a creature of water."

Then get the salt, put your hands on it, and say,

"Blessed be the creature of the earth."

If you prefer, say words you have created for yourself that express purification. Then, mix the salt in with the water.

Relax even more, letting all the disturbances within you flow into the bowl. If you prefer, you can name what you want to send to the water to be transformed: "I send the discontent." I send the stress I had on the road." "I send the fight with my boss."

When feel that you have already sent everything you wanted to, think of the good things you want to attract, and then start splashing the water in the bowl, creating a shower of good energies with what has been transformed.

Purification with a Broom:

For this type of purification, you will need your magick broom. Sweep the sacred space with your broom while singing a song of purification, or make an invocation verbalizing that the space is being purified.

Visualization:

See the circle around you, then, with the eye of your mind, see yourself walking and circling the ritual space, magically cleansing the area to be used. Stop mentally in each quadrant and ask the element associated to assist you in this process.

9. Creating A State Of Relaxation

Relaxing for the ritual to be successful is another factor of paramount importance. Entering a state of deep relaxation is a basic prerequisite that precedes the actual invocatory practice. Here are some examples of relaxation techniques that you can use in rituals:

Visualization to Relax:

After you have done the purification, think about the purpose of your ritual. Let it become firm in your mind. Begin to visualize the four elements of nature in their respective quadrants.

In the north, you see the Earth with its mountains, fields, stones, valleys, trees, and forests.

In the east, see the air with the clouds, whirlwinds, breezes, and your own breath.

In the south, see fire with its flame, the rays of the Sun, volcanoes, lava, and the fire in the center of the Earth.

In the west, see the water with its seas, rivers, fountains, lakes, and rain.

Let the power of the elements come into you and be a part of you.

Now mix your views. What would the joining of earth and water be like? The air and the fire? Air and land?

See in your mind the successive manifestations of nature that take place day by day and how they influence your life, your mood, and your essence. Continue visualizing the elements of nature until you completely relax.

The Sounds of Nature:

Another way to reach a state of deep relaxation is through sounds.

Let the sounds of nature express themselves through you. Reproduce the sounds of earth, air, fire, and water. Mix the sounds of the elements. Keep reproducing these sounds until you feel deeply relaxed. Add a sound to the visualization. While your mind sees a river, reproduce the sound of the river; when your mind visualizes the forest, reproduce the sound of the falling leaves and so on. If you like, sequence your visualization, seeing the leaves being carried in the wind to the divinity that is invoked by you, the river flowing towards the kingdom of the deity, etc.

Relaxing with Colors:

Each color represents a force in nature, and visualizing them is a way to reach a state of deep relaxation.

See the chromatic scale and flow in each of the colors.

See the red, and feel it flowing in you.

See the orange and flow into it.

Then the yellow, feeling yourself navigating through it.

Visualize the green and feel yourself absorbing the energy of color.

Visualize the blue and feel full of this energy.

See the violet and let yourself be carried through the intensity of the color.

Finally see white and feel relaxed, ready to perform your ritual.

Spontaneous Sounds:

Let the sounds flow spontaneously through you, following the energy of the nature of your invocation.

For invocations to the Gods of love, try to let vibrating sounds, like the essence of fire, flow spontaneously through you.

For invocations to deities of prosperity, healing, solidification, concretization, and centering, strong and firm sounds are the most potent (earth).

For invocations seeking harmony, peace, and emotional balance, allow oscillating sounds to form (water).

For creativity, eloquence, or inspiration, let soft sounds flow (air).

Get carried away by the energy of the element of nature most suitable for your invocation

10. Using The 5 Senses

We must always seek to broaden our vision and ritualistic and invocatory possibilities. This is very important, because the more vivid and real the visualizations and meditations that accompany each invocation, the more favorable the results achieved. Use the five senses when performing an invocation ritual, seeking to see, hear, feel, smell, and taste, as if your visualization, which occurs only in your mind, is actually happening in the real world.

Each of the senses is associated with one or more elements:
Touch: Earth
Hearing and Smell: Air
Vision: Fire
Taste: Water

Perceiving Nature Within Us:
A common mistake among Wiccans is to think that nature resides only outside ourselves. It is very common for a person to see trees and mountains when we refer to Earth, but not think about our own body and bones. It is necessary to change this conditioning and perceive the nature that also resides within us. This exercise is done exactly to change this misguided vision.

Close your eyes and relax for a few minutes, and then think of the earth and its attributes. See the Earth in nature, in the fields, in the rocks, in the soil and say: *"The Earth is around me."* Now think of the Earth that resides within you. Where is it? In your bodily mass, in your bones, in everything that is in your body and solid. Then say:

"The earth is my body."

Now think of the air outside, in nature. The clouds, a hurricane, the leaves being carried in the wind. Think of the air inside. Where is it? Feel the wind entering and going out of you. See how your lungs are filled with air. Breathe in and out a few times. Blow on your own body and see that, as the Goddess does, you can also create air from your own body. You are similar to the Goddess. Say it:

"The air is my breath."

Think of the fire that lies in nature. The radius of the sun, the temperature, the heat. Think of the fire inside you. Where is it? Feel the warmth of your own body inside and outside you. Which parts of your body are hotter than others? Feel the inner fire burning within you, like a divine spark, your own spirit. Then say the following words:

"Fire is my spirit."

Think of the water that flows in nature. The rivers, the seas, the waterfalls. Now think of the water inside you. Where is it? Feel your saliva, your tears, your blood flowing and flowing through you. Let your own water purify you, cleanse you. Say it:

"Water is my blood."

Feel harmonized with the four elements.

Recognizing the Senses:

Inside the circle, breathe deeply and notice the different aromas within your sacred space.

Open your eyes and see your circle. Notice the minute details of each instrument, each object. See how the colors are vivid, strong, and different. Take something from your altar like water, wine, or fruit. Notice the different tastes.

Now feel something on your altar. Feel the different shapes, thicknesses, and sizes.

Notice in this exercise the diversity present in nature.

Making the Visualization Real:

Visualize the divinity invoked by you and try to make it as real as possible. Feel the smells present in the scene, mentally hold something that appears in your visualization, and so on, sharpening your five senses. Make your visualization more and more real.

11. Statement Of Desire

The power of the word is very important in magic. Thought is the first step to magick, and thought is expressed through words that invariably translate what we want to achieve at the different levels of our existence.

When we perform an invocation, ritual, spell, or a magical practice, we must pay attention to the way we utter our desire.

Here are some exercises that will help us in this process.

Transforming Thoughts Into Words:

Fix your thoughts on your invocation. Think about the different possibilities that involve accomplishing your goal. Think of the words that most represent your desire and let these words flow from within you. Notice that the more words you say, the more energy you put into your invocation and the more intense your spirit will become. Increase the rhythm of words, speaking faster and faster. Stop thinking about the words, letting them flow with the impulse of your will.

The Different Meanings of the Same Word:

Think of the words that are part of your invocation. Notice the various senses that surround these words. What could happen in your life if these words were misinterpreted and not presented in the way you interpreted or idealized? Example: You go through a difficult time emotionally with your partner and during your ritual you ask the negative situation between you to resolve and come to an end. Of course you would be wishing that the situation would be resolved in the best way and that the harmony between you would be restored. However, simply requesting that such a situation be resolved and come to an end may lead to different interpretations, including the termination of the relationship, the separation of the couple.

Be clear and detailed in the words you use, not giving scope for expressions with ambiguous meanings.

Choosing Powerfully Potent Words:

Which word expresses without equivocation the desire for this invocation and ritual? With your power hand trace this word in front of you, in the air. See the word shining brightly. Imagine that word entering your mouth and you breathe in, growing more and more until you feel compelled to exhale. When you cannot take it anymore, shout your word and visualize it rising to the skies.

12. Power Generation

When we work magically, we generate power through our bodies, voices, thoughts, gestures, and rites.

This power is generated to work our will and fulfill our desires.

Think of the generation of power as the fuel that drives your words to the world of the Gods.

Traditionally, there are 8 ways to do magick and generate power.

1. Ritual

2. A dance

3. Knowledge and use of magical herbs

4. Ability to concentrate the will

5. A trance

6. Psychic control of the forces found in the physical and spiritual body

7. The ability to invoke the Gods

8. A sexual magic, used on specific special occasions

Think for a moment about how you would generate power through these techniques. Invoke the Gods and then dance, sing, direct your will, and realize that you know how to proceed, that you naturally know how to do it through the eight ways to do magic.

13. Releasing The Magic

Releasing the concentrated power at the end of each ritual is something essential for the accomplishment of your will.

There are several techniques for this to happen, but the most important thing is that you have clearly in your mind at the end of each invocation the will that your words reach the goal expressed by them. Before the circle is pulled back, you should stop for a moment and realize the energy it generated. Then intentionally direct such energies to the location, people, or situations you wish to transform through your invocation. Here are some of the most commonly used techniques.

Raising the Cone of Power:

Singing and dancing around the circle, make the melody faster with each turn, always thinking about your goal. Have in your mind your clear purpose and clear scenes, all the while spinning faster and faster. When you feel that you have generated enough power, direct your will to the scene that is in your mind, seeing a large spiral cone ascending to the heavens and going towards your will. You can end the process with an invocation of thanks giving to the Gods and revered forces.

Word of Power:

Think strongly about the purpose of your ritual and invocation and then feel the energy in the circle. Visualize the energy rising to the heavens like a great white, blue, or silver ray. When you feel that the ray is in the fullness of your power, shout a word that expresses your desire: love, health, prosperity, success, peace, etc.

Raising the Power Sphere:

Position your arms horizontally. See that your body mingles

with a great sphere of energy that encompasses it. Think of your desire and then raise your arms, as if with them you were lifting this sphere of energy, raising a large ball. When you're ready, throw this ball at your will. Say a prayer of thanks to the Gods.

Conclusion - Witchcraft

How Can We Live Magically Each Day

Wicca is not something we simply do. It is a way of life, a state of mind, and above all a state of being. Obviously, this feeling does not present itself automatically, and it takes a lot of dedication and work for it to manifest itself fully in us. However, this can be enjoyable when we make our lives a true ritual, making everything we do sacred.

Each daily act can be transformed into a ritual, capable of connecting us with the sacred and filling our lives with peace, harmony, health, and happiness. To begin bringing this everyday magick into your own life, I'll leave you with a few of the following suggestions.

The Act Of Blessing

Try to bless yourself every day as a way to connect with the Goddess and the God. This can be done every morning or night before bed. If you act this way, you will soon be seeing things differently and you will perceive the Gods in the small and great things of your life.

See The Sacred In The Mundane

Try to connect daily with the elements of nature, think of them, and identify their presence in your daily life. Feel the water every time you bathe or drink something. Feel the air element when you see the clouds in the sky or the birds flying. Feel the fire when you feel the rays of the Sun and their heat, and perceive the power of the Earth as you walk to work or school.

See the sacred in the mundane and make your life much more magical.

Cooking Magically

When cooking something for your family, friends, or yourself, there will be the opportunity to put your own energy in to bless this food and bring positive change to all those who feed on it. Do not cook unless you are calm, at peace with yourself, and in a good mood, otherwise your negative energy can be transmitted to the food you are preparing.

Let the cooking function become an act of love, healing, and harmony. As you prepare the food, direct your energy to it, wishing for health, success, and balance for all those who feed on it. As you use fire to heat, water to make sauce, herbs to season, and can feel its wonderful aroma, ask the spirit of the elements to unite in this work alchemical and join their blessings to yours.

In this way, you will be turning the food of your family into pure magick.

Blessing The Food

As a Wiccan, you should be aware of where your food comes from.

Every time you go to eat, visualize where your food came from and the whole process that it has gone through to get to you. Do not forget anyone who may have been involved in this process of bringing food to your table.

If you want to do a small act of thanks giving to the Gods for the food, place your hands over your meal and say:

"Goddess and God
We are grateful for the seeds that grow
By milk, eggs and meats
For the lives that are sacrificed to feed us
For all who plant
For all who harvest and milk
By the sun, rain, wind and earth
We thank all who bring this food to our table.
Blessed be!"

This blessing can be modified according to your will.

As you bless your food, visualize scenes that correspond with the words you utter.

Ritualizing Your Bath

Bathing is a daily ritual done most of the time in an ordinary and carefree way. Make your bath a magical act by adding a meditation as part of this daily routine. If you cannot take 15 minutes of your day to meditate, the bath can become the perfect place for that to happen.

When turning on the shower, let the water run down your body, relaxing all your muscles. Close your eyes briefly and see stones above your shower, trees around you. Turn your shower into your private waterfall and let the water purify and renew your being.

If you have a bathtub, add a few pinches of salt in your bath along with a few drops of your favorite perfume or essential oil. Turn your bathtub into a sacred source of renewal, invoking the healing and renewing power of water.

This can help you get closer to your religion and make your faith stronger. Wicca takes practice, but with the right steps, you will be fully immersed in your new faith.

CPSIA information can be obtained
at www.ICGtesting.com
Printed in the USA
BVHW071633270421
605952BV00009B/260

9 781802 290103